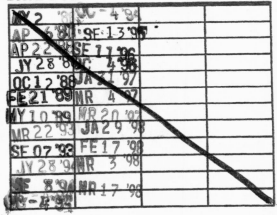

Presidential Influence
in Congress

George C. Edwards III
TEXAS A&M UNIVERSITY

W. H. Freeman and Company
San Francisco

Sponsoring Editor: Richard J. Lamb

Project Editor: Nancy Flight

Manuscript Editor: Paul Monsour

Designer: Sharon H. Smith

Production Coordinator: William Murdock

Illustration Coordinator: Cheryl Nufer

Artist: Donna Salmon

Compositor: Graphic Typesetting Service

Printer and Binder: The Maple-Vail Book Manufacturing
                     Group

Library of Congress Cataloging in Publication Data

Edwards, George C
   Presidential influence in Congress.

   Includes bibliographical references and index.
   1. Presidents—United States.   2. United States.
Congress.   I. Title.
JK585.E33   353.03'72   79-21975
ISBN 0-7167-1161-3
ISBN 0-7167-1162-1 pbk.

Printed in the United States of America

1   2   3   4   5   6   7   8   9

To my grandparents,
Carrie and Oliver Laing

Contents

Preface

This book has been a labor of love. Over the past six years I have been wrestling with the problems of empirically studying the presidency in general and presidential influence in Congress in particular. Although my attention has often been diverted to other research topics, I have always returned gladly to the subject of the presidency. The challenges of empirically analyzing presidential influence in Congress and the importance of the subject have sustained both my interest and my energies.

The book tests propositions about sources of presidential influence in Congress and attempts to explain the behavior of members of Congress toward the president. Some of the questions examined include: Why is there so much conflict between the president and Congress? What difference does it make that the president is his or her party's leader? Does the president have coattails? What influence, if any, does presidential popularity have? How useful is bargaining to the president? How important are presidential legislative skills?

Empirical methods and rigorous analysis are used to investigate these and related questions. This approach has resulted in some surprising findings, such as the lack of presidential coattails, the relative unimportance of presidential legislative skills, the limitations of bargaining, and the responsiveness of Congress members to presidential popularity only among members of their own party.

Quantitative analysis of the presidency is in its nascent stage, and few books or articles have appeared in which empirical methods have been used to test propositions about the president's relationships. I hope this book illustrates the benefits of such an approach. I have endeavored to make the text understandable to readers who are unfamiliar with statistics; thus, it should be of interest to scholars, students of the presidency and Congress, and anyone else interested in the crucial relationships between these two branches of our national government.

During the writing of this book I have incurred many intellectual debts. Chuck Cnudde, Fred Greenstein, Barbara Hinckley, Sam Kirkpatrick, John Manley,

Austin Ranney, Leroy Rieselbach, Doug Rose, Ira Sharkansky, W. Phillips Shively, Steve Wayne, and Tom Wolanin read or commented on parts of the manuscript and on my articles on which the manuscript is based. Tom Cronin and Burdette Loomis read the entire manuscript. All provided sound judgments and helpful advice, and they have my sincere gratitude. Naturally, I alone bear responsibility for what appears in the text.

A very special thanks goes to my editor and close friend, Richard J. Lamb. His talent, confidence, and patience have been of enormous support to me as I have worked on this project.

There are others who also deserve mention. A series of capable assistants, including Earl Bender, Jim Meader, Carl Richard, and Dick Schuldt, have made my computations less burdensome. Both Tulane University and Texas A&M provided computer funds, the former also providing summer grants and the latter meeting the sizable expense of acquiring the Gallup polls analyzed in Chapter 4. Don DeLuca and Ruth Quah of the Roper Center were also most cooperative in helping me to obtain these polls. Charlotte Jones, Edna Lumpkin, and Dee Drummond have plowed through my handwriting with good humor and managed to come up with well-typed pages.

Thanks also goes to the *American Political Science Review, American Journal of Political Science, American Politics Quarterly,* and *Presidential Studies Quarterly* for permission to use material originally published in them.

George C. Edwards III   *October 1979*

Presidential Influence
in Congress

Introduction

This is a book about power. More specifically, it attempts to measure and explain the extent of presidential power or influence[1] in Congress. This is done primarily by examining the effectiveness of various potential sources of such power.

It is important to know how powerful the president is in Congress, why he is that powerful, and how the executive and legislative branches of our national government interact. Such political behavior not only is interesting but also has policy consequences for citizens in the United States and in other nations. Taxes, inflation, energy supplies, welfare payments, consumer protection, defense expenditures, nuclear arms limitations, and much more are all directly affected by the passage or failure of presidential proposals in Congress. Moreover, anyone interested in policy change or systemic reform, even if this interest does not involve special concern for the workings of either of these branches of the national government, needs to understand how they work together, because usually both branches must reach agreement if there is to be major change.

However, we do not know much about why members of Congress do or do not support a president's policies or about how the president can increase congressional support for his proposals. Indeed, we know little about the presidency in general. While we have innumerable descriptions of the institution and its occupants, we lack a fundamental understanding of why the presidency operates as it does and what difference it makes. This presents a striking paradox: The single most important figure in American politics is the one that political scientists understand the least. Thus, to examine and explain presidential influence in Congress is a considerable challenge.

Approaches to Studying the President and Congress

We might divide contemporary scholarship on the president and Congress into three categories. The first, which has had an honored place in political science, focuses on the *legal* setting of the two institutions.[2] The central questions include the following: What are the powers of the president and Congress? What are the constraints on the actions of each? What has determined the boundaries of constitutionally acceptable behavior? It would be difficult to discuss a subject such as presidential influence in Congress without first understanding the answers to these crucial questions.

A second approach to studying presidential-congressional relationships is the *institutional* approach,[3] which describes the institutions and processes involved in interactions between the president and Congress. While this literature once concentrated on the organizational structure and rules of the two institutions, it now addresses the more important topic of describing the behavior of the individuals involved in presidential-congressional relations. Clearly, we must know what these political actors are doing before we can proceed to discuss the significance of their behavior, much less examine analytical questions of relationships such as those pertaining to influence.

Both of these two approaches are employed in this book. However, besides the proper boundaries of constitutionally acceptable behavior, we also want to know what takes place within those limits. Similarly, we want to know not only what behavior occurs but also why members of Congress behave as they do toward the president and how the president's behavior affects support for presidential proposals.

To accomplish these goals we must employ a third approach, which uses *empirical methods,* to test propositions about presidential influence. Concepts must be carefully measured and relationships must be tested by using the most appropriate statistics. We must rely heavily upon logic to analyze our data and to search for alternative explanations of our findings. Finally, to explain presidential influence (or the lack of it), we must emphasize empirical theory, that is, *explanation* of behavior.

By no means have we developed a full-blown theory of presidential influence in Congress. This development awaits many more studies similar to the present one. What we have done is to emphasize the explanation of relationships (or the lack of them) more than past studies have. Sometimes this involves applying existing middle-range empirical theories, such as role theory or incentive theory, as is done in Chapter 5. At other times the explanations are more *ad hoc,* as when we show that bargaining is of little value to the president in influencing Congress. Even here, however, the effort is made to generalize about the relationships across presidents of the past, present, and future.

Thus, our emphasis is on developing and testing propositions about presidential influence in Congress with the goal of explaining this influence and generalizing about it. With this in mind, let us turn to a brief description of the book.

Outline of the Book

We begin our examination of presidential influence in Congress by looking at the varying degrees of success that presidents have had in influencing Congress. Thus, we present data on the success that presidents have had getting their proposals passed, winning votes on which they have taken a stand, having their vetoes sustained, and gaining confirmation of their appointees and ratification of their treaties. In presenting this data we also raise additional questions. The first is over the validity of these measures for determining presidential success in Congress. This discussion anticipates Chapter 2, where a measure is introduced that is utilized throughout the rest of the book.

The second question raised is that of the "two presidencies." Is the president still more successful in Congress in matters of foreign policy than in matters of domestic policy? To answer this question we not only compare presidential success in the two policy areas but also look at some new congressional constraints on the president in his conduct of foreign affairs. One of these constraints concerns executive agreements, an option by which the president can often avoid having to fight for the ratification of treaties in the Senate. Another constraint is the War Powers Resolution, which limits presidential authority to carry out an undeclared war. Both of these issues are symptomatic of a new era in executive-legislative relationships in foreign affairs, and a discussion of them reveals the president's additional burdens in policymaking.

Discussions of issues such as the War Powers Resolution and executive agreements must rely heavily upon the tradition of constitutional law. We need to know the legal limits of presidential and congressional power in foreign policymaking. The same is true in our discussion of the powers that the president usually exercises in domestic policymaking.

The most prominent of these limits is the veto power of the president over congressional bills. In addition to measuring its use and its success, we also want to know on what congressional actions and under what conditions it may be exercised, when has it been exercised, the difference between a regular veto and a pocket veto, and how a veto may be overridden.

A type of unofficial veto that several presidents have employed is the impoundment of funds. In other words, presidents have refused to spend funds appropriated by Congress. To prevent abuses of this technique, Congress passed the Impoundment Control Act of 1974. Once again, we need to understand just how this act limits the president.

The appointment confirmation and treaty ratification powers of the Senate are also examined. We will study how often presidential appointees have been confirmed and how often the treaties negotiated by the president have been ratified, and we will consider the rules under which Congress considers appointments and treaties. We are also concerned with the political interplay between the two branches in these areas.

Aside from the individual issues raised in Chapter 1, we can reach one overall conclusion: The president's proposals often do not pass, and he often loses votes on which he takes a stand. Nevertheless, the president must have the support of Congress to pass his legislation, sustain his vetoes, ratify his treaties, and confirm his appointments. Because he cannot depend on adequate congressional support, the president must influence members of each house.

In Chapter 1 we describe presidential success in obtaining support for White House programs. In Chapter 2 we begin the more significant task of explaining the degree of support that the president receives. To do this, we must examine the sources of conflict between the president and Congress. This will help us to understand why the president often receives inadequate support and therefore needs to influence Congress.

One source of conflict is the different constituencies that the president and each member of Congress represent. The president alone represents the entire nation. This fact naturally leads to a difference of views. We trace this conflict through different stages of policymaking, including predicting the consequences of policy alternatives, evaluating their benefits and costs, and implementing a chosen policy. Moreover, we shall find that reforms designed to make members of Congress more responsive to broader notions of the public interest than those of their constituents are unlikely to be effective. Thus, the source of conflict remains.

A second source of conflict between the executive and legislative branches is the differences in their internal structures. The executive branch is hierarchically organized with one person at the top, while Congress is highly decentralized and lacks an effective integration of information. Thus, the president is likely to have a broader range of information on a policy than a member of Congress has. This may lead not only to different views on a specific policy proposal but also to congressional inability to deal comprehensively with an issue that cuts across several areas of specialization, such as energy. Decentralization in Congress also allows a relatively anonymous member to make irresponsible or self-serving decisions while the highly visible president is held accountable.

Differences in the expertise and information available to members of Congress and the president is a third source of conflict. The president has far more of both available to him, especially regarding foreign and defense policy, for which secrecy is important and few sources of information may exist outside the executive branch. In addition, Congress often does not use the data that are available to it. Again, these differences may lead to different perspectives on issues in the two branches.

The final source of conflict between the president and Congress is their differing time perspectives. Presidents have a limited tenure in office, while members of Congress may spend decades in their positions. If presidents wish to bring about policy changes, they must act quickly. Members of Congress can and do take their time. This sluggishness is aggravated by the decentralization of power in Congress, which necessitates years of negotiation and compromise for most major policy proposals.

Having established the necessity of influencing members of Congress, we turn to a crucial topic for the rest of the book: our approach to studying power. The approach adopted here is to examine the effectiveness of potential sources of influence. This approach has several advantages. It allows us to study where changes in potential sources of influence are related to changes in presidential support in Congress. It also allows us to examine anticipated reactions to presidential behavior and indirect power (where the president influences a third party to influence a second party). Finally, this approach forces us to explain any inferred causation. We must have a theory to relate the source of influence to presidential support.

After presenting our approach to studying power, which is distinguished by its selection of independent variables (the potential sources of power), the next logical step is to present our measurement of the dependent variable (presidential support in Congress). This is measured by using the *Congressional Quarterly*'s Presidential Support Scores. While their validity, reliability, utility, and possible drawbacks are discussed in Chapter 2, it is useful to note here that these measures enable us to calculate the level of support for the president's program of each member of Congress. We are not limited to a measure for the House or Senate as a whole. If this were the case we would only have one figure per chamber per session of Congress and could not examine variability in support among individual members of Congress or groups of members. This would make explanation of behavior very difficult. To examine presidential influence under different conditions, our study covers in most instances the period from 1953 through 1978.

The first source of presidential influence that we examine is political party affiliation (Chapter 3), and the first question that we ask is whether the president receives support from members of Congress of his party beyond what he would receive because of policy agreement. Initially, we show that the president receives more support from members of his own party than from members of the opposition party.

Then we must ask ourselves whether this support is due to shared policy preferences, the pull of party loyalty, or both. The evidence is inconclusive. However, shared party affiliation seems to be a source of influence for the president, especially with regard to foreign policy matters. Because members of the president's party in Congress want their leader to look good, they try not to embarrass him. They may also have personal loyalties or emotional commitments to their party and a distrust of the opposition party.

The crucial question then becomes how the president can use his party affiliation to his advantage. Rarely do the president or members of Congress change their party. Thus, the only way that the president can have more people of his own party in Congress (and thus be more able to exploit party loyalty) is to increase the party's representation there.

One way to do this is to campaign for party candidates in congressional midterm elections. Such presidential efforts over the past quarter century have not been particularly successful. In fact, the president's party usually loses seats in midterm elections. Voters seem willing to blame the president (and thus his party) for bad times, but they do not seem as willing to reward him and his party for good times.

The president's other opportunity to alter the partisan composition of Congress is the coattail effect of his own election campaign(s). To test for the strength of coattails, we must design a study to measure their impact on outcomes in congressional elections. It is not enough to show that a given percentage of voters voted for a congressional candidate because they voted for the presidential candidate of the same party, since this may only increase a representative's already substantial margin of victory and not affect the election outcome at all.

Studying the presidential elections from 1952 to 1976, we find that the coattail effect has declined in recent elections to the vanishing point, primarily because of the decline in electorally marginal congressional districts (those won by narrow margins), districts in which congressional election outcomes might be affected by presidential coattails.

Because a president can do little to manipulate party affiliation and because no president can rely upon his party cohorts for total support, a president must usually adopt a bipartisan approach in dealing with Congress. This is especially true when the opposition party controls one or both houses, as is often the case. Thus, we discuss the necessity for bipartisan politics and the techniques that presidents have used and the problems that they have encountered.

A second potential source of presidential influence in Congress is the president's prestige or popularity. Many authors, most notably Richard Neustadt,[4] have argued that the president's standing with the public is a source of influence. In Chapter 4 we empirically examine this relationship.

Before testing for a correlation between presidential popularity and presidential support in Congress, it is necessary to theorize on just why the former may be a cause of the latter. In other words, we want to be able to explain any relationship that we find. We do not want to throw numbers into a computer and blindly accept whatever comes out, no matter how nonsensical. Two explanations are presented for members of Congress responding to presidential popularity, one based on role theory and the other on the incentive for reelection. Together, these explanations give us confidence that the hypothesized relationship does exist. However, we must still test for the strength of the relationship.

We have two indicators of the president's standing in the public. The first is the Gallup polls, and the second is presidential election results. Separate analyses are carried out for each of these independent variables. After discussing the utility of presidential popularity polls as indicators of presidential popularity, we analyze correlations between them and presidential support in the House and Senate. We first compare the president's average popularity in the entire nation with his average support in the entire House and Senate, finding, however, that we must disaggregate both popularity and support according to party affiliation. In other words, we must compare presidential popularity among Democrats in the public with presidential support among Democrats in each house and then repeat this process with Republicans. Members of Congress appear to respond to the opinions of their electoral supporters rather than to those of all their constituents.

The findings indicate very strong relationships between presidential prestige and presidential support, but we have to search for other explanations for changes in both popularity and support. One such variable is the president's party. Thus, we must control for its influence in our calculations. When we do this we find that the relationship for Republicans disappears. We then try other tests, including separate analyses for Democratic and Republican presidential years. This analysis is quite revealing and, together with other aspects of our examination, leads us to conclude that presidential popularity is indeed a source of presidential influence in Congress.

To look at this relationship from another vantage point, we present a short case study of Richard Nixon in 1973. His support in Congress took a dramatic plunge despite his landslide election, a similar party lineup to that of previous years, an improved legislative liaison operation, and an end to the war in Vietnam. The logical explanation for this decline seems to be the 33 percent decrease in his popularity during the year.

Presidential popularity polls do not measure the president's standing in individual congressional constituencies. One indicator of constituency opinion about the president that can be consistently employed over several years is voting behavior in presidential elections. It is important to point out that what we are doing is examining some of the consequences of presidential elections and not the causes of voting behavior. Most studies of presidential elections focus on explaining the results instead of analyzing their impact.

To carry out our analysis, we develop a model that allows us to control for the influence of constituency party strength on the presidential support of the constituency's representative and the constituency's presidential voting. At the same time, our analysis tests for the direct effect of presidential electoral performance on presidential support and its indirect impact through presidential coattails. Each of the variables is carefully justified and explained, as is the technique of causal modeling used to arrive at our results.

These results show that presidential electoral performance influences presidential support in the House, especially for Democratic presidents. The reasons for this Democratic phenomenon are then discussed, as well as possible explanations for the variance in the strength of the relationships within presidential administrations.

In addition to political party affiliation and presidential popularity, we discuss a large number of more personal potential sources of influence under the title of "Presidential Legislative Skills" in Chapters 5 and 6. These chapters have two goals. The first is simply to categorize and describe the legislative skills of the presidents from Eisenhower to Carter. The second goal is to examine critically some of the more prominent of these skills, such as bargaining and dispensing patronage, to see whether they could systematically serve as broad sources of influence.

In Chapter 5 we examine the president's personal dealings with members of Congress on matters of legislation. We begin with a detailed discussion of the extent of involvement in the legislative process by various presidents, particularly emphasizing Lyndon Johnson, who was extremely active in this regard. Aspects covered include the knowledge of Congress attained by the presidents, their timing in introducing legislative proposals, their consultation with members of Congress in preparing legislation and their giving members notice on pending proposals, their anticipating and preempting of problems, their use of the cabinet in dealing with Congress, their working closely with congressional leaders, their access to members of Congress, and their personal appeals for support. We also raise the question of the tremendous demands that intimate involvement in the legislative process can make on the president's time.

We also focus on bargining, which is often seen as central to presidential-congressional relations.[5] We initially illustrate the types of bargains that take place. More importantly, however, we examine the limits on presidential bargaining with members of Congress. These stem from many sources, including the president's lack of resources (such as favors) with which to bargain, the lack of respectability surrounding bargaining, the lack of willingness of either the president or a member of Congress to bargain on a particular point, and the costs of obtaining bargaining resources from the bureaucracy or other members of Congress who have authority over what the president needs. A president also incurs special costs when bargaining with those who are normally his opponents. Giving them resources strengthens them and will possibly make their opposition more effective in the future. We also note that often neither the president nor powerful members of Congress need to bargain on an issue (they are able to get their way without it) and that much of the impetus for bargaining originates on Capitol Hill and not in the White House.

Next we turn to the issue of professional reputation, examining its potential influence on congressional support of presidential proposals. This concept, also introduced by Richard Neustadt,[6] refers to the president's maintaining both clear, consistent policy views and concern for how members of Congress vote on his proposals. Particular attention is paid to contrasting the good professional reputation of President Johnson with the poor reputation of President Eisenhower.

The chapter ends with a discussion of arm-twisting by the White House, which we show to be generally ineffective. Thus, as with so many other presidential legislative skills, we must be skeptical of its utility.

Chapter 6 begins with an extensive discussion of the multitude of services that the White House provides for members of Congress in order to generate goodwill. These include projects, help with constituents' problems, campaign aid, and patronage. We show the different attitudes toward their use and the different skills in administering them demonstrated by modern presidents. We also emphasize the limited effect of these services in influencing Congress. The value of patronage, for example, is limited by the scarcity of available jobs. In addition, many of the jobs require special skills and thus may not be appropriate for some pleading senator's favorite. Also, most presidential appointees must also be confirmed by the Senate. The use of patronage may also alienate those people who are not appointed and their congressional supporters, and its regular use may lead congressional members to expect presidential largesse that need not be reciprocated.

Other techniques for generating goodwill are discussed, including the many personal amenities that a president can bestow upon a member of Congress. These include notes, phone calls, pens used in bill-signing ceremonies, social events, credit for legislation, and respectful treatment. Naturally, we do not assume that these incidentals directly translate into congressional support.

Other aspects of presidential-congressional relations also deserve attention. These include the president's use of the vice president for congressional relations. Interestingly, the vice president has not usually played an important role in this regard. We also discuss the president's need to be detached (so that he will not take setbacks personally and thus create permanent enemies) and to be flexible and to compromise.

We then turn from direct relationships between the president and Congress to indirect relationships. Since members of Congress usually desire reelection, they must please their constituents. Realizing this, presidents often engage in an "outside" strategy to generate constituent pressure on members of Congress to support presidential legislation.

A president may also try to provide an "umbrella," either a highly respected member of Congress or himself. Members of Congress can justify their support of the president to their constituency by saying that this "sound" public official is also supporting the policy. At other times, a president simply makes sure that members of Congress realize the benefits their constituents will receive from his proposals.

Presidents have been reluctant to appeal to public opinion over the heads of Congress, but they have often worked closely with interest groups to build successful legislative coalitions. We detail both these points as well as other aspects of the outside strategy, including times when public opinion forces the president's legislative hand.

We end Chapter 6 with a detailed discussion of President Carter's legislative skills in terms of the categories presented in Chapters 5 and 6. Carter has hardly been viewed as a master in dealing with Congress. The litany of criticisms includes lack of consultation with Congress and its leaders, lack of advance notice of pending actions, cutting pork barrel projects, unresponsiveness in patronage matters, unwillingness to bargain and compromise, sloppy drafting of legislation, poor timing in introducing proposals, personal effrontery, disregard for personal amenities, inconsistent policy stances and a weak professional reputation, lack of briefings, poor servicing of members' needs, ineffective congressional liaison operation, and general ineptness.

But there is another side to the story. Carter seems to have learned from his mistakes and to have sharpened his legislative skills. The White House organized impressive public relations campaigns on issues such as the Panama Canal treaties and the president's energy program. Moreover, members of Congress have been extensively briefed, and Carter has made numerous personal calls to legislators. At times he has shown more willingness to compromise, but at other times, as on cutting water projects from the budget in 1978, he has stood firm and had his veto sustained. The whole congressional liaison operation seems better organized and more responsive to the needs of Congress. The president has also obtained important support from Republicans in Congress.

The culmination of our discussion of presidential legislative skills occurs in Chapter 7. There we systematically evaluate the importance of these skills as a source of influence in Congress. We relate our description of presidents' legislative skills to the support that the presidents have received in Congress. To control for the fact that the party of the president strongly affects the support that he receives regardless of his skills, we compare only presidents of the same party. Moreover, we disaggregate presidential support by Northern Democrats, Southern Democrats, and Republicans so that we may compare the support of similar groups in Congress over time.

If groups within Congress give presidents with substantial legislative skills, such as Lyndon Johnson, more support than those who are less skilled, such as Jimmy Carter, we have support for the importance of these skills as a source of influence. However, if this does not occur, then we must remain skeptical of their significance despite the conventional wisdom that attributes so much to them.

Surprisingly, perhaps, our comparisons of presidents do not show any pattern by which we can relate legislative skills to presidential support in Congress. We try to find alternative explanations for this finding, but none succeed. Focusing on Johnson and Carter, we find that the latter faces a more aggressive, more decentralized, less deferential Congress in a period of economic instability and distrust of government, all of which serve to make his burden in influencing Congress greater than Johnson's, and not vice versa. We also view the innovativeness of the two presidents' programs but cannot conclude that Johnson's programs required more effective legislative skills to obtain support than did Carter's programs. Nor can differences in popularity account for the lack of differences in the support that the two presidents received.

As a final effort to challenge our finding of the lack of significance of presidential legislative skills, we examine Johnson's close victories. Possibly his skills most played a role in garnering the last few votes necessary to build a winning coalition. However, this hypothesis also fails. Johnson won few close votes, and those that he did win were generally not on major policies.

We conclude that while legislative skills may at times gain support for presidential policies, this is not typical. Thus, what seems to be the most manipulatable source of presidential influence is probably the least powerful.

In the epilogue we survey our results and examine the implications of our findings for presidential-congressional relationships. At this point, however, let us begin our in-depth examination of presidential influence in Congress and proceed carefully over the terrain outlined above.

Notes

1. The terms *power* and *influence* will be used interchangeably in this book.

2. Excellent examples of this orientation to the subject are two recent books by Louis Fisher: *The Constitution between Friends: Congress, the President, and the Law* (New York: St. Martins's, 1978), and *Presidential Spending Power* (Princeton, N.J.: Princeton University Press, 1975).

3. Stephen J. Wayne, *The Legislative Presidency* (New York: Harper & Row, 1978), is a fine example of this approach.

4. Richard E. Neustadt, *Presidential Power* (New York: Wiley, 1976), chap. 5.

5. Ibid., chap. 3.

6. Ibid., chap. 4.

Presidential Success in Congress

1

Before we focus on explaining presidential influence in Congress, let us take a broad view at the end results of that influence. This chapter examines the success of presidents in obtaining passage of their proposals, winning votes, having their vetoes sustained, and gaining confirmation of their appointees and ratification of the treaties they negotiate. In the process we shall see that the president often does not get his way and hence must exercise influence. We shall also learn how the relationship between the president and Congress has shifted over time and how some presidents have attempted to bypass Congress altogether. Finally, we shall discuss some of the constitutional powers that the president may exercise in dealing with Congress and the equally important constitutional constraints on the president.

Presidential Boxscore

One interesting and well-known indicator of presidential success in Congress was the Presidential Boxscore, calculated by the *Congressional Quarterly* up through 1975. It determined how many specific legislative requests made in presidential messages to Congress and in other public statements during the calendar year were ultimately enacted into law. Since most legislation is the result of compromise, *Congressional Quarterly* evaluated final bills to see whether they were generally in accord with presidential requests. Not included in the boxscore were measures advocated by executive officials but not by the president, measures endorsed but not specifically advocated by the president, nominations, suggestions that Congress consider particular topics if they did not require legislation, most legislation dealing with the internal affairs of the District of Columbia, and routine appropriations requests.

Table 1.1

Presidential Boxscore on Proposals Submitted to Congress

YEAR	NO. SUBMITTED	NO. APPROVED	% APPROVED
1953*	44	32	73
1954	232	150	65
1955	207	96	46
1956	225	103	46
1957	206	76	37
1958	234	110	47
1959	228	93	41
1960	183	56	31
1961	355	172	48
1962	298	132	44
1963	401	109	27
1964	217	125	58
1965	469	323	69
1966	371	207	56
1967	431	205	48
1968	414	231	56
1969	171	55	32
1970	210	97	46
1971	202	40	20
1972	116	51	44
1973	183	57	31
1974 (Nixon)	97	33	34
1974 (Ford)	64	23	36
1975	156	45	29

SOURCE: *Congressional Quarterly.*

*The 1953 figures are not comparable to those of later years.

Table 1.1 shows the Presidential Boxscore over a twenty-three-year period. The last column provides the most important information for our purposes. In most cases the percentage of presidential requests approved is below 50 percent. In 1963, 1971, and 1975 (under three different presidents) the boxscore was below 30 percent. In general, presidents had greater success when their party controlled Congress (which occurred in 1953–1954 and 1961–1968). Nevertheless, each president had many failures, and the scores vary considerably both within and between the terms of presidents.

The boxscore has a number of limitations: All requests are weighted equally; a request is counted as approved only if it passes in the same calendar year during which it was submitted (although most important legislation takes two or more years to pass after its introduction); no compensations are made for the facts that some presidents send complex legislation to Congress as one bill while others divide it into several parts and that some anticipate congressional opposition and therefore don't send some bills to the Hill; and no information is given about how individual members of Congress voted. Nevertheless, the boxscore alerts us to the very real problems that all presidents have in obtaining support for their policies in Congress.

Two Presidencies?

In 1966 Aaron Wildavsky published an article that has received a great deal of attention. He argued that since World War II, presidential-congressional relationships have been characterized by "two presidencies": one for domestic policy and the other for defense and foreign policy. In the latter areas presidents have had much more success in dealing with Congress. He argued that foreign and defense policy decisions, because they were perceived as important and irreversible, generally received higher priority from presidents, who thus devoted more effort to getting these policies approved. In addition, the secret nature of these issues limited opposition, as did the general lack of interest, weakness, division, and deference to the president of those who might oppose these policies.[1]

A decade later, however, things looked different. Less secrecy surrounded defense and foreign policy decisions, members of Congress became less deferential to the president, and more persons outside the executive branch were willing and able to challenge the president. The Vietnam war had sensitized Americans to defense and foreign policy and made them more reluctant to view our involvement in world affairs as being urgent or irreversible. At the same time, it had shattered whatever consensus might have existed within the United States on defense and foreign policy. Finally, defense and foreign policy issues were increasingly evaluated in terms of their domestic implications. Our relations with oil-producing nations, for example, could directly affect the price that Americans paid for petroleum, and the sale of wheat to the Soviet Union could raise the cost of many food products at home. Thus, the distinction between policy areas was becoming blurred.[2]

Lance LeLoup and Steve Shull compared Wildavsky's data (covering 1948 through 1964) with similar data for the years 1965 through 1975. Table 1.2 shows their results. As we can see, the difference between the approval rates for domestic policy initiatives and foreign and defense policy initiatives has narrowed considerably. While the approval rates are 70–40 in favor of defense and foreign policy in the earlier period, the comparable figures are 55–46 in the more recent period. Moreover, under the category of domestic policy, 50 percent of the social welfare proposals and 49 percent of the agricultural proposals were passed by Congress between 1953 and 1975. These figures are almost equal to the 55 percent figure for foreign and defense policy over the same time period.[3]

Table 1.2

Percentage of Presidential Proposals Approved by Congress by Policy Area

POLICY AREA	1948–1964	1965–1975
Domestic	40	46
Defense and Foreign	70	55
Defense	73	61
Foreign	59	50

SOURCE: Adapted from Lance T. LeLoup and Steven A. Shull, "Congress versus the Executive: The 'Two Presidencies' Reconsidered," *Social Science Quarterly* 59 (March 1979): 707.

Symptomatic of the new relationship between the president and Congress in defense and foreign policy was the passage of new laws constraining the president. The first law, the Case Act of 1972, dealt with executive agreements. An executive agreement is an agreement made by the president between the United States and another country or countries. Unlike a treaty, it does not necessarily require the consent of Congress (a treaty must receive the votes of two-thirds of the senators present to become law). However, executive agreements, unlike treaties, do not supersede statutes with which they conflict.[4] Otherwise, executive agreements are just as binding as treaties[5] and have been used for such famous compacts as the destroyers-bases deal with Great Britain in 1940, the Yalta and Potsdam agreements in 1945, and the Vietnam peace agreement of 1973.

Presidents have been very careful in their choice of instruments for making international agreements. In recent years treaties have dealt with subjects such as shrimp, the protection of Mexican archeological artifacts, dumping wastes at sea, and the maintenance of lights in the Red Sea; executive agreements have been used to end wars and to establish or expand military bases in other countries. In 1972, as a result of the SALT talks, President Nixon signed a treaty limiting the defensive weapons of the Soviet Union and the United States and an executive agreement limiting the offensive weapons of each country. (The agreement was submitted to Congress, but only because the 1961 law establishing the Arms Control and Disarmament Agency states that any agreement to limit U.S. armed forces or armaments must be approved by legislation or a treaty. Since legislation requires only a simple majority vote, the President opted for it rather than attempting to obtain a two-thirds vote in the Senate.) Thus, although most executive agreements are routine and deal with noncontroversial subjects such as food deliveries or customs enforcement, some implement important and controversial policies.[6]

The State Department has claimed that at least 95 percent of all executive agreements either are made under the authority of previous treaties and statutes or require congressional implementation. Only the remaining few percent are true executive agreements, negotiated by the president under his constitutional authority as commander in chief and as chief executive and representative of the nation in foreign affairs, duties that include receiving ambassadors and other public ministers and executing the laws. However, constitutional authority Louis Fisher has challenged all but the commander in chief rationale as being nebulous and without constraints. Moreover, he points out that administrations have entered into controversial agreements "on the basis of highly questionable interpretations of statutes and treaties." Also, although Congress can theoretically reject some executive agreements by not appropriating the required funds, it is reluctant to do so lest the president (and the United States) be embarrassed and humiliated; also, there may be moral commitments to uphold.[7]

To influence executive agreements, Congress needs to know about them before they are finalized, while options are still open. Even more important, it needs to know that the agreements even exist. In 1969 and 1970, the Senate Foreign Relations Committee discovered that presidents had covertly entered into a number of significant agreements with South Vietnam, South Korea, Thailand, Laos, Ethiopia, Spain, and other countries. In response to these actions Congress passed the Case Act in 1972, which requires the Secretary of State to transmit the text of any international agreement to which the United States is a party, other than treaties, within sixty days. If the president feels publication of an agreement would jeopardize national security, he may transmit the text only to members of the Senate Foreign Relations and House International Relations Committees under an injunction of secrecy that only he (or his successors) may remove.

Unfortunately, Presidents Nixon and Ford did not fully comply with the Case Act. Many agreements were never submitted to Congress and others were submitted after the sixty-day period. Consequently, in 1977 Congress passed legislation requiring any department or agency of the U.S. government that enters into any international agreement on behalf of the United States to transmit the text to the State Department within twenty days of its signing.[8] Neither of these two laws actually limits the president's power to act without Congress in defense and foreign affairs. Yet their passage indicates that Congress is increasingly unwilling to defer blindly to the president's judgment.

The War Powers Resolution of 1973 goes much further than these two laws, empowering Congress to *stop* the president from acting. The Constitution gives Congress the sole power to declare war, a power it has exercised only five times (in 1812, 1846, 1898, 1917, and 1941). Full-scale wars such as those in Korea and Vietnam were not officially declared by Congress. In addition, the president has employed a more limited use of force abroad without a declaration of war or statutory authority on about 200 occasions.[9] Recent instances include the orders of President Eisenhower to invade Lebanon in 1958,[10] of President Kennedy to blockade Cuba in 1962, of President Johnson to invade the Dominican Republic in 1965, of President Nixon to invade Cambodia in 1970, and of President Ford to attack Cambodia to rescue the crew of the *Mayaguez* (a U.S. merchant ship seized by Cambodia) in 1975.

The war in Vietnam, which stirred up deep dissent at home, was the last straw. In 1973 Congress passed the War Powers Resolution over President Nixon's veto. It requires that the president consult with Congress about plans for hostile actions and that he report to Congress within forty-eight hours after ordering U.S. armed forces into hostilities. More significantly, the military action must stop sixty days after the submission of the president's report unless Congress declares war, authorizes the use of force, extends the sixty-day period, or is unable to meet because of an attack upon the United States. At any time Congress can end the use of American armed forces by passing a concurrent resolution (which is not subject to a presidential veto). The president may extend the use of force for thirty additional days if he deems it necessary to protect departing American troops.

The law has aroused considerable debate about just what *consultation* means and whether the president could, in sixty days of hostilities, place the United States in a position from which Congress could not extract it. These and related issues were not resolved by the two applications of the War Powers Resolution since its passage: the evacuations from Southeast Asia in April 1975 and the rescue of the *Mayaguez* from Cambodia in May 1975. Both operations were brief and broadly supported.[11]

Presidential Victories on Votes

Much of the legislation that the president requests from Congress does not even come up for a vote. This, of course, reflects poorly upon the president's influence. However, we can examine the president's success in winning the votes that do occur. Table 1.3, which provides this information for the years from 1953 to 1978, paints a considerably rosier picture than does Table 1.1. Presidents win most of the votes on which they take a clear stand. By that time enough compromises have been made, enough legislators have been persuaded on a proposal's merits, and enough bargains have been struck for the president to obtain a majority vote.

Nevertheless, presidents do not always win. The average annual success rates of presidents from 1953 to 1978 (based on the second column of Table 1.3), shown in Table 1.4, indicate that presidents, especially Republican presidents (who faced Democratic Congresses except in 1953 and 1954), frequently lose votes on issues where they have taken a clear position. Table 1.3 shows considerable variability both within and between administrations. Thus, presidents cannot take for granted that issues on which they take a stand will go in their favor.

We should also note that the figures in Tables 1.3 and 1.4, like those in Table 1.1, tell us nothing about how individual members of Congress voted or why they voted as they did. Since our goal is to explain presidential influence in Congress and not simply to describe its ultimate success, we must consider more than aggregate statistics. But first let us examine three specific areas of presidential interaction with Congress.

Table 1.3

Presidential Victories on Congressional Votes on Which the President
Took a Clear Position

YEAR	CONGRESS		HOUSE		SENATE	
	NO. OF VOTES	% OF VOTES	NO. OF VOTES	% OF VOTES	NO. OF VOTES	% OF VOTES
1953	83	89	34	91	49	88
1954	115	78	38	79	77	78
1955	93	75	41	63	52	85
1956	99	70	34	74	65	68
1957	117	68	60	58	57	79
1958	112	76	50	74	98	76
1959	175	52	54	55	121	50
1960	129	65	43	65	86	65
1961	189	81	65	83	124	81
1962	185	85	60	85	125	86
1963	186	87	71	83	115	90
1964	149	88	52	88	97	88
1965	274	93	112	94	162	93
1966	228	79	103	91	125	69
1967	292	79	127	76	165	81
1968	267	75	103	83	164	69
1969	119	74	47	72	72	75
1970	156	77	65	85	91	71
1971	139	75	57	82	82	70
1972	83	66	37	81	46	54
1973	310	51	125	48	185	52
1974 (Nixon)	136	60	53	68	83	54
1974 (Ford)	122	58	54	59	68	57
1975	182	61	89	51	93	71
1976	104	54	51	43	53	64
1977	167	75	79	73	88	76
1978	263	78	112	70	151	85

SOURCE: *Congressional Quarterly.*

Veto

Congress passes bills for most legislative acts, but it sometimes uses joint resolutions for unusual legislative items. These have the same legal force as bills, and they must be presented to the president for his approval. Unlike these two forms of legislation, constitutional amendments are submitted directly to the states and cannot be vetoed by the president. This was established by the Supreme Court in *Hollingsworth* v. *Virginia* in 1798.[12] Congress also passes concurrent resolu-

Table 1.4

Average Annual Success Rate of Presidents on Congressional Votes

PRESIDENT	AVERAGE ANNUAL SUCCESS RATE (%)
Eisenhower	72
Kennedy	84
Johnson	83
Nixon	67
Ford	58
Carter*	77

*For years 1977 and 1978.

tions, which usually either deal with internal organization and procedures or congressional opinion and therefore do not require presidential response. Similarly, House resolutions and Senate resolutions do not require presidential action, because they usually concern matters principally of interest to the one chamber. Recently, however, Congress has increasingly relied upon concurrent and single-chamber resolutions to veto presidential actions ranging from deferred expenditures to carrying out military activities without a congressional declaration of war.

When Congress passes an item that must be submitted to the president, the president has several options. Within ten days (Sundays excepted) of its presentation,[13] the president may (1) sign the measure, in which case it becomes the law of the land,[14] (2) withhold his signature and return the measure to the house in which it originated with a message stating his reasons for withholding approval, or (3) do nothing.

When the president returns a bill or joint resolution to Congress, he has *vetoed* the measure. It can then become law only if each house of Congress repasses it by a two-thirds majority of those present.[15] Congress may override the presidential veto at any time before it adjourns *sine die*.

The president can veto only an entire bill. Unlike most state governors, he does not have an *item veto,* which allows just specific provisions of a bill to be vetoed. Naturally, as a result of this constraint, members of Congress use a number of strategies to avoid a possible veto of a particular proposal. For example, Congress may add increased appropriations or *riders* (i.e., nongermane provisions) that the president might not want, such as pork barrel projects, to bills that the president otherwise desires. Thus, he must accept these unattractive provisions in order to gain the legislation that he wants. In most such cases, the president does not use his veto.

Some presidents have achieved an item veto in effect by impounding (i.e., not spending) funds appropriated by Congress. Traditionally presidents have used this power discreetly, avoiding major conflicts with Congress. President Nixon's impoundments, however, were not so subtle. The amounts impounded were large, more impoundments were used, the tone of the impoundment messages (when they were issued) were more belligerent, and the impoundments were more clearly intended to alter congressional policy decisions substantially (at one point the president attempted to dismantle the Office of Economic Opportunity by this means). Although his rationales varied, he claimed, in effect, a right not to spend any funds that he had not requested from Congress, regardless of the intent of the law that Congress had passed.[16] Numerous cases regarding impoundments were taken to the courts, including two to the Supreme Court,[17] and the president lost almost all of them.[18]

Litigation, however, is an inefficient way to curb presidential power, since a single case often takes several years to be resolved. Therefore, in response to the excesses of the Nixon administration, Congress passed the Impoundment Control Act of 1974. To "rescind" (i.e., to not spend at all) any funds authorized by law, the president must have the approval of both houses of Congress through a bill or joint resolution passed within forty-five days of continuous session. In effect, Congress must pass a new appropriations bill. Otherwise, the president must spend the appropriated funds. The president may defer spending indefinitely unless either house passes a resolution of disapproval, in which case he must spend the funds as originally specified. Every impoundment, whether routine or controversial, must be reported to Congress.

President Ford continued to attempt impoundments, and the sheer number of his requests overwhelmed Congress, preventing careful consideration of each one. In his short term of office, he requested 330 deferrals and 150 rescissions.[19] This activity was not, however, necessarily to the president's advantage. While Congress was willing to approve rescissions involving little change in government policy, it was very reluctant to approve those involving major changes. Thus, Congress only accepted a small fraction of the requested rescissions. Deferrals are usually of a routine nature, and thus Congress accepted most of those requested by Ford (since the money would eventually be spent). Deferrals involving policy changes, however, had a difficult time gaining congressional assent.[20]

A second type of unofficial item veto occurs when a president signs a bill but states that he will disregard selected provisions or provides interpretations of key clauses. Both actions may significantly modify the bill. President Eisenhower stated that the sections of the 1959 Mutual Security Act dealing with the provision of documents to Congress would not alter the constitutional right of the president to keep secrets. He made a similar statement regarding the Availability of Information Act of 1958, leaving it ineffectual.[21] More dramatically, in 1971 President Nixon signed a bill containing a statement urging the president to set a date for U.S. withdrawal from military actions in Southeast Asia. He said that he would ignore that part of the act, regarding it "without binding force or effect." President Ford, concerned about the concept of the legislative veto, signed two bills in 1976, one dealing with defense appropriations and the other with veterans affairs, but declared that the legislative veto provision in each bill would be treated as a "nullity."[22] The legality of such presidential statements has never been established.

If the president does nothing after he receives a measure from Congress, it becomes law after ten days (Sundays excepted) if Congress remains in session. If it has adjourned during the ten-day period, thus preventing the president from returning the bill to the house of its origination, the bill is *pocket vetoed*. A pocket veto kills a piece of legislation just as a regular veto does.[23] Traditionally somewhat fewer than half of all vetoes have been pocket vetoes. Table 1.5 presents the data for recent presidents.

Presidents have sometimes attempted to use the pocket veto by taking no action on measures sent to them just before Congress went into a temporary recess, claiming that the recess prevented them from returning their veto for congressional consideration. (In 1964 President Johnson pocket vetoed a bill during a congressional recess and then recalled and signed it.) However, in 1974 the U.S. Court of Appeals in the District of Columbia upheld a lower court decision that President Nixon's pocket veto of the 1970 Family Practice of Medicine Act during a short Christmas recess in 1970 was unconstitutional,[24] and the bill became law.

This suit was brought by Senator Edward Kennedy, who also successfully challenged in court another Nixon pocket veto and a similar action by President Ford.[25] In April 1976 Ford's attorney general, Edward Levi, filed a statement in federal district court in Washington saying that the Ford administration would not challenge Kennedy's suit and that the president would not use the pocket veto during congressional recesses as long as an official of Congress was designated to be on hand to receive his vetoes. Thus, since Congress is in session nearly all year, only an adjournment *sine die* will provide the opportunity for a pocket veto.

The last column in Table 1.5 shows that vetoes are rarely used.[26] Not only are the absolute numbers low, but fewer than 1 percent of the bills passed by Congress (which number several hundred per session) are vetoed. The table also shows that presidents who faced Congresses controlled by the opposition party (Eisenhower, Nixon, and Ford) used more vetoes, as we would expect. They were more likely to be presented with legislation that they opposed.

Another important fact regarding vetoes is shown in Table 1.6. Regular vetoes are rarely overridden. Presidents Kennedy, Johnson, and Carter (as of this writing) never had any overridden, and only 3 percent of President Eisenhower's vetoes were not sustained. Twenty-one percent of Nixon's were overridden, which is still a very respectable record. Gerald Ford, sometimes considered an exception to the general pattern, had 75 percent of his regular vetoes sustained despite overwhelming Democratic majorities in both houses of Congress and the post-Watergate assertiveness of Congress.

Despite the low percentage of bills overridden, some very important legislation is passed over the president's veto. In the post–World War II era these include the Taft-Hartley Labor Relations Act (1947), the McCarran-Walter Im-

Table 1.5
Regular and Pocket Vetoes

PRESIDENT	NO. OF REGULAR VETOES	NO. OF POCKET VETOES	TOTAL VETOES
Eisenhower	73	108	181
Kennedy	12	9	21
Johnson	16	14	30
Nixon	24	19*	43
Ford	50	16	66
Carter†	6	13	19

SOURCE: U.S. Senate Library, *Presidential Vetoes, 1789–1976* (Washington, D.C.: Government Printing Office, 1978); "Carter's 19 Vetoes: Inflation Main Target," *Congressional Quarterly Weekly Report,* November 18, 1978.

* Includes two pocket vetoes that were later voided by federal courts.

† For years 1977 and 1978.

migration Act (1952), the McCarran-Wood Internal Security Act (1950), and the War Powers Resolution (1973). In recent years overridden bills have usually concerned appropriations for social welfare programs, with the Democratic Congress supporting higher levels than Republican presidents.

Congress has at times tried to make vetoing a bill difficult for the president when it knew that the veto would be sustained if exercised. In late 1975 both the House and Senate passed different versions of a bill creating a consumer protection agency. The leaders in both chambers knew that President Ford would veto any such bill, so they delayed calling a conference committee to iron out the differences. They felt that as the 1976 presidential election approached, Ford would not veto the bill lest he alienate the bill's supporters. However, he did not change his mind, and a conference committee was never called.[27]

Sometimes presidents choose not to veto a bill either because, as mentioned earlier, they feel the good in the legislation outweighs the bad or because they do not want their veto to be overridden. Thus, President Ford did not veto the 1975 food stamp legislation, which he opposed, because only forty-six members of the House and Senate had supported his own proposal.[28]

When a bill is introduced in either house of Congress, the chamber's parliamentarian classifies it as public or private. Generally, public bills relate to public matters and deal with individuals by classifications or categories, such as college students or the elderly. A private bill, on the other hand, names a particular individual or entity who is to receive relief, such as payment of a pension or a claim against the government or the granting of citizenship. We are usually far more interested in vetoes of public bills, which have broader consequences for society than do private bills.

Table 1.6
Vetoes Overridden

PRESIDENT	NO. OF REGULAR VETOES	NO. OF VETOES OVERRIDDEN	% VETOES OVERRIDDEN
Eisenhower	73	2	3
Kennedy	12	0	0
Johnson	16	0	0
Nixon	24	5	21
Ford	50	12	24
Carter*	19	0	0

SOURCE: U.S. Senate Library, *President Vetoes, 1789–1976* (Washington, D.C.: Government Printing Office, 1978); "Carter's 19 Vetoes: Inflation Main Target," *Congressional Quarterly Weekly Report,* November 18, 1978.

*For years 1977 and 1978.

Up until 1969 presidents usually vetoed more private than public bills. As Table 1.7 shows, most of the vetoes of Eisenhower, Kennedy, and Johnson were of private bills. Things changed, however, under Presidents Nixon and Ford, who vetoed public bills almost exclusively. All of President Carter's 1977 and 1978 vetoes were of public bills. Moreover, all vetoes overridden since 1953 have been of public bills.

The veto is an inherently negative element in the president's arsenal, but sometimes it may be used as a threat to shape legislation. For example, in late 1978 President Carter threatened to veto any bill that allowed tuition tax credits. As a result, Congress seems to have dropped such a provision, which had already passed the Senate.[29] Nevertheless, once exercised, a veto can only say no. At that point, the threat has failed and the chances of the president's legislative proposals passing in the forms that he desires are diminished. Moreover, the threat must be exercised with caution lest it be used too often and be too easily overcome. Thus, while a president's vetoes are normally successful in *stopping* legislation, they are less effective when used as threats to pass his own legislation, and they are utilized only in exceptional cases.

Nominations

The Constitution provides that "ambassadors, other public ministers and consuls, judges of the Supreme Court, and all other officers of the United States whose appointments are not . . . otherwise provided for, and which shall be established by law" shall be nominated by the president "by and with the advice and consent of the Senate." A majority vote of those senators present is required for confirmation. Congress may vest the president, department heads, and judges

Table 1.7

Vetoes of Public Bills

PRESIDENT	NO. OF PUBLIC BILLS VETOED	% OF ALL VETOES
Eisenhower	81	45
Kennedy	9	43
Johnson	13	43
Nixon	40*	93
Ford	61	92
Carter†	19	100

SOURCES: U.S. Senate Library, *Presidential Vetoes, 1789–1976* (Washington, D.C.: Government Printing Office, 1978); "Carter's 19 Vetoes: Inflation Main Target," *Congressional Quarterly Weekly Report,* November 18, 1978.

*Includes two pocket vetoes that were later voided by federal courts.

†For years 1977 and 1978.

with the power to appoint officials who do not require Senate confirmation. Most employees of the federal government obtain their positions in the latter manner.

The only position for which concurrence of the House is required is the office of the vice presidency when it is filled under the provisions of the Twenty-fifth Amendment. In this case a majority of those voting in both houses of Congress is needed to confirm the president's appointment. Only two men, Gerald Ford in 1973 and Nelson Rockefeller in 1974, have ever been appointed vice president, and both were confirmed.

Presidents Truman through Nixon presented over 1.4 million nominations to the Senate. More than 97 percent were confirmed, while 2.7 percent went unconfirmed and less than 0.3 percent were withdrawn. None of the presidents had fewer than 96 percent of their nominations confirmed. While this is a very impressive record, it should be noted that over 90 percent of the nominations were for officer positions in the armed services. In addition, postmasters and some lower-level rural postal officials required senatorial confirmation, making up about one-half of the civilian nominations up through 1969. Foreign Service officers and Public Health Service officials also required confirmation. Except for some postal officials who were involved in patronage politics, most of these military and civilian nominations received only perfunctory attention from senators.[30]

Of more interest are appointments to high-level positions. As Table 1.8 shows, even on appointments to the most important positions in the federal government, the president is rarely rejected. While three of twenty nominees (15 percent) to Supreme Court seats were rejected (Abe Fortas in 1968, Clement Haynsworth in 1969, and G. Harrold Carswell in 1970), no more than 2 percent of the nominations to other positions were rejected, and the figure was less than 1 percent for

Table 1.8

Senate Action on Major Presidential Nominations, 1945–1974

POSITION	NO. NOMINATED	NO. NOT CONFIRMED	% NOT CONFIRMED
Department head	107	1	0.9
Subcabinet official	1,024	1	0.1
Bureau head	322	4	1.2
Independent regulatory commissioner	468	10	2.1
Official of other independent agencies or Executive Office of the President	772	5	0.6
Ambassador	425	1	0.2
International organization representative	182	1	0.5
Major military post	64	0	0
Supreme Court justice	20	3	15.0
Court of Appeals judge	175	0	0
District and other federal courts judge	725	4	0.6

SOURCE: Donald G. Tannenbaum, "Senate Confirmation and Controversial Presidential Nominations: From Truman to Nixon," paper presented at the annual meeting of the American Political Science Association, San Francisco, September 2–5, 1975, p. 5.

most of these. Moreover, Abe Fortas remained on the bench as an associate justice; only his elevation to chief justice was denied by the Senate.

◆ Perhaps the most important reason why the president has been so successful in having his nominations confirmed is that the Senate has not taken its role in this procedure very seriously, at least not until recently. The burden of proof has generally fallen upon those who oppose a nomination. This has been especially true regarding military appointments and civilian appointments to positions in the executive branch and regarding all appointments when the president and Senate majority have been of the same party.

In recent years the Senate has been less passive in evaluating nominations. In 1976, for example, it failed to confirm President Ford's nominations to major positions such as director of the National Bureau of Standards, member of the Securities and Exchange Commission, member of the Consumer Product Safety Commission, assistant secretary of the Air Force, two members of the board of directors of the Tennessee Valley Authority, the president's personal representative on the political status of the Trust Territory of Micronesia, member of the Nuclear Regulatory Commission, chairperson of the Interstate Commerce Commission, comptroller of the Treasury, member of the Federal Power Commission, and two federal judges.[31]

Nevertheless, the Senate was embarrassed the following year when, a few months after confirming Bert Lance's nomination as director of the Office of Management and Budget, it discovered numerous instances of what many considered improprieties in his behavior. Lance resigned soon afterward, but not before the perfunctory nature of most Senate confirmation hearings had been exposed. In the words of Senate Governmental Affairs Committee chairperson Abraham Ribicoff, "There are no established standards to judge nominees; there is no regular, systematic inquiry by committee into the background and integrity of nominees, and the Senate is expected to act without having access to relevant investigative reports prepared on nominees by executive branch agencies." Senator Charles Percy, the ranking Republican on the committee, added, "In too many cases a 'rubber-stamp' endorsement follows perfunctory hearings."[32] These conclusions are supported by several Senate studies of the confirmation process done in recent years.[33]

A second reason why so few major nominations are challenged is that presidents are usually successful in anticipating or testing senatorial reaction to potential nominees. President Nixon never made a planned nomination of John Knowles to be assistant secretary of Health, Education and Welfare in 1969 because of strong opposition voiced by conservative senators and the American Medical Association before the official submission. Usually, however, presidents and their aides make more discreet soundings of both senators and affected interests.[34] Thus, the figures in Table 1.8 do not reflect this senatorial influence, nor do they indicate the number of potential nominees who refuse to be considered because of distaste or concern for the glare of publicity that might attend their confirmation hearings.

Presidents have the power to make recess appointments, in which the nominee begins functioning in his or her position before his or her name has been submitted to the Senate because it is in recess. He must submit the nomination when the Senate reconvenes, however, and the commission of office expires at the end of the next session of Congress if the nomination has not been approved or acted upon.

The Vacancies Act of 1868 and its subsequent amendments have limited the length of *ad interim* appointments made by the president to thirty days. In these appointments, the nominees take office when the Senate is in session but their names are not sent to the Senate for confirmation. These are frequently used for selecting presidential envoys dispatched on diplomatic missions. At various times presidents have extended this period, but, as in so many other instances, President Nixon stretched the rules to their breaking point. In 1973 he appointed Howard Phillips as acting director of the Office of Economic Opportunity, giving him orders to dismantle the agency, which was contrary to legislation passed by Congress. He never submitted Phillips' name to the Senate, and subsequently a federal court of appeals upheld a district court decision that the naming of an acting director for a period extending beyond thirty days was unconstitutional except where confirmation was not required by law or when the Senate was in recess.[35] Phillips had to leave his post.

Recess appointments to the Supreme Court have always been frowned upon by the Senate not only because of the importance of the Court's work but also because of the greater difficulty in questioning a sitting justice as compared with a nominee who has not taken part in a case and who therefore can speak more freely. No such appointments were made for about a century until President Eisenhower made three (Warren, Brennan, and Stewart). In 1960 the Senate adopted a resolution expressing its disapproval of this practice, which subsequent presidents have honored.

When a presidential nomination is not confirmed by the Senate, it is not necessarily voted down on the Senate floor. Nominations can be pigeonholed in committee or voted down in committee and thus never reach the floor. In 1977 the Environment and Public Works Committee voted to reject the nomination of Kent Hansen to the Nuclear Regulatory Commission, voting on the same day to postpone indefinitely the nomination of Marion Edey to the Council on Environmental Quality.[36] Nominations that reach the floor can be recommitted to committee or filibustered, as was the nomination of Abe Fortas to be chief justice.

Nominations may also be withdrawn. Sometimes this occurs after one of the actions cited above has taken place. In 1977 President Carter withdrew the nomination of Donald Tucker to the Civil Aeronautics Board after the Commerce, Science, and Transportation Committee postponed hearings on it indefinitely.[37] On other occasions the ongoing hearings indicate that the nomination will fail or will be confirmed only at considerable political cost, causing embarrassment to the administration and to the affected agency or branch. For these reasons President Nixon withdrew the nomination of L. Patrick Gray to head the FBI and President Carter withdrew the nomination of Theodore Sorensen to head the CIA.

Congress can take other action to limit the president's appointive power. It can mandate fixed terms for officials, an action that both provides an opportunity to review an incumbent's performance and, if the terms are long enough, even denies the president a chance to appoint an official. Two examples are the members of the Federal Reserve Board, who serve fourteen-year terms, and the comptroller general, who serves a fifteen-year term. With their considerably shorter tenures in office, presidents may never appoint a comptroller general or a majority of the Federal Reserve Board. Appointees to many other positions, both civilian and military, serve for fixed periods of time, although for shorter periods than the examples above.

Yet other requirements sometimes limit the president's choice on these appointments. He cannot appoint commissioned officers of the armed services as both the director and deputy director of the CIA. Most regulatory commissions have limits on the percentage of members affiliated with a political party. At least one member of the Railroad Retirement Board must be appointed from a list of people recommended by railroad employees. The special assistant to the secretary of Health, Education and Welfare must be a recognized leader in some medical field.

➤ In addition to the offices that the Constitution requires to be confirmed by the Senate, the Congress can require that the nominees to other offices also be so confirmed. This power to influence the personnel occupying federal positions has most typically been exercised when Congress creates new units of government. At times, however, Congress has enacted laws requiring Senate confirmation of appointees previously chosen entirely at the discretion of the president. In 1973 Congress passed a law requiring confirmation for future directors and deputy directors of the Office of Management and Budget, part of the Executive Office of the President. That same year another law was passed requiring Senate confirmation of newly appointed executive directors of the Council on International Economic Policy. Other such officials include the director of the Federal Bureau of Investigation (1968) and the director of the Office of Procurement within the Office of Management and Budget (1972).

Occasionally Congress eliminates the need for Senate confirmation. In 1965 it accepted a reorganization plan presented by President Johnson that placed the Customs Bureau under civil service regulations. Previously customs collectors and some other customs officials were appointed by the president, generally on the recommendation of his party's senators from the state in which the officials would work. As noted earlier, similar action was taken regarding the Post Office in 1970.

➤ Nonstatutory requirements can also be imposed by the Senate. When Elliot Richardson was nominated as attorney general in 1973, the hearings of the Senate Judiciary Committee elicited clear pledges from the nominee regarding the independence of the Watergate special prosecutor. He took these seriously enough to resign from office when President Nixon ordered him to fire Archibald Cox, the special prosecutor. Richardson's successor, William Saxbe, agreed to even more specific commitments regarding the special prosecutor.

➤ The Armed Services Committee will not confirm anyone for a Pentagon position who owns stock in any corporation other than regulated utilities if the corporation does more than $10,000 a year in business with the Department of Defense. Beginning in 1973, in response to a resolution passed by the Democratic caucus, nominees have been required as a precondition of confirmation to promise to appear and testify before any Senate committee so requesting.

The most important nonstatutory requirement regarding nominees is termed "senatorial courtesy." Senatorial courtesy is the customary manner in which the Senate disposes of state-level federal nominations for such positions as judgeships and U.S. attorneys and marshalls. Under this unwritten tradition, nominations for these positions are not confirmed when opposed by a senator from the affected state if the senator is of the same party as the president. To invoke the right of senatorial courtesy, the relevant senator usually declares the nominee to be "personally obnoxious" or offensive. Other senators then honor their colleague's views and oppose the nomination, regardless of their personal views or the candidate's merits.[38]

The first instance of senatorial courtesy occurred in 1789, when President George Washington failed to have Benjamin Fishbourn confirmed as naval officer of the port of Savannah because of the opposition of Georgia's two senators. Since that time senatorial courtesy has become more and more established. By 1840 senators were virtually naming federal district court judges.[39] In addition, some nominees to national office has been blackballed by a senator from the nominee's home state, and at times senatorial courtesy has been successfully invoked by a senator not of the president's party. Also, on a few occasions, the Senate has failed to observe senatorial courtesy.

Because of the strength of senatorial courtesy, presidents usually check with the relevant senator or senators ahead of time so they won't make a nomination that will fail to be confirmed. In many instances this is tantamount to giving the power of nomination to these senators.[40]

When a president fails to heed the power of senatorial courtesy, the results can be embarrassing. On April 1, 1976, President Ford nominated William B. Poff to a federal judgeship in Virginia. Virginia's Republican senator, William Scott, had previously given notice of his opposition to Poff and of his support for another candidate, Glenn Williams. It is important to note that Scott himself agreed that Poff was qualified for the position. He just felt Williams's philosophy was closer to his own. Thus, on April 15 Scott formally announced his opposition to Poff's nomination in a letter to the Senate Judiciary Committee, simply terming Poff "unacceptable." On May 5 the committee chairperson, Senator James Eastland, moved to table the nomination, and it was tabled without objection.[41]

Treaties

Although mentioned earlier in the discussion of executive agreements, treaties deserve a brief separate discussion here. Historically, the Senate has approved without modification about 70 percent of the approximately 1,600 treaties that have been submitted to it by the president since 1789. Only 16 of those that have come to a vote have been voted down (the most famous probably being the Treaty of Versailles ending World War I and establishing the League of Nations). However, many other proposed treaties have been withdrawn by the president because of opposition in the Senate and thus have never come up for a vote. Nearly 150 treaties have been withdrawn since World War II.[42]

Not only can the Senate ratify treaties without modification or reject them outright, but it can also ratify them with reservations (clarifying or qualifying interpretations) or with amendments (suggested changes or deletions). In early 1978 the Senate ratified two treaties dealing with the Panama Canal. It added a reservation to one of them stating that the United States had a right to use military force, if necessary, to keep the canal open.

Once an addition has been made to a treaty, both the president and the other country or countries who are parties to the treaty must accept it. Such acceptance does not always happen, and many treaties have failed for this reason.[43]

Conclusion

In this chapter we have seen that the president often—but not always—gets his way with Congress. Thus, he must influence Congress to support his policies. In the next chapter we shall examine some of the reasons for conflict between the president and Congress and how we can study presidential influence in Congress.

Notes

1. Aaron Wildavsky, "The Two Presidencies," *Trans-Action* 4 (December 1966): 7–14.

2. For a good example of the revisionist view, see Donald A. Peppers, " 'The Two Presidencies': Eight Years Later," in *Perspectives on the Presidency*, ed. Aaron Wildavsky (Boston: Little, Brown, 1975).

3. Lance T. LeLoup and Steven A. Shull, "Congress versus the Executive: The 'Two Presidencies' Reconsidered," *Social Science Quarterly* 59 (March 1979): 712.

4. *United States* v. *Schooner Peggy*, 5 U.S. (1 Cr.) 103 (1801).

5. See *Altman* v. *United States*, 224 U.S. 583 (1912); *United States* v. *Belmont*, 301 U.S. 324 (1937); *United States* v. *Pink*, 315 U.S. 203 (1942). Executive agreements may not violate the U.S. Constitution. See *United States* v. *Guy W. Capps, Inc.*, 204 F.2d 655 (4th Cir. 1953); *Seery* v. *United States*, 127 F. Supp. 601 (Ct. Cl. 1955); and *Reid* v. *Covert*, 354 U.S. 1 (1957). All these cases are discussed in Louis Fisher, *The Constitution between Friends: Congress, the President, and the Law* (New York: St. Martin's, 1978), pp. 205–208.

6. For more on this point, see Loch Johnson and James M. McCormick, "The Democratic Control of International Commitments," *Presidential Studies Quarterly* 8 (Summer 1978): 275–283; Loch Johnson and James M. McCormick, "Foreign Policy by Executive Fiat," *Foreign Policy* 28 (Fall 1977): 117–138.

7. Fisher, *The Constitution between Friends*, pp. 205, 211–213.

8. Ibid., pp. 208–209.

9. For discussions of these and related matters, see "Congress, the President, and the Power to Commit Forces to Combat," *Harvard Law Review* 81 (June 1968): 1771–1805; Jacob K. Javits, *Who Makes War: The President versus Congress* (New York: Morrow, 1973); Arthur M. Schlesinger, Jr., *The Imperial Presidency* (New York: Popular Library, 1974); Raoul Berger, *Executive Privilege: A Constitutional Myth* (Cambridge, Mass.: Harvard University Press, 1974), chap. 4; Francis Wormuth, "The Vietnam War: The President versus the Constitution," in *The Vietnam War and International Law*, vol. 2, ed. Richard A. Falk (Princeton, N.J.: Princeton University Press, 1969); Clinton Rossiter, *The Supreme Court and the Commander in Chief*, expanded ed. (Ithaca, N.Y.:

Cornell University Press, 1976); Louis Henkin, *Foreign Affairs and the Constitution* (Mineola, N.Y.: Foundation Press, 1972), chaps. 2–4; W. Taylor Reveley III, "The Power to Make War," in The Constitution and the Conduct of Foreign Policy, ed. Francis O. Wilcox and Richard A. Frank (New York: Praeger, 1976); W. Taylor Reveley III, "Presidential War-Making: Constitutional Prerogative or Usurpation?" *Virginia Law Review* 55 (December 1969): 1243–1305.

10. Congress passed a resolution prior to the invasion of Lebanon, but Eisenhower claimed to be acting under his inherent power as president. See Dwight D. Eisenhower, "Special Message to the Congress on the Sending of United States Forces to Lebanon," *Public Papers of the Presidents: Dwight D. Eisenhower, 1958* (Washington, D.C.: Government Printing Office, 1959), pp. 171–173.

11. For discussions of these instances and the War Powers Resolution in general, see Fisher, *Constitution between Friends,* pp. 232–241; Gerald L. Jenkins, "The War Powers Resolution: Statutory Limitations on the Commander in Chief," *Harvard Journal of Legislation* 11 (February 1974): 181–204; Harvey G. Zeidenstein and Hibbert R. Roberts, "The War Powers Resolution, Institutionalized Checks and Balances, and Public Policy," paper presented at the annual meeting of the Southern Political Science Association, Nashville, November 8, 1975; Reveley, "The Power to Make War."

12. 3 Dall. 378 (1798).

13. Congress often refrains from sending legislation to the president immediately after it has passed to give the president time to consider it. Giving the president time is difficult if, for example, he is out of the country when the law is passed.

14. The president may sign a bill after Congress has recessed, *La Abra Silver Mining Co.* v. *United States,* 175 U.S. 423 (1899), or after Congress has adjourned, *Edwards* v. *United States,* 286 U.S. 482 (1932).

15. *Missouri Pacific Railway Co.* v. *United States,* 248 U.S. 277 (1919).

16. See Louis Fisher, *Presidential Spending Power* (Princeton, N.J.: Princeton University Press, 1975), chaps. 7–8, for an historical discussion of the use of impoundments, with emphasis on the Nixon years.

17. *Train* v. *City of New York et al.,* 420 U.S. 35 (1975); *Train* v. *Campaign Clean Water, Inc.,* 420 U.S. 136 (1975).

18. For good discussions of this litigation, see James P. Pfiffner, "Impoundment and the Courts: The Judiciary Enters the Budgetary Process," paper presented at the annual meeting of the Midwest Political Science Association, Chicago, May 1–3, 1975; Louis Fisher, *Court Cases on Impoundment of Funds,* Congressional Research Service, Library of Congress, 74–61 GGR, March 15, 1974.

19. Fisher, *Constitution between Friends,* p. 182.

20. Allen Schick, *The Impoundment Control Act of 1974: Legislative History and Implementation,* Congressional Research Service, Library of Congress, 76–45 S, February 27, 1976.

21. Joseph E. Kallenbach, *The American Chief Executive: The Presidency and the Governorship* (New York: Harper & Row, 1966), pp. 358–359.

22. Fisher, *Constitution between Friends,* pp. 92–93.

23. See, for example, *The Pocket Veto Case,* 279 U.S. 644 (1929).

24. Fisher, *Constitution between Friends,* pp. 96–97. Both houses recessed on December 22, and the Senate returned on December 28 and the House on December 29. The case was *Kennedy* v. *Sampson,* 364 F. Supp. 1075 (D.D.C. 1973) and 511 F.2d 430 (D.C.

Cir. 1974). This decision followed from the case of *Wright* v. *United States,* 302 U.S. 583 (1938), which held that the veto procedure served two fundamental purposes: (1) to give the president an opportunity to consider a bill presented to him and (2) to give Congress an opportunity to consider his objections and override them. Both objectives require protection, which is not provided if the concept of a pocket veto expands indefinitely.

25. *Kennedy* v. *Jones,* Civil Action No. 74–194 (D.D.C.).

26. For an interesting study of the use of vetoes, see Jong R. Lee,"Presidential Vetoes from Washington to Nixon," *Journal of Politics* 37 (May 1975): 522–547.

27. "Consumer Agency in Limbo," *Congressional Quarterly Weekly Report,* February 14, 1976, p. 330; "Consumer Agency Bill," *Congressional Quarterly Weekly Report,* September 18, 1976, p. 2578.

28. "Congressional Finale: Conflict and Compromise," *Congressional Quarterly Weekly Report,* December 27, 1975, p. 2856.

29. "Congress Approves $18.7 Billion Tax Cut," *Congressional Quarterly Weekly Report,* October 21, 1978, p. 3027.

30. Donald G. Tannenbaum, "Senate Confirmation and Controversial Presidential Nominations: From Truman to Nixon," paper presented at the annual meeting of the American Political Science Association, San Francisco, September 2–5, 1975, pp. 2–4.

31. "Major Nominations in Second Session," *Congressional Quarterly Weekly Report,* October 9, 1976, p. 2894.

32. Richard L. Madden, "Senate Re-examining Confirmation Power," *New York Times,* September 14, 1977, sec. 1, p. 31.

33. See U.S., Congress, Senate, Committee on the Operation of the Senate, *Committee and Senate Procedures,* Committee Print (Washington, D.C.: Government Printing Office, 1977); U.S., Congress, Senate, Committee on Commerce, *Appointments to the Regulatory Agencies: The Federal Communications Commission and the Federal Trade Commission (1949–1974),* Committee Print (Washington, D.C.: Government Printing Office, 1976); U.S., Congress, Senate, Committee on Government Operations, *Study of Federal Regulation,* vol. 1, *The Regulatory Appointments Process,* Committee Print (Washington, D.C.: Government Printing Office, 1977); U.S., Congress, Senate, Committee on Foreign Relations, *The Senate Role in Foreign Affairs Appointments,* Committee Print (Washington, D.C.: Government Printing Office, 1971); U.S., Congress, Senate, Committee on the Judiciary, *Advice and Consent to Supreme Court Nominations, Hearings,* Committee Print (Washington, D.C.: Government Printing Office, 1976); U.S., Congress, Senate, Temporary Select Committee to Study the Senate Committee System, *Appendix to the Second Report with Recommendations, Operation of the Senate Committee System: Staffing, Scheduling, Communications, Procedures, and Special Functions,* Senate Report (Washington, D.C.: Government Printing Office, 1977). See also Harriet F. Berger, "Appointment and Confirmation to the National Labor Relations Board: Democratic Constraints on Presidential Power?" *Presidential Studies Quarterly* 8 (Fall 1978): 403–416.

34. See U.S., Congress, Senate, Committee on Commerce, *Appointments to the Regulatory Agencies;* Joel B. Grossmen, *Lawyers and Judges: The ABA and the Politics of Judicial Selection* (New York: Wiley, 1965); Harold W. Chase, *Federal Judges: The Appointing Process* (Minneapolis: University of Minnesota Press, 1972).

35. Ronald C. Moe, "Senate Confirmation of Executive Appointments: The Nixon Era," in *Congress against the President,* ed. Harvey C. Mansfield, Sr. (New York:

Praeger, 1975), pp. 147–148; Fisher, *Constitution between Friends,* pp. 116–117.

36. "Nominations Rejected," *Congressional Quarterly Weekly Report,* October 23, 1977, p. 2239.

37. "Controversial Carter Choice for CAB Post Withdraws," *Congressional Quarterly Weekly Report,* October 8, 1977, p. 2145.

38. For a useful general discussion of senatorial courtesy, see "Ford Judgeship Nomination Derailed," in *Current Guide to American Government, Fall 1976* (Washington, D.C.: Congressional Quarterly, 1976), pp. 91–92.

39. *Powers of Congress* (Washington, D.C.: Congressional Quarterly, 1976), p. 205.

40. See "Ford Judgeship Nomination Derailed."

41. Ibid., p. 92.

42. "Ratification of Panama Canal Agreement . . . Toughest Treaty Fight since Versailles," *Congressional Quarterly Weekly Report,* February 14, 1978, p. 54.

43. Ibid.

Conflict and Influence | 2

In Chapter 1 we described presidential success in obtaining congressional support for the president's programs. In this chapter we shall begin the more important task of explaining this support. We shall first examine sources of conflict between the president and Congress in order to understand why the president needs to influence Congress. We shall then move on to the question of studying presidential influence and present the approach to be taken in the remaining chapters of the book.

Sources of Conflict

The president must influence Congress because he generally cannot act without its consent. Under our constitutional system of separation of powers, Congress must pass legislation and can override vetoes. The Senate must ratify treaties and confirm presidential appointments to the cabinet, the federal courts and regulatory commissions, and other high offices. Yet these facts do not explain the president's need to influence Congress. Theoretically, the two branches could be in agreement.

Likewise, the president and some members of Congress will always disagree because of their personalities or past histories. Yet these differences are not the source of systematic conflict, which lies in the structure and processes of American politics.

Different Constituencies

In "The Federalist No. 46," James Madison wrote, "The members of the federal legislature will likely attach themselves too much to local objects. . . . Measures will too often be decided according to their probable effect, not on the national prosperity and happiness, but on the prejudices, interests, and pursuits of the governments and the people of the individual states."[1] Thus, he focused on the greatest source of conflict between the president and Congress: their different constituencies.

Only the president (and his vice presidential running mate) is elected by the entire nation. Each member of Congress is elected by only a fraction of the populace. Inevitably, the president must form a broader electoral coalition in order to win his office than any member of Congress. Moreover, two-thirds of the senators are not elected at the same time as the president, and the remaining senators and all the House members seem to be increasingly insulated from the causes of presidential victories.[2] In addition, the Senate overrepresents rural states because each state has two senators regardless of its population.[3] Thus, the whole that the president represents is different from the sum of the parts that each legislator represents. Each member of Congress will give special access to the interests that he or she represents. The desires of these interests will receive special consideration, while opposing views will be unlikely to be taken seriously, if they are considered at all.[4]

Let us illustrate the consequences of these different constituencies by looking at the different reactions of the president and Congress to various policies. We shall also look at their behavior at different stages of policymaking.

Predicting policy consequences. One of the principal intellectual tasks in policymaking is to analyze the consequences of alternatives, which requires making predictions about each alternative. Congressional responsiveness to narrow segments of public opinion has influenced these predictions, often to the detriment of public policy.

Congress has recently tried to impose its views on the president in the area of foreign policy more aggressively than it has in the past. In 1974 the Senate attempted to influence the Soviet Union to liberalize its restrictions on the emigration of Jews and other Soviet citizens by making this a condition for international trade benefits. In that same year, Congress cut off aid to Turkey in an attempt to reduce that country's aggressiveness toward Greece and the Greek population on Cyprus. Both tactics were consistent with the desires of outspoken groups in the United States but contrary to the wishes of the president. Also, neither attempt seemed to accomplish its purpose. The Soviet Union and Turkey did not respond as Congress had predicted. The expected consequences of these actions reflected more the desires of a segment of the public than rational policy analysis.

Congressional resposiveness to a few limited interests has also spread resources for some policies too thinly. The Area Redevelopment Administration (ARA) was originally envisioned as a program of business loans to forty or fifty primarily urban labor markets. But the program's resources were widely dispersed when, after only eight months of operation, 900 counties containing one-sixth of the country's population had been deemed eligible for aid. A similar problem occurred with the ARA's successor, the Economic Development Administration.[5]

One way to predict policy consequences is to carry out policy experiments. Once again, with only a very few exceptions, the responsiveness of Congress to certain groups has hindered good policy analysis. The designers of the Headstart preschool programs sought to provide disadvantaged children with early education so that they could compete more effectively when they entered regular schools. The original plan was to involve relatively few children in a year-long program, but pressure to involve more children became so intense that the limited funds permitted only shorter programs. As a result, the original policy was not tested.[6]

A similar problem occurred with the Model Cities program, which was originally conceived as an experiment to concentrate funds on one central city to see if it could be rebuilt and rejuvenated. But many cities wanted to be models, and President Johnson did not feel Congress would pass a bill that would only aid one or a few cities. By the time the bill left the executive branch, it included provisions for sixty-six cities. Unsatisfied, Congress increased the number to 150 in the first year and to over 250 by the second. The available funds were spread so thinly that judging the program as it was originally intended was impossible.[7]

Responsiveness to narrow segments of public opinion hinders policy experimentation in more general ways. People may oppose policy if its benefits are distributed by chance. But this randomness is necessary if policymakers are to base their decisions on an experiment in which a sample of the target population that receives aid is compared in the target population with those who do not. Concern for only a segment of public opinion also inhibits the use of long-term experiments. Several years may elapse between a program's conception and the analysis of its results, but the time perspectives of most members of Congress regarding the distribution of new benefits are in months (they are even shorter if the benefits are seen as burdening any specific group). This encourages broad legislative action in the short run, not cautious policy experimentation.

Benefits and costs.   After predicting policy consequences, decision makers need to evaluate their benefits and costs. But few members of Congress are interested in cost-benefit evaluation because it is technical and time-consuming and offers few political payoffs. Since the public provides few incentives for close attention to policy evaluation, Congress does little to enhance its capabilities in this area. Even the new Congressional Budget Office lacks the staff to evaluate specific policies in depth.[8]

Indeed, the study of important issues does not have a high priority in Congress. The principal reason for this is, once again, responsiveness to vested interests. Efforts to please constituents through casework, private bills, tax loopholes, local projects, and local politicking take up most of a representative's time. As David Mayhew argues, members of Congress spend their days advertising, position taking, and credit claiming. They consequently spend less time on committee work and mobilizing their colleagues on votes because these activities have little interest to the public and therefore offer few political advantages.[9]

Some members of Congress ease the burdens of policymaking by making responsiveness to narrow interests a firm decision rule. Richard Fenno reports that the House Interior Committee passes all member-sponsored, constituency-supported bills, and the House Post Office and Civil Service Committee supports the maximum possible pay increases and improvements in employee benefits and opposes rate increases for mail users.[10]

Sometimes the decision rule may be less clear, but the results are the same. Members of Congress publicly refuse to support the closing of expensive, little-used post offices in their constituencies even though they privately acknowledge that their existence is poor policy and keeps the postage costs for their constituents high.[11] While one might argue that post offices also serve a social welfare function by providing a meeting place in rural areas, no serious analysis uses this argument. Opposition to closing these post offices is based on pleasing constituents.

Similarly, members of Congress support pork barrel projects with high cost-benefit ratios in order to please constituents, especially contractors, unions, and merchants, and thus enhance their reelection possibilities. Reelection platforms are commonly based on a variant of "Congressman _____ Delivers!"[12] While these projects can also be viewed from a social welfare perspective, they do not seem to further social goals and their primary beneficiaries tend to be the well-off. Of course, not everyone in Congress gains from each project. But the concentrated benefits and dispersed costs provide significant incentives for supporting these projects (just as logrolling provides incentives for members to support each other's projects) and little incentive to oppose them.[13]

Because of its large expenditures in particular congressional districts, defense policy is especially susceptible to decision making that pays little heed to benefits and costs. As one candid congressman with a military contractor in his district put it, "I like to build lots of those nuclear subs."[14] In 1976 the *Congressional Quarterly* reported that the Defense Department had announced 2,764 base closings, reductions, or realignments in the United States and Puerto Rico since 1969. The federal payroll would have been reduced by over one-half million employees if these changes had been instituted. To avoid problems with Congress, the department has tried to keep these decisions secret until the last minute and to avoid announcements at election time when members of Congress are especially vulnerable to constituency pressure. These strategies, however, often fail to prevent Congress from torpedoing these plans, and the Pentagon has had so many decisions overturned that it has stopped keeping track.[15]

Other examples of congressional responsiveness to constituency interests rather than to a cost-benefit analysis for the country as a whole include continued aid to federally impacted school districts long after the dislocations of the federal impact have ended (much of this aid goes to wealthy school districts), support for building hospitals despite a surplus of hospital beds, using grants-in-aid to build sewer and water facilities in a wide range of localities despite the original intent to use them to help suburban areas control growth,[16] and appropriations for western recreational areas although people are concentrated in the East (senators are concentrated in the West).

In September 1977 the National Railroad Passenger Corporation (Amtrak), a quasi-governmental corporation, requested an appropriations supplement of $18 million from Congress, warning that it would have to cut service if it did not receive the funds. However, the House members of the congressional conference committee handling the bill agreed only to an additional $8 million. Therefore, in November Amtrak sent a letter to all members of Congress outlining its financial position, listing ten routes that might be eliminated on the basis of congressionally mandated criteria. Five days later its board voted to suspend the Floridian (Chicago-Miami train) and to move into the final phase of studying whether to drop or consolidate five western routes. These actions, naming specific routes, were quickly followed by congressional action to provide the funds that Amtrak requested, with House delegations from the states served by the Floridian providing strong support. In addition, the conferees removed from their conference report language implying that Congress would not continue to bail Amtrak out of its financial problems and language urging the corporation to use congressionally mandated criteria for establishing the desirability of routes. Later that day Amtrak announced that it was not suspending any routes for the time being.[17]

This concern for narrow constituency interests was perhaps displayed most blatantly by Senate Finance Committee chairperson Russell Long. He told Deputy Treasury Secretary Robert Carswell "most of these senators will vote for or against a formula by just looking at how their state makes out . . . how much money they do or do not get. . . . All you have to do is show a senator a sheet of paper, here is how your state makes out under this formula." On the same bill Senator Edmund Muskie told a reporter, "If you spread the money around broadly enough, you can buy just about any vote."[18]

When Congress does attempt to use cost-benefit analysis, it frequently distorts it. It has mandated, for example, that benefits must exceed costs for water projects. Yet, to help insure that certain projects are funded, it supports, against the president's wishes, the projects' sponsoring agencies (such as the Army Corps of Engineers or the Bureau of Reclamation), which overestimate benefits and underestimate costs.[19] In 1974 Congress agreed to increase the "discount rate" by which future benefits are estimated (thus decreasing their estimates), but it exempted all current projects from the increase.

President Carter's first real battle with Congress in 1977 was over the water projects. He wanted to end several projects for which he felt the costs exceeded the benefits. After a substantial battle, a compromise was reached in which he got about half of what he wanted. The following January Secretary of Interior

Cecil Andrus told a press conference, "If you think I'm going to walk up to the Hill with another hit list and go through the agony and heartburn I went through last year, I can only say, 'I'm not stupid.'"[20]

It is not only in dealing with particularized benefits for their constituencies that members of Congress are responsive to parochial public opinion and may ignore or give little attention to policy consequences for the general welfare. Congress has also passed legislation to increase the minimum wage in response to the demands of organized labor, despite considerable evidence that this policy would have detrimental consequences for those whom it was ostensibly designed to aid.[21]

A 1976 Senate Commerce Committee report on appointments to the FCC and FTC found that persons with experience in or strong opinions about the relevant regulated industry are unlikely to be appointed because of the opposition of some groups in the public.[22] Therefore, those ultimately appointed are less effective regulators. Presidential executive reorganization proposals are regularly vetoed by Congress in response to the demands of organized interests. Lyndon Johnson wrote that in 1966 many members of Congress told him that they understood the need for a tax increase to fight the inflation that would result from spending on the war in Vietnam and on Great Society programs, yet they would not vote for one because of fears of constituency reactions.[23]

Implementation. After legislation becomes law, policymaking is not over for Congress, or at least it should not be. Congress has a clear responsibility for overseeing the implementation of these laws. Yet members of Congress have little interest in what the public cares or knows little about (such as administrative procedures). The incentives for overseeing are weak because overseeing usually holds little promise of political visibility for the members of Congress, and local interests or the bureaucracy that provides constituents with services may be irritated by this overseeing.[24]

The area in which Congress does become involved in implementation is, as we would expect, the area of particularized benefits ("casework") and not of broad policy questions. (The desire to provide casework benefits may also provide incentive to keep the bureaucracy decentralized, a policy that is contrary to the president's wishes. Decentralization makes intervention in the bureaucracy easier.) On occasion, Congress hinders the implementation of policies. Federal agencies are frequently reluctant to withhold funds from state and local governments that fail to follow policy guidelines because they fear irritating members of Congress who represent the affected locations.[25]

Insulation for the public interest. Members of Congress are aware that, given the chance, their colleagues will appeal to their constituents with policies that would work against the common good. Therefore, Congress has made some attempts to limit responsiveness to narrow segments of public opinion. For instance, Congress has removed itself from making specific tariff decisions in order to avoid making policies that historically have had disastrous consequences for the American economy. Many other decisions, particularly those of a regulatory nature, are made by persons in less visible parts of the government system, such as executive agencies and regulatory commissions.

Members of the House taxing and spending committees are chosen in part for their relative insulation from public opinion. Once bills reach the floor, the Ways and Means Committee likes to function under closed rules (which do not allow amendments), and the Appropriations Committee provides as little time as possible for representatives to study spending bills before voting on them. Congress has also established separate committees to consider authorizations and appropriations. At least in the House, the Appropriations Committee is expected to cut authorizations and "guard the Treasury" against the ravages of the more constituency-oriented authorization committees, in which committee assignments reinforce the power of particular interests. [26]

Even in appropriations committees, however, public opinion often reigns. Fenno reports that bureaus with specific constituency support do better in appropriations decisions than do others, and that the Senate is more generous in its spending decisions than the House because the former is subject to more constituency pressure. [27] Likewise, Ferejohn found that the public works budget received fewer cuts after the Public Works Subcommittee of the House Appropriations Committee was manned by members with constituency interests in the projects. [28] Thus, when vague demands for budgetary responsibility clash with specific demands for expenditures, the latter seem to win.

Potential of reforms.   In recent years reformers have advocated that Congress be "opened up" and made responsive to a broader range of public opinion. They have proposed decentralizing committee power by ending the seniority system and forming subcommittees for each committee. They have also proposed to decrease the secrecy of deliberations by opening committee meetings to the public and by increasing public voting in committees and on the floor.

Unquestionably, public participation in American politics is extremely low and no contrary trend is in sight. A recent Harris Poll found that only 33 percent of adults had ever written to their U.S. representative and even fewer (25 percent) to their U.S. senator. Even fewer ever had a personal conversation with members of Congress (22 percent with a House member and 13 percent with a Senator). [29] While some may argue that recent reforms will encourage more people to communicate with their representatives in Congress, only the most optimistic expect more than a very small fraction of the population to send its views to Washington.

So members of Congress respond to those people with special interests in legislative actions. [30] While certain strains of democratic theory argue that intensity of preference should be considered in gauging public opinion, it is exactly this influence by narrow interests that most reformers are attempting to reduce or eliminate.

Of course, representatives can theoretically be responsive to the public's desires without direct communication with the public, but there is little evidence that legislators will support desires that are not actively expressed over demands that are unless the expressed demands are substantively extreme. Also, increased openness in the system may allow "watchdogs" like Ralph Nader and Common Cause to spot abuses of closed politics, such as tax loopholes. But such groups have not effectively altered either major policies or the basic aspects of congressional policymaking.

In sum, congressional responsiveness to parochial public opinion is an important source of conflict between the president and Congress. Institutional reforms to make Congress more responsive to public opinion are unlikely to alleviate these problems (and might even aggravate them) because the problems are rooted in fundamental aspects of our political system, such as geographic representation, weak parties, and frequent elections—not in tyrannical committee chairpersons, the seniority system, and secrecy. If there is to be a significant change in congressional behavior, it will have to originate with public opinion—and no such change is in sight.

Internal Structure

The internal structures of the executive and legislative branches also cause differences between the president and Congress. The executive branch is hierarchically organized, facilitating the president's examining a broad range of viewpoints on an issue and then weighing and balancing various interests. This structure also helps the president to view the trade-offs among various policies. Since one person, the president, must support all the major policies emanating from the executive branch, he is virtually forced to take a comprehensive view of those policies.

Members of Congress frequently do not take such a broad view. Each house of Congress is highly decentralized, with each member jealously guarding his or her independence and power. The party structure, unlike the situation in many countries, is not a unifying force within the U.S. legislature.[31] Most members of Congress gain their party's nomination by their own efforts, not the party's. Because virtually anyone can vote in party primaries, party leaders do not have control over those who run under their parties' labels. Moreover, candidates are largely responsible for providing the money and organization for their own election, precluding party control over another aspect of electoral politics. Party leaders also have few ways to enforce party discipline among those who are elected. What sanctions might be applied, such as poor committee assignments, are rarely used because legislators are very hesitant to set precedents that could be used against themselves.

Thus, while the structure of Congress ensures that a diversity of views will be heard and that many interests will have access to the legislative process, it does not follow that *each* member will hear all the views and see the proponents of each interest. Indeed, the decentralization of Congress almost guarantees that the information available to it as a whole is not a synthesis of the information available to each legislator. The Congress as a whole does not ask questions—individual members do. Thus, not all members receive the answers.[32]

Indeed, one of the functions of decentralizing power and responsibility in Congress is to allow for specialization in various policy areas. However, because of specialization, legislators make decisions about many of the policies with which Congress must deal in form only. In actuality they tend to rely upon the cues of party leaders, state party delegations, relevant committee leaders of their party, and other colleagues to decide how to vote.[33]

The different structures would not necessarily lead to a divergence of viewpoints between the president and Congress if the people who influenced the votes of each legislator represented the full range of views in the chamber, but they do not. Committees attract members from constituencies having special interests in subject areas of the committee or who have ideological interests of their own to promote: Westerners head for the Interior and Insular Affairs Committee in the House and the Environmental and Public Works Committee in the Senate, representatives from farming constitutencies gravitate toward the Agricultural Committees, urban legislators desire seats on the Banking, Housing and Urban Affairs and the Human Resources Committees in the Senate and the Banking, Finance and Urban Affairs and the Education and Labor Committees in the House. Supporters of increased defense spending want to be on the Armed Services Committees, and so on.[34] Thus, the committees' members are frequently unrepresentative of each house. Moreover, the individuals or state party delegations who serve as cue givers are chosen because they represent constituencies or maintain ideologies that are similar to those of the member who is consulting them. They also do not represent a cross section of viewpoints.

Another cause of the lack of information integration in Congress is the practice of members of one committee deferring to members of another committee who are reporting a bill in exchange for the same deference to their own committee's legislation. Thus, members representing special interests have a disproportionate say over policy regarding those interests—policy that might not be enacted if committees were fully representative of each chamber. This in turn can easily lead to a series of policies being passed that are more favorable to special interests than would be the case in absence of reciprocity.

Even the congressional experts in a given area fail to integrate information among themselves. In 1977 President Carter proposed that Congress pass a law reforming the rate structure of electric power companies. At the year's end Senator J. Bennett Johnston said that the Senate had not studied the complex subject sufficiently to make a decision, his subcommittee having held only a few hours of hearings over three days. The extensive hearings of the House Interstate and Foreign Commerce Committee's Subcommittee on Energy and Power, held over a two-year period, made little or no impact on the Senate, although Johnston was aware of them. The Senate required its own hearings before it was willing to move on the president's proposals.[35]

Besides not considering the full range of available views, members of Congress are not generally in a position to make trade-offs between policies. Because of its decentralization, Congress usually considers policies serially, that is, without reference to other policies. Without an integrating mechanism, members have few means by which to set and enforce priorities and to emphasize the policies with which the president is most concerned. This latter point is especially true when Congress is controlled by the opposition party.

In addition, Congress has little capability to examine two policies, like education and health care, in relation to each other. Not knowing that giving up something on one policy will result in a greater return on another policy, members have little incentive to engage in trade-offs. The new Budget Committees have a broader scope than other committees and are involved in making some trade-offs between policies and setting some priorities. But they deal only with direct expenditures (and then usually only with increases over past expenditures) not taxes (except for general revenue estimates), tax expenditures, treaties, natural gas deregulation, or other important areas. Moreover, they only recommend general limits on spending, leaving it up to the more parochial subject-area committees to go into specifics. The House committee is composed of temporary members whose permanent committee assignments undoubtedly limit their scope.

Another related area of presidential-congressional conflict caused by the decentralization of Congress is its lack of ability to deal comprehensively with major policy domains. Congress distributes its workload among committees, but committee jurisdictions do not usually cover entire policy areas. For example, no one congressional committee handles either energy, welfare, economic stability, or national security (the last requiring a coordination of defense policy and diplomacy).[36] When President Ford submitted his omnibus energy program to Congress in 1975, it was divided and parceled out to four committees in the House and nine in the Senate, all jealous of their prerogatives. Different committees in each house have authority over the Bureau of Reclamation, the Corps of Engineers, and the Soil Conservation Service, all of which are involved in water resource policy, a seemingly specific area. None of the involved committees wants to give up authority over "their" agency, and none of the groups interested in these policies want to lose their special access to the committees.[37] No congressional mechanism coordinates the decisions of the six committees involved. In another instance, President Carter's hospital cost control bill was assigned to four committees, two in the House (Ways and Means and Commerce) and two in the Senate (Finance and Human Resources). Also, in early 1978, three different House committees reported seabed mining legislation and had to spend their time negotiating among themselves.[38]

Recently the House has established temporary committees to handle energy and welfare legislation. While these committees have been helpful, the programs that they propose may be turned over to the relevant regular committees. For example, the special House committee handling President Carter's welfare proposals had to return its decisions to the Agriculture, Ways and Means, and Education and Labor Committees before the House could consider them. Thus, the piecemeal approach ultimately reigned.

The Ad Hoc Committee on Energy, which handled President Carter's energy proposals, received the decisions of five separate committees and then put them in a package before they went to the floor, adding its own amendments. This process, however, may have hindered passage of the president's proposals. Because all the relevant interests represented in the House did not have access to the committee, the House-passed bill ran into serious problems in conference committee negotiations with the Senate, where deliberations on the programs were less centralized and more open. The House committee had failed to combine both benefits of hierarchy, a comprehensive approach to a policy area and a wide-ranging consideration of the relevant interests.

Thus, the special overview committees have not been the final solution to Congress's inability to deal comprehensively with a policy area. This failure was acknowledged in 1979, when the representative who chaired the special House committee on welfare reform in the Ninety-fifth Congress (1977–1978) declared that the idea had not worked.[39]

The hierarchical structure of the executive branch, with the president at the pinnacle, forces the president to take responsibility for the entire executive branch. Moreover, when the president exercises power, it is clear who is acting and who should be held accountable. Congress, on the other hand, is not responsible for implementing policies, and each member is relatively obscure compared with the president. Since Congress is so decentralized, any member can disclaim responsibility for policies or their consequences. This fact helps us understand the fascinating spectacle of members of Congress running for reelection by campaigning *against* Congress.[40] It may also help to explain why polls continually show public respect for Congress to be extremely low[41] despite the fact that incumbents win reelection with ever greater consistency (especially House members). Representatives are not being held accountable for their collective decisions.[42] With increased openness, Congress may also increase its efforts to avoid accountability. Anyone who has witnessed a congressional campaign is aware that members of Congress do not go out of their way to articulate specific views on controversial issues. Likewise, they prefer to deal with controversial issues in Congress indirectly and procedurally, following the dictum that "no one ever got defeated for something he didn't say." The "end-of-the-war" vote in the House in 1972 was actually a vote on a motion to table a motion that would instruct conferees to insist on the House version of the defense authorization bill in the light of the Legislative Reorganization Act of 1970.[43]

The important point for us, however, is that representative can make irresponsible or self-serving decisions and then let the president take the blame. Congress is usually more interested in the immediate distribution of the benefits of policies to their constituents than in the ultimate consequences of policies. The short-run results please the interested parties and can easily be attributed to congressional actions; long-term effects are more obscure, as are their causes. Thus, members of Congress gain points for reelection while evading accountability for their actions. This is yet another source of conflict with the president.

Information and Expertise

A third source of conflict between the president and Congress is the difference in information and expertise available to them.[44] Despite the substantial increase in congressional staff in recent years, including the expansion or addition of analytic units such as the General Accounting Office, the Congressional Research Service in the Library of Congress, the Office of Technology Assessment, and the Congressional Budget Office, members of Congress rarely have available to them expertise of the quantity and quality that is available to the president.

Aside from the fact that the executive branch includes nearly 5 million civilian and military employees plus hundreds of advisory committees while Congress employs only about 30,000 persons (including supporting agencies), the expertise of the two branches differs. Members of Congress tend to hire generalists, even on committee staffs. Sometimes these individuals develop great expertise in a particular field, but more often they are only amateurs compared with their counterparts in the executive branch. Many are selected to serve legislators' needs and desires, which have little to do with policy analysis, and neither house has a merit system, a tenured career service, or a central facility for recruiting the best available talent.[45]

Congress is especially at a disadvantage in matters concerning foreign policy and national security policy, matters in which the president relies on classified information that is generally unavailable to Congress. Furthermore, Congress is often overwhelmed by the complexity of domestic policy. When the Senate considered reform of the U.S. Criminal Code in early 1978, it had to rely almost totally upon the Judiciary Committee, and throughout the debate it accepted hundreds of committee amendments offered in single packages.[46]

In addition, Congress is often reluctant to use data that are available. In 1973 Comptroller General Elmer B. Staats remarked, "We have trouble getting people on the Hill to read General Accounting Office reports despite the summaries and précis of our findings" (the General Accounting Office is Congress's primary unit for overseeing the executive branch). This view is supported by A. Ernest Fitzgerald, the Pentagon management specialist who first revealed the huge cost overruns on the Air Force's C-5A transport plane. He argues that many members of Congress preferred to stay ignorant of the facts so that they would not have problems in justifying continuance of the program.[47] There is also reason to believe that when Congress passed the Occupational and Safety Health Act (OSHA), it ignored the evidence suggesting the limited efficacy of government standards in decreasing industrial accidents.[48]

Because the president and Congress have different information and expertise available to them, they may well see issues from different perspectives. The president's views will generally be buttressed with more data and handled more expertly. This may give him different views and more confidence in his views.

Time Perspectives

The Constitution limits the president to a maximum of ten years in office and eight years if he does not complete the unfinished term of a predecessor. If presidents are activists—and virtually all modern presidents are forced to be in one way or another—they can waste no time in pushing for the adoption of their policies. For example, in his first year in office, President Carter proposed a new Department of Energy, reform of the welfare system, reform of the financing of the social security system, several energy policy proposals, executive branch reorganization legislation, public jobs, ending expenditures for the B-1 bomber, several water resource projects, and the Clinch River breeder reactor, legislation to hold down hospital costs, an air pollution bill, new housing programs, a series of election laws, food stamp reform, a strip-mining bill, a wiretap bill, two Panama Canal treaties, a tax cut, common-site picketing for labor unions, a new minimum wage bill, user fees for inland waterways, new target prices for some agricultural commodities, and the creation of the largest number of new federal judgeships in history. All of these proposals were in addition to routine legislation for maintaining ongoing programs.

Congress has a different timetable. Its members tend to be careerists and therefore do not have the same compulsion to enact policies rapidly. This sluggish approach is aggravated by the decentralization of Congress. Because no one has the authority to push through legislation, a great deal of negotiating and compromising must take place on all but a few noncontroversial (and usually unimportant) issues. This process can take years. President Nixon proposed revenue sharing in 1969; it passed in 1972. President Truman proposed a national health plan in 1948; a limited version (Medicare) was passed in 1965.

Moreover, the decentralization of Congress provides "veto points" at virtually every stage of the legislative process. At these points intense minorities can rule over weak majorities. An extreme example of this occurred in 1960 when both the House and Senate passed aid-to-education bills but, as is usually the case, in different forms. Thus, they needed a conference committee to iron out the differences since a bill must ultimately pass both houses in exactly the same form to become law. But the conference committee never met and the bill died because the House Rules Committee, by a vote of 7 to 5, refused to allow the bill to go to conference. Thus, a small group was able to overrule the desires of the president, the House, the Senate, and the American public. Senate filibusters, in which a minority of senators keep the majority from voting on a bill, are also well-known forms of this veto point phenomena.

The most obvious consequence of Congress's sluggishness in handling legislation is that the president is not likely to get much of what he wants now until later, if at all. In a nationally televised interview after his first year in office, President Carter commented that it was easier for him to study and propose an energy policy to Congress than it was for Congress to pass it.[49] Thus, he had to exert influence on Congress. A second consequence is that presidential policies may be passed too late to become fully effective. For example, when John Kennedy became president, he inherited a slumping economy. His economic advisers advised a tax cut to stimulate the economy, which Kennedy proposed to Congress in late 1962. The bill did not pass until January 1964, denying the economy a much needed stimulus for an entire year. And this action was taken quite soon for Congress. The Senate would probably have held the bill longer if it had not been spurred by the assassination of the president.

Presidential-Congressional Conflict in Perspective

The argument being made here is not that the president's proposals should always be adopted by Congress. Presidents are not always or even usually wise, nor do they prevent political realities from overcoming rational policy analysis or withhold support for policies that primarily benefit their electoral coalitions. Presidents are quite capable of making errors in their judgments about trade-offs and policy consequences and of not utilizing the options, information, and expertise available to them. Moreover, problems within the executive branch inhibit rational policy analysis.[50] Presidents can also procrastinate in proposing or reacting to others' solutions to national problems, either because of lack of interest or time or because of irresponsibility. Conversely, members of Congress are not, at least not usually, merely parochial and selfish representatives of special interests, with no concern for the general welfare.

The point is that the structure of American government exerts strong pressure on the two branches to represent different sets of interests and to view policies differently. This in turn sets the stage for conflict and virtually compels a president to try to influence Congress.

Now that we have seen why the president needs to influence Congress, we shall move on to the question of *how* we ought to study this influence. This discussion will pave the way for the remaining chapters, in which we analyze various sources of presidential influence.

Approach to Studying Power

The discussion of power comes naturally to the political scientist, yet we know little about it, especially in regard to our most important governmental institutions. As Prof. John Manley recently wrote, "The prevalence of the concept in political science is exceeded only by its failure to yield any widely accepted or firmly supported generalizations."[51] Regarding the president, we cannot even agree whether he is in a relatively weak position[52] or an "imperial" one.[53] Despite our ignorance, little is being done to increase our understanding of power and its consequences. Even the recent eight-volume *Handbook of Political Science* includes no article on power or influence.[54] Yet power remains a central concern of our discipline. The research presented here, by attempting to measure and explain power relationships, will hopefully yield some insights into presidential influence in Congress.

The fundamental approach to studying presidential power taken in this book is to examine the effectiveness of potential *sources* of influence. This approach has several important advantages for the study of power relationships. First, to attribute power to the president, it is necessary to see whether members of Congress give him more support under some conditions than under others. In other words, we must see whether changes in potential sources of influence are related to changes in the support among representatives for the president. Otherwise, we have no basis for inferring presidential power. Just because someone votes for presidential legislation does not mean that he or she was influenced by the president. Instead, there simply could have been agreement on the issues. Without systematic data on congressional preferences in the absence of influence, we must look at either changes in the behavior of representatives over time or differences between their behaviors during a session of Congress and see whether the differences are related to presidential power sources after we have controlled for other possible influences.

At first glance, focusing on sources of presidential power may seem to exclude the possibility of considering anticipated reactions, but this is not so. A president need not wield a power source before a vote that he wishes to influence in order for that power source to be considered useful and worthy of study. It is only necessary that the source exist and that its potential use exist in the minds of members of Congress. For example, it may be understood that a president will provide campaign aid to those who have given him support in the previous session of Congress. Thus, those desiring such aid will anticipate the president's reaction to their support of his policies.

Similarly, the president does not have to exercise a power source directly upon those whom he desires to influence in order for us to study its utility or for it to be considered a power resource. For example, the president can use his legislative liaison office, an institutional power source, to activate important constituents of members of Congress whom he wants to influence, asking the constituents to influence their representative or senator on his behalf.

It is also not necessary for the president to determine the extent of his power sources for them to be usefully examined. His popularity is a product of numerous forces, many of which are beyond his control,[55] and patronage jobs are severely limited by law. Yet both factors can be related to presidential success in obtaining congressional support for his policies.

Another advantage of this approach is that it forces us to explain inferred causations. In hypothesizing about a potential source of influence, one must provide a theory to relate it to the outcomes of presidential support. This theorizing, in addition to empirical work in general, is what is so desperately needed in the presidential literature.

The sources of influence studied here are not the same as the "bases" of power (rewards, coercion, expertise, legitimacy, and reference), articulated most notably by French and Raven,[56] which are sometimes used to study power. These are really general types of power sources rather than ones that we can operationally define. Moreover, a concept such as reward is too broad to reflect the many types of rewards that a president may give, which range from jobs to invitations to state dinners, or the many ways in which a president may use them, from explicit bargaining to general helpfulness with constituent problems. Conversely, a concept such as referent power, which is based on personal identification with an individual, is of little value to us because the president rarely has a personal relationship with a member of Congress. Furthermore, these bases of power come from the literature on social psychology and therefore focus on interpersonal power relations. Thus, they fail to cover sources of indirect power, such as presidential popularity.

One further comment is necessary. Very few scholars have ever applied empirical methods to the study of the presidency itself (as opposed to studies of voting in presidential elections or mass attitudes towards the president), especially in regard to testing propositions. In a recent study of the literature for the Ford Foundation, Hugh Heclo found a lack of basic empirical research on the presidency.[57] To quote John Manley again, Richard Neustadt's observations about presidential power "were so felicitous and so well argued that they passed into political science more as copybook maxims than as hypotheses to be tested."[58] It is almost as if the behavioral resolution passed presidential scholars by, leaving them to rely upon historical anecdotes. This research should help to recify this situation. It centers on identifying, measuring, and relating variables, employing methods such as regression analysis and causal modeling.

The Dependent Variables

The dependent variables in this study are Presidential Support Scores from 1953 through 1978, calculated by the *Congressional Quarterly* (CQ). They allow one to measure the level of support for a president's program provided by each representative and senator or by any group of them; thus, one is not limited to a measure for the House or Senate as a whole. It is important to reiterate that what we are examining here is the president's success in gaining support from senators and representatives for his legislative program and not his success in passing legislation per se. A measure for the latter would give us only one figure per session of Congress and mask any variability in support among individual members of Congress or groups of members. This would make explanation of congressional behavior very difficult.

In addition, these indexes of presidential support satisfy the test of reliability, since the same criteria for formulating them have been used since 1953. Separate indexes of support based on roll-call votes have been calculated for each member of Congress annually. Thus, no sampling procedures were used or needed. We have a universe of members with which to work in the 1953–1978 period. Furthermore, for 1955 through 1970, separate indexes for domestic and foreign policy have been calculated, which allow power relations in different policy areas to be examined.

The *CQ* analyzes all the public statements and messages of the president to determine what legislation he personally desires or does not desire. Only issues on which the president has taken a personal stand are included in the indexes. Moreover, *CQ* includes votes only if the legislation that the president originally supported is voted on in a similar form; issues are excluded if they have been so extensively amended that a vote can no longer be characterized as reflecting support of or opposition to the president. Furthermore, the position of the president at the time of the vote serves as the basis for measuring support or opposition, because the president may have altered his earlier position or changed his view after the vote took place. Finally, key votes to recommit, reconsider, or table are also included, and appropriations bills are included only if they deal with specific funds that the president requested be added or deleted. This latter point helps distinguish between the president and the institutionalized presidency. Thus, the indexes of presidential support are valid.

Nevertheless, these indexes present some problems. First, they are based solely on roll-call votes. Many significant decisions are made by committees, party leaders, non-roll-call votes, and so on.[59] The roll-call votes used here, however, are all significant decisions, and although no systematic evidence exists on this point, it is reasonable to argue that the most important votes on a president's programs are roll-call votes. Moreover, roll-call votes are the only systematic data that are available, and they cover a wide range of issues.

Another problem is nonvoting. Support scores are lowered by absent members of Congress because the *CQ* makes no attempt to interpret nonvoting; it assumes that most absences are due to illness or official business. This explanation may be generally correct, but some absences occur when members of Congress desire to support or oppose the president but do not want to express their position publicly. There is simply no way to know how to interpret absences. Thus, we are forced to assume that the reasons for nonvoting balance out and are evenly distributed throughout each house. This assumption is probably safe since members from each region have similar rates of voting participation on these sets of roll calls. Moreover, those who were unable to participate in voting because of prolonged illness, death, or resignation were eliminated from the analysis. For each of the other members of Congress, presidential support is calculated by dividing the number of votes supporting the president's position by the number of votes on which the president has taken a stand.

A final concern is that of weighting. Both between sessions and within each session, each vote is weighted equally, because even if we knew the president's complete set of priorities (which we do not) and even if he had a comprehensive set of priorities (which he does not), each member of Congress responds to presidential requests with his or her own set of priorities (to the degree that the member has one). Since we cannot assume that the issues the president cares about most and therefore fights hardest for are those issues that members of Congress care about most, we cannot assume that these issues are the best tests of presidential influence. The president's task in such cases is not necessarily especially difficult.

Another reason that the varying degrees of presidential effort to influence Congress are not a particularly serious problem is that direct involvement of the president and his staff is only one of several sources of influence. A number of potential sources, such as popularity and party affiliation, are not manipulatable on a given issue but nevertheless may be important influences on congressional voting. Moreover, this involvement is frequently strategic rather than tactical. In other words, much presidential activity toward Congress is aimed at generating general goodwill and not at gaining a particular person's vote on a particular issue. Thus, we should not assume that presidential efforts are dominant in determining congressional votes.

One way to study presidential influence that has been suggested is to locate the major obstacles to presidential success and then assess the degree to which the president overcomes them. For example, the opposition of the Conservative Coalition (Republicans and Southern Democrats) is a major hurdle for a liberal Democratic president such as Kennedy or Johnson.

However, using a measure such as the percentage of votes won by a president when opposed by the Conservative Coalition has serious limits.[60] Most obviously, such a measure is not very useful in examining the influence of conservative Republican presidents, for whom the Conservative Coalition is not an obstacle. Moreover, such a measure does not help us understand presidential influence except at the most rudimentary level. It provides only another boxscore of aggregate presidential success (and then only success in overcoming the particular obstacle). We cannot examine individual behavior and therefore are hindered in explaining such behavior.

A third problem is that success in overcoming an obstacle may depend more on the size of the obstacle than on the president's influence. For example, President Johnson's substantial success in overcoming Conservative Coalition opposition in 1965 and 1966 was largely due to the fact that the size of the coalition was substantially reduced by the loss of thirty-eight Republican seats in the 1964 election. Thus, a measure showing increased presidential success over this obstacle is not very illuminating.

A final problem with a measure such as overcoming Conservative Coalition opposition is an element of circularity: We look at presidential success in overcoming an obstacle only when he has failed to prevent the obstacle from developing (in the case of the Conservative Coalition, it develops when a majority of Republicans and Southern Democrats oppose the president on a roll-call vote). We necessarily ignore occasions on which the president might have prevented its development through his influence on individual members of Congress.

One final point should be made about Presidential Support Scores. There is no evidence that presidents have varied in their use of "posturing," that is, trying to inflate their degree of congressional support by proposing popular but frivolous legislation or by withholding unpopular legislation. While some of each has undoubtedly occurred, there seem to be no systematic differences between presidents. Thus, we need not control for posturing in our study.

Notes

1. James Madison, "The Federalist No. 46," in *The Federalist* (New York: Modern Library, 1937), p. 307. For the views of Presidents Kennedy and Nixon, respectively, see Theodore C. Sorenson, *Kennedy* (New York: Bantam, 1966), p. 387; Richard M. Nixon, *RN: The Memoirs of Richard M. Nixon* (New York: Grossett and Dunlap, 1977), p. 762.

2. See, for example, Walter Dean Burnham, "Insulation and Responsiveness in Congressional Elections," *Political Science Quarterly* 90 (Fall 1975): 412–413; the discussion on presidential coattails in Chapter 3; Albert D. Cover and David R. Mayhew, "Congressional Dynamics and the Decline of Competitive Congressional Elections," in *Congress Reconsidered,* ed. Lawrence C. Dodd and Bruce I. Oppenheimer (New York: Praeger, 1977); David R. Mayhew, "Congressional Elections: The Case of the Vanishing Marginals," *Polity* 6 (Spring 1974): 295–317; Morris P. Fiorina, *Congress: Keystone of the Washington Establishment* (New Haven: Yale University Press, 1977); John A. Ferejohn, "On the Decline of Competition in Congressional Elections," *American Political Science Review* 71 (March 1977): 166–176; Albert D. Cover, "One Good Term Deserves Another: The Advantages of Incumbency in Congressional Elections," *American Journal of Political Science* 21 (August 1977): 523–542.

3. I use the term *overrepresents* because each person living in a rural state has more influence on the election of a senator by virtue of being one of a small number of voters. Thus, rural voters have more representatives per person than urban voters.

4. See John W. Kingdon, *Congressmen's Voting Decisions* (New York: Harper & Row, 1973), p. 34; George C. Edwards III, "Presidential Influence in the House: Presidential Prestige as a Source of Presidential Power," *American Political Science Review* 70 (March 1976): 101–113; George C. Edwards III, "Presidential Influence in the Senate: Presidential Prestige as a Source of Presidential Power," *American Politics Quarterly* 5 (October 1977): 481–500; Duncan MacRae, *Dimensions of Congressional Voting* (Berkeley: University of California Press, 1958), p. 264; Aage R. Clausen, *How Congressmen Decide: A Policy Focus* (New York: St. Martin's, 1973), pp. 126–127, 182, 188; Warren E. Miller and Donald E. Stokes, "Constituency Influence on Congress," *American Politi-*

cal Science Review 57 (March 1963): 49–50; Lewis A. Dexter, "The Representative and His District," in *New Perspectives on the House of Representatives,* 2nd ed., ed. Robert L. Peabody and Nelson W. Polsby (Chicago: Rand McNally, 1969); Gregory Markus, "Electoral Coalitions and Senate Roll-Call Behavior: An Ecological Analysis," *American Journal of Political Science* 18 (August 1974): 595–608; Bruce I. Oppenheimer, "Senators' Constituencies—Suggestions for Redefinition," paper presented at the annual meeting of the American Political Science Association, Chicago, September 1971; Christopher H. Achen, "Measuring Representation," *American Journal of Political Science* 22 (August 1978): 475–510; Charles S. Bullock III and David W. Brady, "Party, Constituency, and U.S. Senate Voting Behavior," paper presented at the annual meeting of the Southern Political Science Association, New Orleans, November 1977; Richard F. Fenno, Jr., "U.S. House Members in Their Constituencies: An Exploration," *American Political Science Review* 71 (September 1977): 915; Morris P. Fiorina, *Representatives, Roll Calls, and Constituencies* (Lexington, Mass.: Lexington Books, 1974).

5. Eugene Bardach, *The Implementation Game: What Happens after a Bill Becomes a Law* (Cambridge, Mass.: M.I.T. Press, 1977), p. 79.

6. Alice M. Rivlin, *Systematic Thinking for Social Action* (Washington, D.C.: Brookings Institution, 1971), p. 84.

7. Edward C. Banfield, "Making a New Federal Program: Model Cities, 1964–68," in *Policy and Politics in America,* ed. Allan P. Sindler (Boston: Little, Brown, 1973); Hubert H. Humphrey, *The Education of a Public Man: My Life and Politics* (Garden City, N.Y.: Doubleday, 1976), p. 409.

8. "Congressional Budget: Toughest Test Ahead," *Congressional Quarterly Weekly Report,* September 6, 1975, p. 1925.

9. David R. Mayhew, *Congress: The Electoral Connection* (New Haven, Conn.: Yale University Press, 1974).

10. Richard F. Fenno, Jr., *Congressmen in Committees* (Boston: Little, Brown, 1973), chap. 3.

11. Interview with Postmaster General Benjamin F. Bailar, 1976.

12. See, for example, "The New Senate Class: Big and Independent," *Congressional Quarterly Weekly Report,* December 30, 1978, p. 3499.

13. This point is nicely made by John A. Ferejohn, *Pork Barrel Politics* (Stanford, Calif.: Stanford University Press, 1974). See also "Water Policy: Battle over Benefits," *Congressional Quarterly Weekly Report,* March 4, 1978, pp. 566, 569–570.

14. Quoted in Robert Sherrill, *Why They Call It Politics* (New York: Harcourt Brace Jovanovich, 1972), pp. 104–105.

15. "Turning Screws: Winning Votes in Congress," *Congressional Quarterly Weekly Report,* April 24, 1976, p. 951. For other critical comments about Congress's handling of defense policy based on constituency interests, see Les Aspin, "The Defense Budget and Foreign Policy: The Role of Congress," *Daedalus* 104 (Summer 1975): 155–174.

16. Charles L. Schultze, *The Politics and Economics of Public Spending* (Washington, D.C.: Brookings Institution, 1968), pp. 134–135.

17. "Amtrak Derails Supplemental," *Congressional Quarterly Weekly Report,* December 3, 1977, p. 2542. See also "Congress Forbids Amtrak to Cut Train Service," *Congressional Quarterly Weekly Report,* November 12, 1977, pp. 2403–2404.

18. "Carter Fiscal Aid Plan Faces Overhaul in Congress," *Congressional Quarterly Weekly Report,* May 20, 1978, p. 1268.

19. For discussions of the use of cost-benefit analysis in Congress, see Robert H. Haveman, *The Economic Performance of Public Investments* (Baltimore: Johns Hopkins University Press, 1972); Ferejohn, *Pork Barrel Politics*. For a classic discussion of congressional control of an executive pork barrel agency, see Arthur A. Maass, "Congress and Water Resources," *American Political Science Review* 44 (September 1950): 576–593.

20. "Water Policy: Battle over Benefits," p. 565.

21. William R. Keech, "Electoral Politics and the Meaning of Partisanship in Federal Minimum Wage Policy," paper presented at the annual meeting of the American Political Science Association, San Francisco, September 4, 1975.

22. U.S., Congress, Senate, Commerce Committee, *Appointments to the Regulatory Agencies: The Federal Communications Commission and the Federal Trade Commission,* Committee Print (Washington, D.C.: Government Printing Office, 1976).

23. Lyndon B. Johnson, *The Vantage Point: Perspectives of the Presidency 1963–1969* (New York: Popular Library, 1971), p. 440.

24. See, for example, Morris S. Ogul, *Congress Oversees the Bureaucracy: Studies in Legislative Supervision* (Pittsburgh: University of Pittsburgh Press, 1976); Seymour Scher, "Conditions for Legislative Control," *Journal of Politics* 25 (August 1963): 526–551.

25. Martha Derthick, *The Influence of Federal Grants* (Cambridge, Mass.: Harvard University Press, 1970), pp. 207–208.

26. For the best discussion of House taxing and spending committees, see John F. Manley, *The Politics of Finance: The House Committee on Ways and Means* (Boston: Little, Brown, 1970); Richard F. Fenno, Jr., *The Power of the Purse: Appropriations Politics in Congress* (Boston: Little, Brown, 1966).

27. Fenno, *The Power of the Purse,* pp. 370–371.

28. Ferejohn, *Pork Barrel Politics,* p. 193.

29. U.S., Congress, Senate, Committee on Government Operations, Subcommittee on Intergovernmental Relations, *Confidence and Concern: Citizens View American Government,* Part I, Committee Print (Washington, D.C.: Government Printing Office, 1973), p. 256.

30. See, for example, Catherine E. Rudder, "Committee Reform and the Revenue Process," in *Congress Reconsidered,* pp. 124–126, 132.

31. For a thorough treatment of "responsible parties," see Austin Ranney, *The Doctrine of Responsible Party Government* (Urbana: University of Illinois Press, 1962).

32. Thomas R. Wolanin, "Congress, Information and Policy Making for Postsecondary Education: Don't Trouble Me with the Facts," *Policy Studies Journal* 4 (Summer 1976): 386–387.

33. See, for example, Kingdon, *Congressmen's Voting Decisions;* Donald R. Matthews and James A. Stimson, *Yeas and Nays: Normal Decision-Making in the U.S. House of Representatives* (New York: Wiley, 1975).

34. See Kenneth A. Shepsle, *The Giant Jigsaw Puzzle: Democratic Committee Assignments in the Modern House* (Chicago: University of Chicago Press, 1978).

35. "Senate Rejection of Carter Energy Proposals Attributed to Belief They Were Unwise," *Congressional Quarterly Weekly Report,* October 22, 1977, p. 2234.

36. For similar comments regarding foreign economic policy, see William J. Lanouette, "Who's Setting Foreign Policy—Carter or Congress?" *National Journal,* July 15, 1978, p. 119.

37. For a recent example of committee jurisdictional jealousies, see "Senate Approves Committee Changes," *Congressional Quarterly Weekly Report,* February 12, 1977, pp. 279–284.

38. "Committees Tangle over Seabed Mining," *Congressional Quarterly Weekly Report,* February 25, 1978, pp. 525–526.

39. "Administration Narrows Welfare Reform Plan to Meet '78 Objections," *Congressional Quarterly Weekly Report,* February 10, 1979, p. 237.

40. Fenno, "U.S. House Members in Their Constituencies," p. 914.

41. For example, a Harris poll taken at the end of 1977 found that Congress had the "confidence" of only 15 percent of the American people (up from 9 percent in 1973). See William Claiborne, "U.S. Institutions Rising in Public Esteem," *New Orleans Times-Picayune,* January 8, 1975, sec. 1, p. 31.

42. For a discussion of this point, see Richard F. Fenno, Jr., "If, As Ralph Nader Says, Congress Is 'the Broken Branch,' How Come We Love Our Congressmen So Much?," in *Congress in Change: Evolution and Reform,* ed. Norman J. Ornstein (New York: Praeger, 1975); Glenn R. Parker and Roger H. Davidson, "Why Do Americans Love Their Congressmen So Much More Than Their Congress?" *Legislative Studies Quarterly* 4 (February 1979): 53–61.

43. Aspin, "The Defense Budget and Foreign Policy," p. 165.

44. Johnson, *Vantage Point,* pp. 440–441.

45. James L. Sundquist, "Congress and the President: Enemies or Partners?" in *Congress Reconsidered,* pp. 234–235.

46. "Senate Debates Only Tiny Part of Bill," *Congressional Quarterly Weekly Report,* February 4, 1978, p. 287.

47. "The President versus Congress: The Score since Watergate," *National Journal,* May 29, 1976, p. 739. See also Aspin, "The Defense Budget and Foreign Policy," p. 164.

48. Albert L. Nichols and Richard Zeckhauser, "Government Comes to the Workplace: An Assessment of OSHA," *Public Interest* No. 49 (Fall 1977): 50.

49. National televised interview, December 28, 1977.

50. For a lengthy discussion of these, see George C. Edwards III and Ira Sharkansky, *The Policy Predicament* (San Francisco: W. H. Freeman and Company, 1978), chaps. 4–8.

51. John F. Manley, "White House Lobbying and the Problem of Presidential Power," paper presented at the annual meeting of the American Political Science Association in Washington, D.C., September 1977, p. 3.

52. Richard E. Neustadt, *Presidential Power* (New York: New American Library, 1964).

53. Arthur M. Schlesinger, Jr., *The Imperial Presidency* (New York: Popular Library, 1974).

54. Fred I. Greestein and Nelson W. Polsby, eds., *Handbook of Political Science* (Reading, Mass.: Addison-Wesley, 1975).

55. See, for example, Richard A. Brody and Benjamin I. Page, "The Impact of Events on Presidential Popularity: The Johnson and Nixon Administrations," in *Perspectives on the Presidency,* ed. Aaron Wildavsky (Boston: Little, Brown, 1975); John E. Mueller, *War, Presidents and Public Opinion* (New York: Wiley, 1973), chaps. 9–10; Samuel Kernell, "Explaining Presidential Popularity," *American Political Science Review* 72 (June 1978): 506–522.

56. John R. P. French, Jr., and Bertram Raven, "The Bases of Social Power," in *Studies in Social Power,* ed. Dorwin Cartwright (Ann Arbor: University of Michigan Press, 1959).

57. Hugh Heclo, *Studying the Presidency* (New York: Ford Foundation, 1977).

58. Manley, "White House Lobbying," p. 1.

59. See Clausen, *How Congressmen Decide,* pp. 19–20, for the view that roll call votes reflect less visible decisions. See also Joseph K. Unekis, "From Committee to the Floor: Consistency in Congressional Voting," *Journal of Politics* 40 (August 1978): 761–769.

60. For an interesting study using this measure, see Manley, "White House Lobbying," pp. 39ff.

3 | *Party as a Source of Influence*

The political party affiliation of members of Congress is the most commonly discussed factor in explaining their votes. In this chapter we shall examine the question of whether the shared party affiliation of the president and some members of Congress serves as a source of influence for him. We shall also investigate the possibilities of the president acting to increase the effectiveness of party as a source of influence and of his helping to increase his party's representation in Congress.

Presidential Party Affiliation as a Source of Influence

Quite naturally, the president's party affiliation is a source of influence in Congress, since it affects only congressional members of the president's party. It must move these legislators from their normal positions to positions that are more consistent with those of the president. That members of the president's party are more open to his influence is clear from research done by John Kingdon. When he asked members of the House in early 1969 who played a role in their decision making, 42 percent of Republicans spontaneously mentioned the Nixon Administration, a high figure for spontaneous mentions. Only 14 percent of the Northern Democrats and 12 percent of the Southern Democrats gave a similar response. Moreover, one-third of the Republicans replied that the administration played a major or determining role in their decisions, about five times the figure for Democrats.[1]

Party Support of the President

Tables 3.1 and 3.2 show the annual average support for the president given by members of the House and Senate, respectively, according to party affiliation.

58

Table 3.1

House Members' Average Percentage Presidential Support by Party, 1953–1978

	DEMOCRATS			REPUBLICANS		
YEAR	OVERALL POLICY	DOMESTIC POLICY	FOREIGN POLICY	OVERALL POLICY	DOMESTIC POLICY	FOREIGN POLICY
1953	49	——	——	74	——	——
1954	45	——	——	71	——	——
1955	53	47	69	60	64	50
1956	52	50	75	72	72	69
1957	50	51	47	54	51	61
1958	55	53	63	58	59	55
1959	40	35	67	68	71	57
1960	44	40	54	59	59	58
1961	73	73	73	37	32	52
1962	72	73	70	42	42	41
1963	73	74	69	32	34	21
1964	74	73	75	38	39	36
1965	74	74	77	42	42	42
1966	64	64	61	38	38	34
1967	69	70	67	46	47	40
1968	64	64	66	51	52	50
1969	48	47	64	57	58	51
1970	53	53	56	66	67	56
1971	47	——	——	72	——	——
1972	47	——	——	64	——	——
1973	36	——	——	61	——	——
1974	44	——	——	57	——	——
1975	38	——	——	63	——	——
1976	32	——	——	63	——	——
1977	63	——	——	42	——	——
1978	60	——	——	35	——	——

The tables show that members of the president's party in Congress consistently give him strong support. This is especially impressive when we remember that three Republican and three Democratic presidents are covered here, and the presidents of each party varied considerably in their policies, personalities, and political environments. Nevertheless, their fellow party members supported them with their votes.

Tables 3.3 and 3.4 show the average support given by members of each party in the House and Senate to presidents of each party according to *CQ*'s overall, domestic, and foreign policy scores. Comparing the set of figures in the last column in each table shows that in every instance except one, members of the

Table 3.2

Senators' Average Percentage Presidential Support by Party, 1953–1978

| | DEMOCRATS | | | REPUBLICANS | | |
YEAR	OVERALL POLICY	DOMESTIC POLICY	FOREIGN POLICY	OVERALL POLICY	DOMESTIC POLICY	FOREIGN POLICY
1953	47	——	——	67	——	——
1954	40	——	——	71	——	——
1955	56	36	71	72	68	75
1956	39	30	58	72	75	67
1957	52	44	63	69	64	76
1958	45	43	54	67	69	62
1959	38	32	54	72	73	71
1960	42	38	54	65	64	69
1961	65	65	67	37	34	46
1962	63	60	70	40	38	44
1963	63	65	61	44	40	52
1964	62	64	58	45	45	45
1965	65	66	61	48	45	58
1966	57	54	63	43	38	62
1967	61	60	64	53	49	61
1968	48	48	51	47	46	51
1969	47	40	66	66	64	72
1970	45	43	58	62	60	80
1971	41	——	——	65	——	——
1972	44	——	——	67	——	——
1973	37	——	——	61	——	——
1974	39	——	——	56	——	——
1975	47	——	——	68	——	——
1976	39	——	——	63	——	——
1977	70	——	——	52	——	——
1978	66	——	——	41	——	——

president's party support his policies more than members of the opposition party do. (See Table 3.5 for the number of members of Congress in each party.)

In most instances these differences in support are quite substantial, reaching as high as 30 percent. The one instance in which the pattern is reversed is House foreign policy support under Republican presidents. On these issues Democrats provided the president 5 percent greater support on the average than Republicans did. This finding is easily explained. Recent Republican presidents have taken activist, internationalist foreign policy stances. Traditionally, Democrats in Congress have been more likely to hold such views than Republicans. Thus, by simply voting their views, Democrats in the House have given Republican presi-

Table 3.3

Average Support by House Members for Presidents according to Party

HOUSE MEMBERS	% SUPPORT
Democratic Presidents	
Democratic	
Overall Policy	69
Domestic Policy	71
Foreign Policy	70
Republican	
Overall Policy	40
Domestic Policy	41
Foreign Policy	40
Republican Presidents	
Democratic	
Overall Policy	46
Domestic Policy	47
Foreign Policy	62
Republican	
Overall Policy	64
Domestic Policy	63
Foreign Policy	57

NOTE: Overall policy covers 1953 through 1978; domestic and foreign policy covers 1955 through 1970.

dents more support than Republicans. As we shall see, however, this does not mean that party affiliation has not been a source of influence for Republican presidents in foreign policy. Without the pull of the president's party affiliation, Republican support might have been much lower.

The Strength of Party Affiliation as a Source of Influence

Studying political party affiliation as a source of presidential influence is very difficult because it is hard to tell whether a member of the president's party votes for the president's policies because of shared party affiliation or because of agreement with the president's policies. Without doubt, members of the same party share many policy preferences and have similar electoral coalitions supporting them. For example, much of the support that a liberal Democratic president receives from Northern Democrats for liberal policies is due to policy agreement. In this case there is little ground for attributing influence to the president's party affiliation, nor is there much need for influence. The president has simply taken stands that are in accord with the normal policy positions of this group of fellow party members.

The most common way of examining the influence of the president's party affiliation on members of Congress is to see how a member's voting behavior differs under presidents of different parties. Of course, as discussed above,

Table 3.4

Average Support by Senators for Presidents according to Party

SENATORS	% SUPPORT
Democratic Presidents	
Democratic	
Overall Policy	62
Domestic Policy	60
Foreign Policy	62
Republican	
Overall Policy	45
Domestic Policy	42
Foreign Policy	52
Republican Presidents	
Democratic	
Overall Policy	44
Domestic Policy	38
Foreign Policy	53
Republican	
Overall Policy	66
Domestic Policy	67
Foreign Policy	72

NOTE: Overall policy covers 1953 through 1978; domestic and foreign policy covers 1955 through 1970.

much of any change in presidential support will be due to agreement or disagreement with the president's policies. Thus, some authors have examined changes in congressional voting on policy scales that are independent of the occupant of the White House. Issues are selected for study on which the policy stands of Democratic and Republican presidents are expected to be the same. Thus, changes in the voting of members of Congress can reasonably be attributed to the president's party affiliation.

Mark Kesselman compared the voting on foreign aid bills of representatives serving in both the Eighty-first Congress (1949–1950) and the Eighty-sixth Congress (1959–1960) and in both the latter Congress and the Eighty-seventh Congress (1961–1962). In the first comparison, approximately one-fifth of the members of the House shifted their stances under the new president (Eisenhower). Some Democrats shifted to isolationism in the absence of an internationalist president of their own party, and some Republicans became more internationalist under the stimulus of an internationalist Republican president. The converse trend was found for the 1960–1961 Republican to Democratic presidential transition.[2]

Charles Tidmarch and Charles Sabatt did a similar study for the Senate, examining changes in senators' voting on internationalist/isolationist scales between 1960 and 1961 and between 1968 and 1969. Corroborating Kesselman's findings, they found that under a Democratic president, several Democratic

Table 3.5

Number of Members of Congress by Party for Tables 3.1–3.4

YEAR	HOUSE		SENATE	
	DEMOCRATS	REPUBLICANS	DEMOCRATS	REPUBLICANS
1953	208	217	47	46
1954	213	218	47	45
1955	230	203	49	47
1956	228	202	46	47
1957	229	199	47	46
1958	226	195	49	46
1959	279	152	64	34
1960	276	151	64	34
1961	257	172	64	34
1962	255	174	64	33
1963	251	172	66	33
1964	251	175	66	33
1965	282	147	66	32
1966	281	146	67	32
1967	245	184	64	36
1968	242	183	63	36
1969	234	176	57	42
1970	239	178	57	41
1971	254	173	56	42
1972	252	174	55	42
1973	233	183	58	41
1974	230	184	57	39
1975	286	144	61	38
1976	282	141	62	37
1977	285	141	61	37
1978	276	142	60	38

senators became more internationalist and several Republican senators became isolationist. There was little net change among Democrats when Nixon became president, but 20 percent of the Republican senators moved to a more internationalist position, matching the president's policies.[3]

Aage Clausen has employed his well-known policy dimensions for purposes similar to the purposes of these studies. For representatives and senators serving in the last two Eisenhower Congresses (1957–1960) and the two Congresses of the Kennedy-Johnson administration (1961–1964), he compared their mean positions on each of his policy dimensions. He repeated this procedure for the last Kennedy-Johnson Congress (1963–1964) and the first Nixon Congress (1969–

1970). Of his five policy dimensions, only the one termed "international involvement" showed any change in representatives' behavior.[4] When he and Carl Van Horn compared the Eighty-eighth Congress (1963–1964) with the Ninety-first and Ninety-second (1969–1972), they again found changes on this dimension. In both studies Republicans were more supportive of international involvement under a Republican president than under a Democratic president, while Democratic representatives displayed the opposite tendencies.[5]

In their study of House voting from 1949 through 1972, Herbert Asher and Herbert Weisberg found that on foreign aid issues, Northern Democrats' support remained fairly stable, Southern Democrats' support increased slightly under Democratic presidents, and Republicans' was significantly greater under Republican presidents. Most of these changes, however, seem to be due to members who had not served under administrations of different parties, because 85 percent of the representatives who served in at least two successive administrations between 1949 and 1972 did not change their voting with the change in administration.[6]

Although these data provide some basis for attributing influence to the president's party affiliation in the area of foreign affairs, they are not as conclusive as the data in the studies previously cited. The authors suggest that this may be due to the fact that, unlike the other scholars, they only examined votes on final passage of legislation. Since these votes are more visible to the public than earlier votes, such as those on amendments, Asher and Weisberg suggest that representatives may be less willing to support the president on these votes.[7] It is important to note, however, that the votes preceding final passage votes are often crucial in determining both the substance of legislation and its likelihood of passage.

It is not hard to understand the role of presidential party as a source of influence in foreign policy. Since most members of Congress are relatively free from constituency and interest group pressure in this area, they are less inhibited in following a president of their own party. Also, because the president has a greater personal responsibility for foreign affairs than domestic affairs, his prestige is more involved in votes on foreign policy. Thus, his fellow party members in Congress have more reason to support him in these matters to avoid embarrassing him.

In their study Asher and Weisberg also found that Republicans often increased their support for increasing the national debt ceiling during a Republican administration. Democrats, voting their policy views, continued to support increasing the debt.[8] Similarly, Clausen and Van Horn found changes in their "government management" policy dimension, which concerns government involvement in the economy. Under a Republican president, Republicans are more supportive of activist federal policies while Democrats are less supportive.[9]

In domestic policy areas such as civil rights, agricultural assistance, and social welfare, two factors depress the influence of the president's party affiliation. One is constituency. The constituency of a member of Congress is more likely to have

opinions on these issues. When constituency opinion and the president's proposals conflict, as they often do for Southern Democrats on matters concerning civil
rights, members of Congress are more likely to vote with their constituencies.[10]

The second important factor has already been mentioned: policy agreement
between the president and his party members in Congress. As long as the new
president sends proposals to Capitol Hill that are consistent with the policy
stands taken by most of the members of his party under the previous president,
there will be little need to influence these members. Thus, we would expect little
change in the voting of members of Congress as measured by policy scales. If the
president's party has been divided, then there will be more need and more
potential for party affiliation to be a source of influence.

Despite these somewhat negative arguments, additional evidence supports the
role of presidential party affiliation as a source of influence in Congress. In his
in-depth study of the House in the early months of 1969, John Kingdon found
several votes on which a substantial number of Republicans switched their votes
from the previous year to vote with the new Republican president. These votes
included increasing the national debt, opposing farm payment limitations, and
support for foreign aid and the poverty program. In addition, the president
generally had a small group of party members who were ready to change their
votes to support his position if such an action was necessary on close ballots.
Similarly, many Democratic representatives switched their votes and opposed
foreign aid and the proposed surtax when they no longer had the pull of a
Democrat in the White House.[11] Malcolm Jewell found a similar switch in voting
on foreign policy issues, especially among Republicans, after Eisenhower succeeded Truman.[12]

We should keep in mind that the necessary use of policy scales in the studies
mentioned above raises some problems of interpretation because the scales measure congressional support for certain policies rather than congressional support
for the president. This is particularly true of Clausen's work, in which policy
dimensions were developed as a result of an admirable effort to learn how
representatives approached the broad range of issues with which they were faced,
and then were used for a purpose inappropriate to their design, that is, to measure
congressional reaction to the president. Although Clausen does not indicate
which votes are included in his dimensions, they must include many votes on
which the president took no position, and they may not include all the votes on
which he did take a position. Since the president may not have taken a stand on
many of the votes that were studied by Clausen,[13] we cannot infer a lack of
presidential party influence from the lack of movement on several of Clausen's
policy dimensions. Moreover, even if members of Congress do not alter their
levels of support for certain policy dimensions, the dimensions may shift to the
left or right as a result of the president's policy proposals. Such a shift could mask
significant changes in voting behavior.

In conclusion, the president's party affiliation seems to be a source of influence
in Congress, although a limited one. It is strongest in the area of foreign affairs,

in which members of Congress have fewer forces acting on them compared with domestic policy. In domestic matters, party affiliation plays its greatest role when the president's policies are contrary to the normal stances of his party and when constituency pressures are lax enough to allow members of the president's party in Congress to respond to the pull of a member of their party in the White House.

Using Party as a Source of Influence

How does the party of the president change the votes of at least some congressional members of his party? First, members of the president's party have an incentive to make him look good by not losing votes, because his standing in the public may influence their chances for reelection (to be discussed below), and they do not want to embarrass "their" administration. Second, they may have personal loyalties or emotional commitments to their party and their party leader, which the president can translate into votes when necessary. Thus, members of the president's party vote with him when they can, giving him the benefit of the doubt, especially if their own opinion on an issue is weak.[14] As Speaker of the House "Tip" O'Neill said in 1977, "We loved to send Jerry Ford's vetoes back to him. But we have a Democratic President now, and who needs that?"[15] (One presidential aide described as "just amazing" how often members vote for the administration's proposals not on substance but on loyalty and a desire to be helpful.[16]) These two factors are buttressed by distrust of members of the opposition party, who are seen as always willing to undercut the president.[17]

The members of the president's party also receive more communications from the White House than do the members of the opposition party. This further enhances the relationships between the president and these legislators. Moreover, the president can more effectively threaten to withhold favors from members of his own party than from members of the opposition party, since the latter do not expect to receive many favors anyhow.[18]

Presidential Midterm Campaigning

Given that party affiliation is a source of influence, what can a president do to manipulate it for his own purposes? Once members of Congress are elected, they almost never change their party affiliation, and the rare instances when they do have not resulted from presidential urgings. Thus, if presidents are to alter the party composition of Congress, they must help to elect additional members of their party. One way to accomplish this goal is to campaign for candidates in midterm congressional elections.

Campaign Efforts

President Eisenhower once stated, "Frankly, I don't care too much about the congressional elections." This was due to lack of support in the past from some

Republicans in Congress and a personal liking for some Democratic candidates.[19] In 1970 President Nixon ordered Vice President Agnew and other leading Republicans to refrain from going after Democratic senator Gale McGee of Wyoming and to support his Republican opponent only nominally because McGee had provided Nixon with strong support for his foreign policies. Similarly, the Republican opponent of Senator Harry Byrd, Jr., a conservative Virginian, received little White House aid.[20]

Sometimes presidents are so unpopular that the candidates of their party do not want their support. President Johnson adopted a low profile during the 1966 campaign because of his lack of public support (below 50 percent in the Gallup Poll). In 1974, before he resigned, President Nixon wanted invitations to campaign for Republicans to prove that he wasn't political poison, but he had few offers as the Watergate crisis reached a head.[21]

Nevertheless, modern presidents have often taken an active role in midterm congressional elections. In the 1954 campaign Eisenhower had a cabinet meeting televised. He also supported Vice President Nixon's campaign activities, mobilized the cabinet to stump the country, made several trips to states with close senatorial contests, and broadcast a national appeal for a Republican Congress.[22] In the 1958 campaign, Vice President Nixon carried the brunt of the speaking chores, but the president made several major speeches to promote a Republican Congress.[23] Thus, the "nonpolitical" Eisenhower became the most active presidential midterm campaigner in history. However, in 1962 President Kennedy was even more active, despite having to cut his campaigning short in October because of the Cuban missile crisis.[24]

In 1970, President Nixon was heavily involved in the congressional elections. He chose Vice President Agnew to carry the main burden of making speeches and offered him the services of several White House aides and speech writers. Nevertheless, behind the scenes Nixon was running the show, making strategic decisions such as selecting issues to raise and to avoid, labeling particular Democratic candidates as "radicals," encouraging people (mostly representatives) to run for the Senate, and deciding whom to support.[25] He also made numerous campaign speeches. (The strident tenor of the White House campaign hurt Nixon's chances of having his welfare reform program passed in the remainder of the congressional session following the election. The Democrats viewed the president with bitterness and vindictiveness and were in no mood to go along.)[26] President Carter was also an active campaigner in 1978, speaking on behalf of Democratic candidates all across the country.

Success of the President's Party in Midterm Elections

Presidential efforts in midterm elections have had quite limited success. We can look as far back as Woodrow Wilson's efforts in 1918, which were rewarded by the loss of both houses of Congress. Similarly, the Republicans lost both houses in 1954 and met with near disaster in 1958, losing forty-seven seats in the House

Table 3.6

Changes in Congressional Representation of the President's Party in Midterm Elections

YEAR	HOUSE		SENATE	
	LOSSES	GAINS	LOSSES	GAINS
1954	18	0	1	0
1958	47	0	13	0
1962	4	0	0	4
1966	47	0	3	0
1970	12	0	0	2
1974	47	0	5	0
1978	11	0	3	0

and thirteen in the Senate. Democrats under Kennedy did better in 1962, actually gaining four Senate seats, but they lost forty-seven in the House and three in the Senate under Johnson in 1966. In 1970 the Republicans held losses under Nixon to twelve in the House and gained two seats in the Senate. In 1974, however, they lost forty-seven seats in the House and five in the Senate under President Ford. Under President Carter, the Democrats had marginal losses in 1978, losing eleven seats in the House and three in the Senate. Table 3.6 summarizes this data.

Why the president's party usually loses seats in Congress in midterm elections in not clear. Certain events may contribute to such losses. For instance, President Nixon's taped 1970 election eve speech was angry, hard-line, and heavily political. It also suffered from poor-quality film and a poor soundtrack. In contrast, Senator Edmund Muskie made a "cool" and generally well-received election eve speech for the Democrats.[27] But such events cannot account for the systematic losses over time, which are independent of the occupant of the presidency.

Early research indicated that the president's party generally lost seats in Congress in midterm elections primarily because of changes in the composition of the electorate between the presidential and midterm elections. In the latter, it was argued, voter turnout was smaller and those who did vote voted largely along party lines. Those voters who had been stimulated to enter the electorate or to cross party lines primarily because of the attractiveness of the winning presidential candidate and who also voted for the congressional candidates of the president's party either did not vote at all or voted for the other party's congressional candidates in the subsequent midterm elections. In either case the candidates of the president's party lost the bonus of having the president on the ticket and thus were more likely to lose their seats in midterm elections.[28]

An important elaboration of this argument was made by Barbara Hinckley. She presented data indicating that the number of House seats lost by the president's party in the midterm election is related to the strength of the president's coattails in the preceding election. Representatives whom the president helped to victory, especially those in close elections, were particularly vulnerable to a switch in the party winning the seat in the midterm election. Thus, we should expect larger losses for the president's party following landslide victories, which presumably would reflect a strong coattail effect.[29] The results in Table 3.6 seem to confirm this view, since large losses of House seats (forty-seven) followed the presidential landslide victories of 1956, 1964, and 1972, while considerably fewer losses occurred after close presidential elections.

Despite the plausibility of this reasoning, it has several limitations. Although turnout is lower in midterm elections than in presidential elections, recent evidence shows that "the differences between presidential and off-year electorates are relatively unimportant." The degree of party voting is about the same in both elections, as is the participation of Independents (who have, at least traditionally, been considered less interested in politics).[30] Therefore, the losses sustained by the president's party in midterm elections are unlikely to be primarily accounted for by differences in voter turnout and party voting. In addition, we have already noted that incumbents in Congress are less and less likely to lose their seats, no matter who helped them gain them. We shall see in the next section that the effect of presidential coattails on congressional elections has steadily diminished.

Recent research has yielded different explanations. Both Edward Tufte and Samuel Kernell have found that the president's popularity correlates fairly strongly with the aggregate national vote received by candidates for the House of the president's party. Tufte also found significant correlations between real disposable income and the midterm vote for House candidates of the president's party. Of course, these trends take place within the confines of party voting, so that it takes a substantial increase in presidential popularity, for example, to increase by a small amount the aggregate vote percentage received by candidates for the House of the president's party.[31]

Kernell has carried the analysis further and suggested a reason why both Democrats and Republicans receive smaller percentages of the total congressional vote in midterm elections when the president is of their own party (even if the president is relatively popular, as he was in 1954, 1962, and 1970). He argues that negative opinions disproportionately influence political behavior and that the electorate votes *against* policies and incumbents more than it votes *for* new policies and candidates. The president is the only highly visible national actor and therefore is a prominent reference for choosing a candidate. Thus, a greater proportion of the voters who disapprove of the president are likely to vote than of those who approve, especially if the voters are Independents or of the opposition party. Moreover, disapproval of the president is a stronger source of party defection than approval, and defectors from party voting occur disproportionately within the president's party, primarily among his detractors. Because voting turnout is low in midterm elections, a relatively small amount of negative voting may have significant consequences. About the only thing a president can do to counteract this effect is to be popular so that few voters will have negative opinions about him.[32]

This discussion inevitably raises the question of the president's ability to influence his popularity (or, as Tufte suggests, the economy), which we shall address in the next chapter, where we examine presidential popularity as a source of influence in Congress. In the meantime we can conclude that presidents have not been overly successful in helping to win congressional seats for their party in midterm elections.

Presidential Coattails

Presidential coattails are part of the lore of American electoral behavior. Politicians project them, journalists attribute them, historians recount them, and political scientists analyze them. Yet their extent and consequences remain undetermined. In the following pages we shall attempt to understand this concept better.

Previous Coattail Studies

There have been two basic types of studies of presidential coattails. The first type has relied upon aggregate voting data, comparing the results in congressional districts for presidential and congressional candidates of the same party to discover (1) the extent to which one ran ahead of the other,[33] (2) whether both won, lost, or split the district,[34] (3) the relationship between the vote percentages of the two candidates,[35] (4) the likelihood of the congressional candidate winning his or her district if the presidential running mate received a certain percentage of the vote,[36] and (5) whether both candidates in a district gained or lost over previous elections.[37]

Aggregate voting studies have the advantage of examining a complete record of actual voting behavior in every constituency. Thus, the data is comprehensive and accurate. Aggregate data also permit an analysis of the differences between constituencies at any one time and within the same constituency over time. The principal disadvantage of these studies is that they do not (and cannot) examine voter motivations. This is important, for very different motivational factors can produce similar election results.[38] There are many reasons for voting a straight party ticket, the appeal of a presidential candidate being only one. Others include party loyalty, the appeal of individual issues, and the appeal of individual candidates. Additional problems in interpreting election results arise from the fact that just a small amount of split-ticket voting may produce split results in a congressional district.[39] Finally, the extent of coattails is not clear just from the degree to which a president runs ahead of congressional running mates.[40]

The second major category of presidential coattail studies is comprised of studies based on survey data.[41] These studies have focused on voter motivations. Basically, they have attempted to determine the boundaries of the potential coattail vote by finding and comparing the people who voted a straight party ticket, at least for the presidential and congressional candidates, and those who did not vote primarily on the basis of party identification but who voted for a congressional candidate on the basis of the personal appeal of the presidential candidate of the same party.

Survey studies are strongest where aggregate voting studies are weakest: on the question of voters' motivations. It is very difficult, however, to separate different motivations. Party identification and the appeal of candidates and issues often overlap. Moreover, expensive panel studies are needed to determine which candidate a voter decided upon first, and these are rarely available. Even if they were, there would be the problem of handling simultaneous decisions. As we would expect, survey studies are weakest in the area of constituency-level data, since they are based on national samples. Thus, it is not possible to study results in individual constituencies.

Major Concerns

One aspect common to coattails studies of both categories above is an attempt to discover if and to what extent coattails exist. By the same token, none of the studies attempt to measure the impact of the presidential vote on outcomes in congressional elections. That is the focus of this research.

Presidential coattails have their greatest significance in their impact on the outcomes of congressional elections. If a presidential candidate raises or lowers a representative's normally substantial vote by a few percentage points by being on the ballot, the consequences will be relatively unimportant. But if the coattails of a presidential candidate change the party of the occupant of a congressional seat, the implications for public policy can be significant, especially if a number of congressional districts change party affiliations. Congresspersons of each party tend to vote differently; those of the president's party give him more support. Also, new House members are primary agents of change in public policy.[42]

In his analysis of the 1972 election (in which few House seats changed parties although President Nixon won in a landslide) Walter Dean Burnham argues that incumbents are increasing insulated from electoral effects, such as an adverse presidential landslide. Therefore, he continues, coattails have been "virtually eliminated" by the breakdown in the party system and the increased electoral advantages of incumbents.[43] This argument of decreasing coattail impact provides an additional concern for this study. Not only do we want to measure the impact of coattails on outcomes in congressional elections in a given year, but we also want to examine the impacts over time to learn whether the electoral effects of presidential coattails and congressional elections are becoming increasingly dissociated.

The Model

If presidential coattails influence congressional election outcomes, the better the president runs in a district, the greater should be the chances of a House candidate from his party winning the seat in that district. In our model, the presidential vote in each district is operationalized as the percentage of the total presidential vote received by the winning presidential candidate. The outcome in a House election is operationalized as a dummy variable, with "1" representing "Democrat" and "0" representing "Republican." So that winning presidential and congressional candidates are matched, the signs for the relationship between the presidential vote and congressional outcomes are reversed in years when a Republican wins the presidency. In this way both parties can have the potential to show a positive coattail relationship. In essense, the signs appearing in the tables have been standardized so that a minus indicates a negative relationship. Our study covers the seven presidential elections from 1952 through 1976.

Other factors influence the outcome of House elections besides the presidential vote. The level of support for a political party in a congressional district undoubtedly influences the presidential vote in that district. Similarly, the strength of a party in a constituency will influence which party wins the constituency's congressional seat. Therefore, we must control for the influence of constituency party strength.

The variable of constituency party strength should be an accurate representation of party strength for candidates for national office and not of the results of a deviant election. Its measurement should also be taken as closely as possible to the most recent presidential and congressional elections. At the same time party strength must not be measured in terms of the most recent presidential vote in the constituency to avoid reciprocal causation between it and the president's vote.

With these considerations in mind, constituency party strength is operationally defined as the average of the Democratic party's percentage of the vote in the elections for the three national offices (president, senator, and representative) in each constituency. Using these three components allows us to triangulate the measurement of constituency party strength, thereby including elections from different years and allowing us to average out the results of deviant elections. To avoid the problem of reciprocal causation, data are used from the presidential election *previous* to the election measured in the presidential vote variable. An example of the data comprising the index of constituency party strength is as follows: For the 1960 presidential election, the three components of the variable are the 1958 House election, the 1956 or 1958 senatorial election (whichever is most recent), and the 1956 presidential election.

Special care was taken to insure that the data used for any given district over a period of years actually represented the voting that took place in that district. Reapportionment created some problems because new districts were created and others were renumbered. If a district was entirely new, with no history of voting, it was eliminated from the analysis. If a district was only two years old and therefore did not have a history of presidential or senatorial voting (usually the former), the existing voting statistics were averaged together to arrive at the measure of constituency party strength. Finally, if the district changed its number, the most recent data for the district was matched with older data from the same district having the old district number.

The relationships involved in the analysis that follows are displayed in Figure

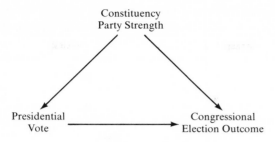

Figure 3.1
Paths of influence among constituency party strength, presidential vote, and congressional election outcome.

3.1. All the figures in the tables below represent the relationships between the presidential vote and congressional election outcomes while controlling for constituency party strength.

Analysis

Table 3.7 shows the impact of the presidential vote on outcomes in all congressional districts. Before examining the data, two general points should be made regarding the figures. First, unstandardized regression coefficients are used because we are comparing data sets with different variations. Second, the t test for statistical significance is calculated for each figure. Although we are dealing with universes of data, significance tests can aid us by providing parameters of true relationships. If the relationships discussed below cannot pass tests of significance, then we can be confident they are really nonexistent. This is especially true since the large N's involved should make it easier for the relationships to pass significance tests.

The figures in Table 3.7 indicate that the effect of presidential coattails on congressional election outcomes was statistically significant in each presidential election from 1952 through 1968, although the impact steadily declined. By 1972 no coattail effect was apparent. This is also the case for President Carter in 1976. The strongest coattail impact, which occurred in 1952, can be interpreted as follows: For every 1 percent of the vote received by the president (Eisenhower), the probability of a representative from his party (Republican) being elected increased 1.3 percent. The 1956 results indicate that for every 1 percent of the vote received by the president, the probability of a representative of his party being elected increased 0.8 percent, and so on. The impact is generally weak.

These findings are consistent with the view that coattails are no longer a significant factor in congressional elections, but before accepting this view, we should be sure that the results are reflecting the true relationships. The figure in Table 3.7 may mask relationships because the North and the South are not

73

Table 3.7
Effect of Presidential Coattails on Congressional Election Outcomes in All Districts

YEAR	N	b
1952	420	.013*
1956	435	.008*
1960	436	.008*
1964	421	.007*
1968	435	.006*
1972	419	−.001
1976	431	.005

* Significant at .05 level.

differentiated in the computations. We would expect coattails to be weak in the South because of the one-party system there. Democratic candidates have traditionally won almost all the House seats regardless of the success of the Democratic presidential nominee. This situation may artificially depress a strong relationship existing in the North. Thus, we should separate the eleven states of the Confederacy from the rest of the states and calculate the coattail effects for both regions.

Table 3.8 displays the results of these computations. The second column shows that the impact of the presidential vote on outcomes in congressional elections in the North has steadily diminished since 1952 and that it has not been statistically significant since 1956. These findings clearly support the argument that the coattail effect has diminished over time.

The last column of Table 3.8 indicates that the coattail effect in the South has not been statistically significant except in 1968 and 1976. This is as expected, given the noncompetitive nature of most congressional elections in the South throughout the period covered. The exceptional case of 1968 cannot be explained by Republican gains, since the party only picked up two seats in the South. Rather, it seems to be related to George Wallace's impressive showing in the presidential election. He carried five of the eleven southern states and won over 25 percent of the vote in five others. Most of this vote would have gone to Richard Nixon if Wallace had not been on the ballot.[44] Therefore, the vote that Nixon did receive came from true Republicans, the same voters most likely to vote for Republican candidates for the House. If most of the Wallace vote was added to the Nixon vote in each district, the 1968 results would be masked, because those who ranked Wallace over Nixon generally voted for the Democratic congressional candidates, as evidenced by the Democratic House victories.

Similarly, President Carter's statistically significant, albeit weak, 1976 coattails in the South did not result in any net gain for Democrats. The explanation for his seeming coattail effect appears to be the extremely poor performance of George McGovern in the South in 1972. He ran more poorly there than any modern Democratic presidential candidate. Thus, our measurement of consti-

Table 3.8

Effect of Presidential Coattails on Congressional Election Outcomes by Region

YEAR	NORTH		SOUTH	
	N	*b*	*N*	*b*
1952	318	.018*	102	−.001
1956	329	.010*	106	.002
1960	330	.006	106	−.003
1964	324	,002	97	.001
1968	329	−.001	106	.009*
1972	316	−.003	103	.002
1976	323	.000	108	.013*

*Significant at .05 level.

tuency party strength (the expected party vote for Democratic candidates) is unnaturally low. The low constituency party strength variable allows Carter's 1976 presidential vote to explain more of congressional electoral outcomes.

Most of the findings in Tables 3.7 and 3.8 are consistent with common impressions of coattail strength. We would expect some coattail effect in 1952 when the Republicans gained twenty-two seats in the House, but little impact in 1960 when the Democrats lost twenty seats in spite of Kennedy's victory. Similarly, only five new Republican seats accompanied Nixon's 1968 election and only twelve accompanied his 1972 landslide; furthermore, many of these victories were largely due to the reapportionment following the 1970 census.[45] The Democrats gained only two House seats to garnish President Carter's 1976 victory. Thus, we would not expect much coattail effect in these elections.

Table 3.8 indicates that the coattail effect in the North in 1956 was fairly sizable despite the fact that the Democrats actually gained two seats in the face of Eisenhower's landslide. This is not as unreasonable as it may seem. The president's coattails may have helped Republicans in the House *retain* their seats and stemmed the rising Democratic congressional tide (which appeared in full force in 1958), even if they were not effective in winning new Republican seats.

Also, part of the strength of the measured coattail effect in 1956 might be spurious due to the high correlation between constituency party strength and the presidential vote. The absolute value of the zero-order correlation is .87, the highest for any of the equations in this study. This strong relationship may have helped to increase the relationship between the presidential vote and congressional election outcomes. The multicollinearity problem simply reduces our confidence in the measurement of the coefficient.

The 1964 Election

The biggest surprise is the low figures in both tables for 1964, an election in which the Democrats picked up thirty-eight seats. The data for the Northern states in this election shows that Johnson ran well nearly everywhere: The standard deviation for the presidential vote variable is the lowest of any of the seven elections examined. In fact, Johnson won 113 districts that elected Republicans to the House.[46] Conversely, thirty-three Democrats won congressional seats in districts carried by Goldwater. Thus, one-third of the districts were split, a figure exceeded only in 1972. This indicates that Democrats in both the North and South won or lost largely independently of whether Johnson ran well. In addition, only in northern districts in which Johnson won with at least 60 percent of the vote were Democratic candidates likely to win,[47] and these were generally districts that had been Democratic in previous years—hardly an indicator of a strong coattail effect.

There is also a freakish quality to the Democratic successes in the House races in the 1964 election. Twenty-eight of the forty-seven Democratic freshmen who won districts that had been represented by Republicans in the preceding Congress won with 52 percent of the vote or less, and all but two won with 56 percent or less. In addition, twenty-three of the thirty-nine Republcan incumbents who were defeated had won their previous election with 57 percent of the vote or less (fourteen had 55 percent or less). Yet we cannot attribute even victories in close races in marginal districts to Johnson's landslide.

In 1964, 52 percent of the public were registered Democrats.[48] This was the party's highest rating ever and a 6 percent net increase over 1962. Another 9 percent of the public said that they were independents who were closer to the Democrats (a 2 percent gain over 1962). Meanwhile, the Republicans were at a modern all-time low of 24 percent (a 4 percent decline from 1962). To a large degree, this increase in Democratic party identification among voters likely accounted for the Democratic victories in marginal districts.

It is also noteworthy that nearly half (eighteen) of the thirty-nine defeated Republican incumbents had gone out of their way to be identified with Senator Goldwater by signing a full-page preconvention advertisement in the *New York Times* (June 17, 1964), endorsing his nomination. The very high percentage of defeats for these signers is not attributable to their conservativeness or their lack of support for the liberal policies of President Johnson, because their equally conservative colleagues who were not so closely identified wtih Goldwater were defeated at a considerably lower rate. Moreover, there was no relationship between changes in the congressional vote and changes in the presidential vote from previous elections in the districts of nonsigners.[49] Instead, the defeat of the signers seems to be due to identification with Goldwater. Voters here seem to have voted *against* the senator, whose image in the public was "phenomenally unfavorable,"[50] rather than for the president.

The arguments that at least some voters may vote for the congressional candidate of one party because they disapprove of the leader of the other party is supported by the research of Sam Kernell.[51] He cites evidence that congressional candidates of the president's party believe that the president's unpopularity can work against them in midterm elections; thus, they try to avoid association with an unpopular president. More significantly, he found that disapproval of the president was a more powerful influence on voting turnout and choice in midterm elections than approval was.

In sum, considerable evidence refutes the conventional wisdom that presidential coattails had a strong effect on congressional election outcomes in 1964. This evidence supports the findings in Table 3.8 of a weak coattail effect that year.

Why Has the Coattail Effect Vanished?

Clearly, the coattail effect on congressional elections has been minimal for some time. Why? We might attribute this to the decreasing frequency of party voting.[52] However, while there has been an increase in split-ticket voting,[53] party voting has never been the cause of the coattail effect. As we noted earlier, for there to be a coattail effect, voters must vote for a congressional candidate who is of the party of their presidential choice on the basis of the presidential candidate's appeal and not on the basis of party loyalty.

Another explanation for the decreasing impact of the presidential vote on outcomes in House elections cites the fact that the percentage of electorally competitive districts has declined since the mid-1950s.[54] If House seats are less competitive, then presidential candidates will have to have stronger coattails to affect the outcomes in House elections.

While lack of competitiveness seems to be the immediate cause of the diminished impact of coattails, how do we explain the decrease in competition? First, there is increasing evidence that members of Congress have been quite responsive to public opinion in recent years[55] and may be becoming more so.[56] If this is true, then voters should have less reason to vote for opposing candidates.

Second, representatives seem to be devoting more attention to their constituents[57] by adopting an ombudsman role. To aid themselves in this effort, they are increasingly employing mobile offices, "hot lines," and computer terminals plugged into government data banks. With an expanded federal bureaucracy, representatives can provide more services for their constituents and probably receive more constituent complaints about the bureaucracy in need of remedies. This work is good publicity and should aid the representatives in their reelections. In addition, some voters may be viewing representatives primarily as ombudsmen and are thus placing more value on Washington experience in their voting decisions.[58] This also would help the reelection of incumbents.

Implications

The reduced coattail impact has two important implications for public policy. The first is that presidents have lost a potential source of influence in Congress. Since representatives of the president's party are generally more amenable to his persuasion and support his proposals more than representatives of the opposition party, it is to a president's advantage to carry members of his party into Congress on his coattails. But it appears that he is no longer able to do this.

A second implication is that it is more difficult for a president to bring about major policy changes because he does not have a large number of representatives in his debt. Moreover, the lack of a coattail effect has made it safer for congressional candidates to ignore national issues in their campaigns and to focus on local concerns and such nonsubstantive matters as their attendance records and family life. Therefore, a president is less likely to take office with a substantial number of backers who have strongly committed themselves to his programs in the campaign.

We shall end our discussion of coattails in the form of a caveat. This study has not attempted to explain outcomes in congressional elections per se, but rather to learn whether and to what degree presidential coattails influence them. A full explanation of the broader question of congressional election outcomes awaits further analysis.

Bipartisanship

Despite the president's advantage in dealing with members of his party in Congress, a president is often forced to solicit bipartisan support for several reasons. First, the opposition party may control one or both houses of Congress. Even if the president received total support from all members of his party, he would still need support from some members of the opposition. For instance, since 1953 the Republicans have controlled the executive branch and the Democrats have controlled the legislative branch in fourteen years (1955 through 1960 and 1969 through 1976).

For a bipartisan approach to be successful depends upon restraining partisanship to avoid alienating the opposition. President Eisenhower, who faced a Democratic Congress in six of his eight years as president, and his staff consciously attempted to follow such an approach. (Eisenhower was also not inclined towards partisanship.)[59] He cultivated Democratic votes, especially on foreign policy,[60] and was fairly successful.

Nixon and Ford also faced Democratic-controlled Congresses. They tried to steer a middle course between the Eisenhower soft sell and the more partisan approaches of Kennedy and Johnson. They wanted to maximize Republican strength while appealing to conservative Democrats by taking an issue-oriented, ideological line as well as a party line.[61] In the 1972 elections, Nixon did not adopt a heavily partisan line, hoping for a majority based on principles rather than just party.[62]

A second reason for bipartisanship is that no matter how large the representation of the president's party in Congress, he cannot always depend upon it for support. Tables 3.1 and 3.2 clearly show that members of his own party frequently oppose the president. As we shall see in Chapter 7, Southern Democrats support Democratic presidents less consistently than do Northern Democrats. This is especially true regarding civil rights legislation, as Table 3.9

Table 3.9

Votes on Final Passage of Major Civil Rights Legislation
Supported by Democratic Presidents

LEGISLATION	HOUSE			SENATE		
	Repub-licans	Northern Democrats	Southern Democrats	Repub-licans	Northern Democrats	Southern Democrats
24th Amendment (poll tax), 1962	132–15	132– 1	31–70	30–1	39–1	8–14
1964 Civil Rights Act	138–34	141– 4	11–92	27–6	43–1	3–20
1965 Voting Rights Act	112–24	188– 1	33–60	30–2	42–0	5–17
1968 Open Housing Act	100–84	137–13	13–75	29–3	39–0	3–17

SOURCE: Adapted from "GOP Played Key Role in Civil Rights Laws," *Congressional Quarterly Weekly Report,* April 29, 1978, p. 1050.

NOTE: Figures to left of dash are yes votes; those to right are no votes.

illustrates. Southern Democrats overwhelmingly opposed each piece of legislation listed in the table, and the president would have lost the vote each time without the support of Republicans.

Civil rights is not the only policy area in which Democratic presidents have needed Republican support. When John Kennedy was elected president, an aide in the White House legislative liaison office made a detailed study of the prospects for his program in the House. He concluded that they were "very bleak" despite the clear Democratic majority there.[63] Lyndon Johnson concluded at the beginning of his presidency that as a progressive president, he would need help from the leaders of both parties to pass his domestic legislation.[64] Thus, he regularly consulted Republican congressional leaders and restrained evidence of partisanship in public forums.

Johnson worked very closely with Senate Republican leader Everett Dicksen. They had many intimate, one-to-one conferences, which Johnson regarded as essential for gaining the necessary Republican support for controversial legislation. The president gave Dirksen the same preferential treatment given to Democratic Senate Majority Leader Mike Mansfield and spoke to Dirksen frequently, sometimes as often as ten times a day.[65] Kennedy did not share the rapport with Dirksen that Johnson had but still had the senator to the White House monthly and talked to him on the phone slightly more often.[66] In some instances the senator provided Kennedy with crucial support.[67]

Republican presidents have also had trouble gaining support from members of their party in Congress. President Eisenhower was plagued in his first term by Senator Joseph McCarthy's irresponsible charges against his administration and by Senator John Bricker's attempts (nearly successful) to pass a constitutional amendment limiting the president's use of executive agreements. In the House, Representative John Taber, chairperson of the House Appropriations Committee, fought him on mutual security (foreign aid) funds, and Representative Daniel Reed, chairperson of the House Ways and Means Committee, did the same on income tax legislation. More generally, he had trouble gaining support from the basically conservative congressional Republicans for his internationalist foreign policy and his moderate domestic policies.[68] President Nixon went to the highly unusual step of helping to defeat Republican senator Charles Goodell of New York in the 1970 election because of the senator's politically liberal opposition to the president's policies.

The primary reason that party discipline in Congress is relatively weak is that the parties are highly decentralized; no one controls those aspects of politics that are of vital concern to members of Congress: nominations and elections. Members of Congress are largely self-recruited, gain their party's nominations by their own efforts and not the party's, and provide most of the money and organizational support needed for their elections. Presidents can do little to influence the results of these activities, and usually they don't even try.[69] As President Kennedy said in 1962, "Party loyalty or responsibility means damn little. They've got to take care of themselves first.They [House members] all have to run this year—I don't and I couldn't hurt most of them if I wanted to . . . and there's little the National Committee can do to help them."[70]

Nor do presidents control their party's machinery in Congress. Committee chairpersons and ranking minority members have traditionally been determined by seniority, and the chairpersons always come from the majority party in the chamber, which often is not the president's. The few exceptions to the seniority rule in recent years were not in any way inspired by the White House (which was controlled by Republicans while both houses of Congress were controlled by Democrats). For all practical purposes, the president plays no role at all in determining the holders of these important positions.

Party leaders, who at least theoretically are to serve as liaisons with the president, are not always dependable supporters. They certainly are not simple extensions of the White House. As one presidential aide said of Senate Majority Leader Byrd in 1977, "God, is he independent. He ain't our man—he's the Senate's man."[71] Presidents do not lobby for candidates for congressional party leadership positions and virtually always remain neutral during the selection process; at most they may occasionally express a preference for one of the candidates.[72] They have no desire to alienate important members of Congress, whose support they will need.

Presidents also do not control the actions of party leaders or consistently receive their support. Eisenhower was unable to convince House Minority Leader Joseph Martin either to bring several younger Republicans to the weekly White House legislative strategy meetings[73] or to give former Majority Leader Charles Halleck a significant role in party affairs.[74] He was opposed by many Republican party leaders on his school aid, foreign trade, budgetary, and foreign policies.[75] Senate Majority Leader Mike Mansfield broke with President Johnson over the war in Vietnam and sustained his opposition for the rest of Johnson's term of office.

Yet other problems confront a president trying to mobilize his party in Congress. If the president's party has just won the presidency, it will have to adjust from its past stance as the opposition. This is not always easily done.[76] Moreover, when a new party gains control of the White House, committee and party leaders will be less influential because they will be expected to take their lead on major issues from the White House. This may also make party discipline more difficult. Finally, the pressures to be "president of all the people" rather than a highly partisan figure should not be overlooked. This role expectation of being above the political fray undoubtedly constrains presidents and inhibits overtly partisan actions.

Despite the frequent necessity of a bipartisan strategy, it is not without costs. Bipartisanship often creates a strain with the extremists within the president's party as a Republican president tries to appeal to the left for Democratic votes and a Democratic president to the right for Republican votes. While the Republican right wing and Democratic left wing may find it difficult to join a coalition in favor of alternatives to their own president's policies, they may complicate a president's strategy by joining those who oppose his policies.

Conclusion

We have seen that party affiliation is a source of influence for the president. Members of Congress of his party tend to give him more support than members of the opposition party. While much of this support is due to shared policy preferences, on some issues the pull of party affiliation provides the president with additional support. Unfortunately for the president, however, he can do little to increase the number of his party's representatives in Congress, since midterm campaigning by the president and presidential coattails have little impact, and he cannot always rely on support from his party. Thus, even a president whose party controls Congress must often make bipartisan appeals and depend upon other sources of influence.

Notes

1. John W. Kingdon, *Congressmen's Voting Decisions* (New York: Harper & Row, 1973), pp. 175–176.
2. Mark Kesselman, "Presidential Leadership in Foreign Policy," *Midwest Journal of Political Science* 5 (August 1961): 284–289; Mark Kesselman, "Presidential Leadership in Congress on Foreign Policy: A Replication of a Hypothesis," *Midwest Journal of Political Science* 9 (November 1965): 401–406.
3. Charles M. Tidmarch and Charles M. Sabatt, "Presidential Leadership Change and Foreign Policy Roll-Call Voting in the U.S. Senate," *Western Political Quarterly* 25 (December 1972): 613–625. In each group except Republicans under Nixon, a few senators moved in a direction opposite to what would be expected.

4. Aage R. Clausen, *How Congressmen Decide: A Policy Focus* (New York: St. Martin's, 1973), chap. 8.

5. Aage R. Clausen and Carl E. Van Horn, "The Congressional Response to a Decade of Change: 1963–1972," *Journal of Politics* 39 (August 1977), pp. 632, 635, 653.

6. Herbert B. Asher and Herbert F. Weisberg, "Voting Change in Congress: Some Dynamic Perspectives on an Evolutionary Process," *American Journal of Political Science* 22 (May 1978): 409–416.

7. Ibid., p. 414.

8. Ibid., pp. 406–409.

9. Clausen and Van Horn, "The Congressional Response," pp. 637–640.

10. For example, see Kingdon, *Congressmen's Voting Decisions,* p. 112.

11. Ibid., pp. 173–175, 178.

12. Malcolm E. Jewell, *Senatorial Politics and Foreign Policy* (Lexington, Ky.: University of Kentucky Press, 1962), pp. 31–33, 36, 41–46.

13. See Kingdon, *Congressmen's Voting Decisions,* p. 184.

14. Ibid., pp. 172, 175, 178, 180. See also Donald R. Matthews, *U.S. Senators and Their World* (New York: Norton, 1973), p. 140.

15. "Shadowboxing," *Newsweek,* June 6, 1977, p. 15.

16. Lawrence O'Brien, *No Final Victories* (Garden City, N.Y.: Doubleday, 1974), p. 106. See also Lawrence O'Brien, "Larry O'Brien Discusses White House Contacts with Capitol Hill," in *The Presidency,* ed. Aaron Wildavsky (Boston: Little, Brown, 1969), p. 482.

17. Kingdon, *Congressmen's Voting Decisions,* pp. 172–173.

18. Ibid., pp. 180–181, 184, 186.

19. Arthur Larson, *Eisenhower: The President Nobody Knew* (New York: Scribner's, 1968), p. 35. See also Dwight D. Eisenhower, *Mandate for Change: 1953–1956* (New York: Signet, 1963), pp. 519, 522–523. See also Dwight D. Eisenhower, *Waging Peace: 1956–1961* (Garden City, N.Y.: Doubleday, 1965), pp. 380–381, where Eisenhower almost apologizes for making a political speech.

20. William Safire, *Before the Fall: An Inside View of the Pre-Watergate White House* (New York: Doubleday, 1975), pp. 318, 540.

21. Jack Anderson, "Kissinger Fears Assad Might 'Jump the Tracks,'" *New Orleans States-Item,* April 12, 1974, p. A-11.

22. Robert Donovan, *Eisenhower: The Inside Story* (New York: Harper & Row, 1956), p. 277; Eisenhower, *Mandate for Change,* pp. 518–523; Sherman Adams, *Firsthand Report* (New York: Popular Library, 1962), pp. 167–168. While the purpose was to show what good hands the country was in, the impact of the event is unclear. The participants were stilted and unreal.

23. V. O. Key, Jr., *Politics, Parties and Pressure Groups,* 5th ed. (New York: Crowell, 1964), pp. 566–567.

24. Arthur M. Schlesinger, Jr., *A Thousand Days: John F. Kennedy in the White House* (Boston: Houghton Mifflin, 1965), pp. 757–758; Theodore Sorensen, *Kennedy* (New York: Bantam, 1966), pp. 391, 399.

25. Safire, *Before the Fall,* pp. 317–322; Rowland Evans, Jr., and Robert D. Novak, *Nixon in the White House: The Frustration of Power* (New York: Vintage, 1972), pp. 318–322, 328–330, 336–345. Also see Mark J. Green, James M. Fallows, and David R. Zwick, *Who Runs Congress?* (New York: Bantam, 1972), p. 101.

26. Daniel P. Moynihan, *The Politics of a Guaranteed Income: The Nixon Administration and the Family Assistance Plan* (New York: Vintage, 1973), p. 531.

27. Safire, *Before the Fall,* pp. 336, 339; Evans and Novak, *Nixon in the White House,* pp. 344–345.

28. Angus Campbell, "Voting and Elections: Past and Present," *Journal of Politics* 26 (November 1964): 745–757: Key, *Politics, Parties and Pressure Groups,* pp. 568–569; Angus Campbell, "Surge and Decline: A Study of Electoral Change," *Public Opinion Quarterly* 24 (Fall 1960): 397–418.

29. Barbara Hinckley, "Interpreting House Midterm Elections: Towards a Measurement of the In-Party's 'Expected' Loss of Seats," *American Political Science Review* 61 (September 1967): 694–700.

30. Robert B. Arsenau and Raymond E. Wolfinger, "Voting Behavior in Congressional Elections," paper presented at the annual meeting of the American Political Science Association, New Orleans, September 4–8, 1973, pp. 10–11.

31. Edward R. Tufte, "Determinants of Outcomes in Congressional Elections," *American Political Science Review* 69 (September 1975): 812–826; Samuel Kernell, "Presidential Popularity and Negative Voting: An Alternative Explanation of the Midterm Decline of the President's Party," *American Political Science Review* 71 (March 1977): 44–66.

32. Kernell, "Presidential Popularity and Negative Voting."

33. Charles Press, "Voting Statistics and Presidential Coattails," *American Political Science Review* 52 (December 1958): 1041–1050.

34. Milton C. Cummings, Jr., *Congressmen and the Electorate: Elections for the U.S. House and the President, 1920–1964* (New York: Free Press, 1966), chaps. 1–2.

35. Malcolm Moos, *Politics, Presidents and Coattails* (Baltimore: Johns Hopkins University Press, 1952), pp. 110–111.

36. Milton C. Cummings, Jr., "Nominations and Elections for the House of Representatives," in *The National Election of 1964,* ed. Milton C. Cummings, Jr., (Washington, D.C.: Brookings Institution, 1966), pp. 231–233; Charles M. Tidmarch and Douglas Carpenter, "Congressmen and the Electorate, 1968 and 1972," *Journal of Politics* 40 (May 1978): 479–487.

37. Charles Press, "Presidential Coattails and Party Cohesion," *Midwest Journal of Political Science* 7 (November 1963): 320–335.

38. Warren E. Miller, "Presidential Coattails: A Study in Political Myth and Methodology," *Public Opinion Quarterly* 19 (Winter 1955–56): 368; Angus Campbell and Warren E. Miller, "The Motivational Basis for Straight and Split Ticket Voting," *American Political Science Review* 51 (June 1957): 293–312.

39. Cummings, *Congressmen and the Electorate,* p. 51.

40. Miller, "Presidential Coattails," pp. 354–356.

41. Miller, "Presidential Coattails, pp. 353–368; Campbell and Miller, "The Motivational Basis for Straight and Split Ticket Voting," pp. 293–312; William B. Moreland, "Angels, Pinpoints, and Voters: The Pattern for a Coattail," *American Journal of Political Science* 17 (February 1973): 170–176.

42. See, for example, David W. Brady and Naomi B. Lynn, "Switched Seat Congressional Districts: Their Effect on Party Voting and Public Policy," *American Journal of Political Science* 21 (August 1973): 528–543; Asher and Weisberg, "Voting Change in Congress," pp. 391–425; Clausen and Van Horn, "The Congressional Response," pp. 624–666; Clausen, *How Congressmen Decide.*

43. Walter D. Burnham, "Insulation and Responsiveness in Congressional Elections," *Political Science Quarterly* 90 (Fall 1975): 412–413.

44. David A. Mazmanian, *Third Parties in Congressional Elections* (Washington, D.C.: Brookings Institution, 1974), p. 71; Philip E. Converse, Warren E. Miller, Jerrold G. Rusk, and Arthur C. Wolfe, "Continuity and Change in American Politics: Parties and Issues in the 1968 Election," *American Political Science Review* 63 (December 1969), pp. 1090–1092.

45. Congressional Quarterly, *Current American Government: Spring 1973* (Washington, D.C.: Congressional Quarterly, 1973), p. 10.

46. Walter DeVries and Lance Tarrance, Jr., *The Ticket Splitter: A New Force in American Politics* (Grand Rapids, Mich.: Wm. B. Eerdmans, 1972), p. 30.

47. Cummings, "Nominations and Elections," p. 233.

48. Richard Brody, "Change and Stability in the Components of Partisan Identification," *DEA News*, No. 13 (Spring 1977), p. 13.

49. Robert A. Schoenberger, "Campaign Strategy and Party Loyalty: The Electoral Relevance of Candidate Decision-Making in the 1964 Congressional Elections," *American Political Science Review* 63 (June 1969): 515–520.

50. Philip E. Converse, Aage R. Clausen, and Warren E. Miller, "Electoral Myth and Reality: The 1964 Election," *American Political Science Review* 59 (June 1965), pp. 330–331.

51. Kernell, "Presidential Popularity and Negative Voting."

52. Burnham, "Insulation and Responsiveness," p. 413 fn.

53. Robert B. Arsenau, "Motivational Conflict and Split Ticket Voting," paper presented at the annual meeting of the American Political Science Association, San Francisco, September 2–5, 1975,

54. David Mayhew, "Congressional Elections: The Case of the Vanishing Marginals," *Polity* 6 (Spring 1974): 295–317.

55. Kingdon, *Congressmen's Voting Decision*, chap. 2. See also our discussions in Chapter 2 and Chapter 4.

56. Barbara S. Deckard, "Political Upheaval and Congressional Voting: The Effects of the 1960s on Voting Patterns in the House of Representatives," *Journal of Politics* 38 (May 1976): 326–345.

57. Richard F. Fenno, Jr., *Home Style: House Members in Their Districts* (Boston: Little, Brown, 1978).

58. Morris P. Fiorina, "The Case of the Vanishing Marginals: The Bureaucracy Did it," *American Political Science Review* 72 (March 1977): 177–181; Glenn R. Parker and Roger H. Davidson, "Why Do Americans Love Their Congressmen So Much More Than Their Congress?" *Legislative Studies Quarterly* 4 (February 1979): 53–61.

59. Larson, *Eisenhower*, pp. 34–36; Abraham Holtzman, *Legislative Liaison: Executive Leadership in Congress* (Chicago: Rand McNally, 1970). p. 240; Eisenhower, *Mandate for Change*, p. 245; Stephen J. Wayne, *The Legislative Presidency* (New York: Harper & Row, 1978), p. 142.

60. Randall B. Ripley, *Majority Party Leadership in Congress* (Boston: Little, Brown, 1969), p. 125. See also Jewell, *Senatorial Politics and Foreign Policy*, p. 78.

61. Wayne, *The Legislative Presidency*, p. 156.

62. Safire, *Before the Fall*, pp. 547, 550, 685.

63. Wayne, *The Legislative Presidency,* p. 174, fn. 17.

64. Joseph A. Califano, Jr., *A Presidential Nation* (New York: Norton, 1975), p. 155.

65. Ibid., pp. 155–156. See also Eric Goldman, *The Tragedy of Lyndon Johnson* (New York: Dell, 1974), pp. 83–84, 385–387; Jack Bell, *The Johnson Treatment* (New York: Harper & Row, 1965), p. 40; Neil MacNeil, *Dirksen: Portrait of a Public Man* (New York: World, 1970), pp. 274, 276–281.

66. MacNeil, *Dirksen,* pp. 225, 281. Nevertheless, Kennedy sought bipartisan support less than did Johnson. See also Holtzman, *Legislative Liaison,* p. 241.

67. See, for example, Bell, *The Johnson Treatment,* pp. 38–39.

68. See, for example, Eisenhower, *Mandate for Change,* p. 246; Gary Reichard, *The Reaffirmation of Republicanism: Eisenhower and the Eighty-third Congress* (Knoxville: University of Tennessee Press, 1975), p. 121.

69. William H. Riker and William Bast, "Presidential Action in Congressional Nominations," in *The Presidency,* ed. Wildavsky.

70. Sorensen, *Kennedy,* p. 387.

71. "Jimmy's 'Oracle,'" *Newsweek,* October 3, 1977, p. 27.

72. Eisenhower, *Mandate for Change,* pp. 274, 363, 530; Eisenhower, *Waging Peace,* p. 384; Donovan, *Eisenhower,* p. 112; Emmet Hughes, *The Ordeal of Power* (New York: Atheneum, 1975), pp. 128–129; Dan Rather and Gary Gates, *The Palace Guard* (New York: Harper & Row, 1974), p. 303. An exception seems to have been Johnson's recommendation (as vice president) of Hubert Humphrey for majority whip in the Senate. See Hubert H. Humphrey, *The Education of a Public Man: My Life and Politics* (Garden City, N.Y.: Doubleday, 1976), p. 242.

73. Eisenhower, *Waging Peace,* p. 384.

74. Eisenhower, *Mandate for Change,* pp. 529–530. However, Eisenhower did insist that Halleck attend White House congressional leadership meetings despite his ouster as majority leader.

75. See, for example, Hughes, *The Ordeal of Power,* pp. 126–128; Ripley, *Majority Party Leadership in Congress,* p. 122, 126–127; Donovan, *Eisenhower,* p. 242; Adams, *Firsthand Report,* p. 368; Marquis Childs, *Eisenhower: Captive Hero* (New York: Harcourt Brace, 1958), p. 248; Jewell, *Senatorial Politics and Foreign Policy,* pp. 62–63.

76. See, for example, Nixon's discussion of budget deficits with Republican representatives in Safire, *Before the Fall,* p. 276. See also Joe Martin, *My First Fifty Years in Politics* (New York: McGraw-Hill, 1960), p. 229.

4 | *Presidential Prestige as a Source of Influence*

In a representative democracy, the people are ultimately supposed to hold the power. Thus, the president's standing with the public should be a source of influence. If the public voices its support for a particular presidential policy, we would expect Congress to listen. Since the public rarely expresses clear opinions on policy, however, a significant question is whether the president's prestige or popularity (the terms will be used interchangeably) does serve as a source of influence in Congress.

Views of the Relationship

The most noted proponent of the view that presidential popularity engenders presidential support in Congress is Richard Neustadt, who cites presidential prestige as a primary source of presidential power. Operating mostly in the background, Neustadt argues, presidential popularity sets the limits of what Washingtonians will do for or to the president; widespread popularity gives the president leeway and decreases resistance to his policies.[1]

Abraham Lincoln once declared, "Public sentiment is everything. With public sentiment nothing can fail, without it nothing can succeed." This view is echoed by Eisenhower aide and authority on the presidency Emmet John Hughes:

> Beyond all tricks of history and all quirks of Presidents, there would appear to be one unchallengeable truth: the dependence of Presidential authority on popular support. . . . And the judgments of all historians of the Presidency concur that the loss of the people's trust is the one mortal disaster from which there can be no real recovery.[2]

President Eisenhower was an extremely popular president, and observers have concluded that this helped him to preempt challenges from congressional Democrats[3] and to bring around Republicans like Senator Everett Dirksen, who switched his allegiance to the president at the peak of the latter's popularity, probably in part to be associated with Eisenhower in the 1956 election.[4] On the 1955 tax cut proposal, which Eisenhower opposed, Vice President Nixon told Republicans in Congress that they would not be defeated in the 1956 election on the basis of their vote on the tax cut per se. "What will count," he said, "is whether you were for or against the President."[5]

In his memoirs, President Johnson stated that "Presidential popularity is a major source of strength in gaining cooperation from Congress."[6] He told aide Jack Valenti early in his presidency, "I keep hitting hard because I know this honeymoon won't last. Every day I lose a little more political capital. That's why we have to keep at it, never letting up. One day soon, I don't know when, the critics and the snipers will move in and we will be at stalemate. We have to get all we can, now, before the roof comes down."[7] Thus, in February of 1965, following his landslide victory, he assembled the congressional liaison officials from the various departments and told them that his victory at the polls "might be more of a loophole than a mandate" and that since his popularity could decrease rapidly, they would have to use it to their advantage while it lasted.[8]

Johnson followed his own advice. At the end of the extraordinarily productive 1965 session of Congress, he tried to push the District of Columbia home rule bill through Congress, a feat that several presidents had attempted unsuccessfully. When asked by an aide why he was working seven days a week on the bill when the same liberal majority would be returning in January, he replied that he knew the odds were greatly against his success and that it was the only chance he would have. Despite the returning liberal majority, "they'll all be thinking about their reelections. I'll have made mistakes, my polls will be down, and they'll be trying to put some distance between themselves and me. They won't want to go into the fall with their opponents calling 'em Lyndon Johnson's rubber stamp."[9]

Richard Nixon, whose problems with presidential popularity we shall examine in detail below, agreed with his predecessor about the importance of the president's standing in the public, stating, "No leader survives simply by doing well. A leader survives when people have confidence in him when he's not doing well."[10]

President Carter's aides were quite explicit about the importance of Carter's popularity in their efforts to influence Congress. One stated that the "only way to keep those guys [Congress] honest is to keep our popularity high."[11] *Congressional Quarterly* found that the president's legislative liaison officials generally agreed that their effectiveness with Congress ultimately depended upon the president's ability to influence public opinion. As one of them said, "When you go up to the Hill and the latest polls show Carter isn't doing well, there isn't much reason for a member to go along with him. There's little we can do if the member isn't persuaded on the issue."[12] Another White House aide was even more explicit: "No president whose popularity is as low as this President's has much clout on the Hill."[13]

The view from Congress was much the same. When Carter was high in the polls, Speaker "Tip" O'Neill said Congress would have a hard time overriding any of his vetoes because of his broad public support.[14] When he was low in the polls a year later, Representative John Anderson, chairperson of the House Republican Conference, found that Carter's influence on the Hill had eroded.[15]

Two Explanations for the Relationship

Although numerous authors and observers have argued that presidential prestige is an effective tool in influencing members of Congress, they have provided only very general explanations of this relationship. I suggest that there are at least two explanations: The first is derived from role theory, and the second is based on the incentive for reelection.

Davidson's study of roles in the Eighty-eighth Congress (1963 and 1964, which were the middle years of our study) found that 82 percent of the members of the House considered the primary or secondary aim of their activities ("purposive" role) to be that of a "tribune." In other words, discovering and reflecting public opinion were very significant functions of their positions. Davidson also found that 69 percent of the members of the House replied that to some degree they adopted the role of "delegate." That is, they felt they should accept instructions from their constituents.[16] There is no reason to think that senators view their roles differently, especially since so many of them have previously served in the House.

In addition, Davidson, O'Leary, and Kovenock show that "the public expects Congress to cooperate with the president and to expedite major aspects of his legislative programs."[17] Presumably the strength of this expectation is related to the strength of the public's support for the president. Thus, if members of Congress respond to expectations (whether their own or the public's), they should increase their support for the president as the public increases its support for him.

Many other purposive and representational roles may exist besides those that have been examined in the literature. Moreover, the role studies of Congress have not shown that role perceptions necessarily lead to behavior consistent with those roles.But the significant point is that role theory plausibly explains why presidential popularity influences support for the president's policies.

The second explanation is based on the incentive for reelection. In other words, members of Congress may choose to be close to or independent from the president, depending on his popularity, to increase their chances of reelection. The leading exponent of this view of presidential influence is Richard Neustadt. He argues that the "essence of a President's persuasive task with congressmen . . . is to induce them to believe that what he wants of them is what their own appraisal of their own responsibilities requires them to do in their interest, not his."[18]

Several components must fit together to make this a reasonable model. First, most of those involved in governing must have interests that lie beyond the realm of policy objectives. This seems to be particularly true of national leaders, who usually are politically ambitious and have long political careers.[19]

Second, members of Congress must gauge and be concerned about the president's standing with the public outside of Washington.[20] One reason for this interest is the lack of reliable information on public preferences. Few people communicate with these legislators, and few of the communications that are received relate to issues. Moreover, communications that do deal with issues generally come from sources that are not representative of the general public, and the opinions expressed are frequently too obscure or arrive too late to affect the behavior of a member.[21] Furthermore, the views expressed in newspapers are not representative, quality opinion polls cost too much for all but a few members of Congress to use, and questionnaires sent out under the franking privilege are frequently unreliable because the questions are sometimes "loaded" and the response is usually unrepresentative. In sum, despite numerous sources of constituency information, members of Congress "suffer from an 'information gap'; they face grave difficulties in discovering what are the preferences of their constituents."[22] Consequently, the president's popularity provides members of Congress with a guide to the public's views. As the central figure in American politics, the president is the object of a constant stream of comment and evaluation by all segments of society, including those segments that are unlikely to articulate specific policy preferences.

The third component of the incentive-to-reelection model is that members of Congress must anticipate the public's reactions to their behavior toward the president and his policies. This is true, according to Newstadt, because dependent people must consider popular reaction to their actions.[23] Davidson point out that "many Congressmen are hypersensitive to anticipated constituent reaction, regardless of the real threat that may be involved." Therefore, "most members are keenly aware that constituents impose certain boundaries on their activities."[24] Fenno agrees, adding that members of Congress are unsure about various things, such as who voted for them in the last election, population shifts, the effects of redistricting, and their next challenger.[25]

Further evidence of representatives' concern for public reactions to their behavior comes from research by Miller and Stokes and by Cnudde and McCrone. This research shows that even though the public is generally ambiguous about the substance and communication of their policy preferences, its representatives in the House behave in accordance with what they believe the public's views to be.[26] Likewise, Kingdon argues that legislators overestimate their visibility and the issue orientation of the electorate and therefore attempt to anticipate the reactions of the electorate.[27] Moreover, even though voters may be unclear about how their representatives voted on specific issues, they may well hold general images of members of Congress.[28]

Not only is there evidence that members of Congress anticipate voter reaction to their actions, but there is recent evidence that they would be wise to anticipate voter reaction to their support for the president. Burnham and the *Congressional*

Quarterly found that members of Congress defeated in the 1974 elections had supported Richard Nixon significantly more than did their colleagues who won reelection.[29] Others have found that the public assesses Congress in terms of the public's evaluation of the president,[30] while yet others have discovered a direct connection between the president's popularity and the public's voting for Congress.[31]

Thus, given the visibility of the president and the potential importance of presidential prestige as an indicator of constituency preferences, and given the phenomena of anticipated reactions, it is plausible that members of Congress are concerned with public reactions to their behavior toward the president. Johnson aide Harry McPherson states that members of Congress "listened hard for evidence of how the President stood in their states in order that they might know how to treat him."[32] Richard Nixon tells us that presidential popularity polls affect the ability of presidents to lead because politicians pay attention to them.[33]

Finally, for the incentive-to-reelection model to hold, members of Congress must act in response to the president's prestige. This is the major question here. We now have reason to believe that they will respond to public opinion about the president because they feel they ought to, because it is in their interest to do so, or both.

Others who have posited a relationship between presidential prestige and presidential support in Congress have based their conclusions on insight and selected examples, and have not systematically marshalled empirical data to test their hypotheses.[34] We shall do this here. Two useful indicators of presidential standing in the public are available to us: presidential popularity polls and presidential election results. We shall carry out separate analyses using each indicator as the primary independent variable.

Popularity Polls

The Variable

We can use public opinion polls from 1953 through 1976 as indicators of the president's popularity with the public. The Gallup Poll[35] has been asking exactly the same question concerning the president's popularity for over two decades: "Do you approve the way President _____ is handling his job?"[36] Clearly, this question does not relate to specific policies, but it does fit the general nature of public opinion. As Neustadt has written, "Presidential standing outside Washington is actually a jumble of imprecise impressions held by relatively inattentive men."[37] The wording of the question is also consistent with the general indexes of presidential support (Presidential Support Scores) that we are using as dependent variables. In other words, members of Congress can be expected to respond only in a general way to presidential popularity.

In addition, the question has been asked several times yearly. In the period covered by this study, the question was asked no fewer than eight times in one year and on an average of fifteen times.[38] Thus, it seems likely that presidential popularity in any year has been accurately tapped by the Gallup Poll.

Since the *CQ*'s Presidential Support Scores are computed annually, we must average the Gallup polls for each year to get a comparable measure of presidential prestige among the public. However, there is another good reason for averaging the polls. As Neustadt points out, "since the general public does not govern, presidential influence is shielded from the vagaries of shifting sentiment."[39] Thus, sharp, short-term fluctuations are not likely to alter the basic attitudes of members of Congress toward supporting the president.

The question arises whether a president's popularity and public support for his programs are separate concepts. A number of political observers have argued that there is little connection between a president's prestige and the public understanding of and support for his programs.[40] Numerous authors have shown, however, that significant changes in presidential popularity occurred concomitantly with major social, economic, and political changes having widespread consequences, such as unemployment, inflation, and war.[41] This is strong evidence that presidential popularity and policy are related. In addition, Neustadt points out that "sharp changes in the popularity of men whose public manners were substantially unaltered" have taken place. While the personality of a president can affect his prestige, serving as "a cushion and a prop," what people experience in their own lives is more important in altering the prestige of a president.[42]

On a more abstract level, Schlesinger argues that Kennedy's popularity "was packed with a whole set of intellectual implications which were preparing the nation for legislative change."[43] Moreover, Stokes writes that the candidacy of a particular man for president "has implications reaching beyond sheer popular appeal. A candidate for the nation's great office is a focus for popular feelings about issues and questions of group benefit as well."[44] Thus, it is reasonable to believe that the Gallup Poll taps not only presidential popularity but also general views on programs. Therefore, it would be logical for a member of Congress to use presidential prestige as an indicator of constituents' views when considering how to vote on the president's requests.

A remaining question of importance is how members of Congress learn of presidential prestige. Because of the high visibility of the Gallup polls, we can assume that members of Congress are aware of the changes in the overall level of presidential prestige. However, the figures for presidential popularity among particular groups within the population may not be sufficiently visible for us to assume that all members of Congress could use them as cues when voting on presidential requests. Nevertheless, we can view the results of the Gallup polls as indicators of what members of Congress hear of presidential prestige from all sources including constituents, the media, and fellow party elites as well as from the polls themselves. While any one of these additional sources of information may constitute a biased sample, together they provide members of Congress with a triangulation of presidential prestige, increasing the reliability of what they hear.

Analysis

Table 4.1 shows the relationships between overall presidential popularity as measured by the Gallup Poll and congressional support for the president's overall, domestic, and foreign policies. Since our theory predicts that members of Congress will respond in a general way to shifts in presidential popularity rather than in an exact way, we shall employ the correlation coefficient (r) to test for the hypothesized relationships. This statistic will tell us whether presidential popularity and presidential support in Congress vary together.

The results show that there are respectable correlations between the variables except for domestic policy support in the House.[45] The .50 correlation for the overall House score indicates, however, that this low domestic policy score would have been higher if we had measures of domestic policy support over the full twenty-four years instead of only sixteen. Since the overall support score is based on more domestic than foreign policy issues, the two should correlate fairly closely when measured over the same period of time. At any rate, the substantial correlations indicate that presidential prestige does have an influence on presidential support.

Table 4.1 shows the relationship between the president's popularity in the entire country and presidential support in the entire House and Senate. Several authors have suggested, however, that members of Congress do not necessarily heed all the voters who live within their districts or states; in effect, they choose which groups within their constituencies they will represent. These groups are generally part of the members' electoral coalitions. In addition, members of Congress are likely to communicate with these groups most frequently.[46] Thus, rather than responding to overall presidential prestige, members of Congress may respond to presidential prestige among these groups because of role perceptions or an interest in electoral security. Thus, this reasoning is congruent with both explanations discussed earlier.

Table 4.1
Correlations between Overall Presidential Popularity and Presidential Support

	OVERALL POLICY 1953–1976	DOMESTIC POLICY 1955–1970	FOREIGN POLICY 1955–1970
House	.50	− .01	.44
Senate	.40	.37	.40

In earlier research I found that presidential popularity among common demographic groups, such as those according to sex, age, religion, education, occupation, income, and city size, often either did not vary among different categories of the variable or was highly correlated with a related variable. From these variables I selected occupation as the most representative and most internally differentiated. I then dichotomized it as high and low socioeconomic status and related it to presidential support. I also divided the population by party affiliation and related this variable to presidential support. Since the latter relationships were the stronger and more significant, presidential popularity among party groups will serve as our indication of constituency opinion here.[47]

Party affiliation is the best indicator of sources of support for members of Congress. Thus, we should expect members of Congress to be more responsive to presidential prestige within their electoral bases (i.e., Democratic members should be more responsive to Democratic party identifiers and Republican members to Republican party identifiers). The reasons for this may be role perceptions, pragmatic concerns about reelection, or both.

Tables 4.2 and 4.3 present the results of correlating presidential prestige among party-identified groups in the public with the presidential support of their fellow partisans in Congress. Each of the twelve correlations is substantial (only one falls below .66), fulfilling our expectations of stronger relationships when both presidential popularity and presidential support are disaggregated by political party. Also worth noting is that presidential popularity among Democrats and Republicans in the public correlates at $-.48$, indicating that Democrats and Republicans in Congress respond to two different sets of opinion. All the correlations (not shown) between Democratic public opinion and Republican congressional support and between Republican public opinion and Democratic congressional support are negative; in fact, all but those between presidential popularity among Republicans in the public and Democratic foreign policy support in Congress are strongly negative.

The fact that Independents occupy a middle position in regard to correlations with elected representatives of the two parties, as shown in Table 4.4, further supports our findings. Independents do not consistently support one party, and, in general, they vote less frequently and have had less well developed ideas politically than those people who identify with either major party.[48] Thus, it is

Table 4.2

Correlations between Presidential Prestige among Democrats in the Public and Presidential Support among Democrats in Congress

	OVERALL POLICY 1953–1976	DOMESTIC POLICY 1955–1970	FOREIGN POLICY 1955–1970
House	.88	.83	.67
Senate	.86	.82	.44

Table 4.3

Correlations between Presidential Prestige among Republicans in the Public and Presidential Support among Republicans in Congress

	OVERALL POLICY 1953–1976	DOMESTIC POLICY 1955–1970	FOREIGN POLICY 1955–1970
House	.75	.73	.72
Senate	.83	.84	.66

more difficult and less profitable for members of Congress to respond to the views of Independents than to the views of supporters of their own parties.

Several possibilities could modify our findings. First, we have assumed that members of Congress follow public opinion about the president rather than shaping it. If the reverse was true, then presidential support among members of Congress could not be a response to presidential prestige. That some members of Congress, particularly key members, do affect public opinion seems plausible, but the extent is unmeasured and perhaps unmeasurable. Nevertheless, most members of Congress are not highly visible to their constituents[49] and are unlikely to influence the president's popularity among them very much.

Another possibility is that a third factor influences both presidential prestige and presidential support. If so, the relationship between the two variables would be spurious. One such possibility is that members of each party in the public and in Congress react to the president on the basis of his legislative proposals. In this case presidential programs rather than popularity would determine presidential support. This reasoning, however, assumes that both the public and members of Congress respond to presidential programs similarly, which is unlikely given their differences in background, responsibilities, and access to information on presidential proposals. In addition, this line of reasoning assumes that public and congressional evaluations of the president are based *solely* on his legislative programs. Thus, the president's failure to propose programs, his policies that are

Table 4.4

Correlations between Presidential Prestige among Independents in the Public and Presidential Support among Democrats and Republicans in Congress

	OVERALL POLICY 1953–1976	DOMESTIC POLICY 1955–1970	FOREIGN POLICY 1955–1970
House			
Democrats	.17	−.23	.21
Republicans	.06	.17	.30
Senate			
Democrats	.21	−.21	.33
Republicans	.17	.29	.07

not voted on by Congress (such as administrative decisions and much foreign policy), and his handling of other matters (Watergate, State of the Union messages, etc.) would have little influence on presidential popularity or support. These assumptions are difficult to accept.

The possibility that both the public and members of Congress respond similarly to the president's general performance seems equally unlikely. The differences between the two groups precludes our making such an assumption. Moreover, representatives would have to translate their general evaluations into specific votes on legislative proposals, which in turn would match changes in the public's general approval of the president. This is hardly likely.

Another possibility—and one worthy of testing—is that most of the variance in both presidential popularity and presidential support is due to changes in the party occupying the White House, as occurred between 1960 and 1961 and between 1968 and 1969. In other words, we might expect that the party of the president would influence his public popularity and congressional support.[50] Thus, the strong correlations between presidential prestige and presidential support might be due to the influence of presidential party on both.

To test this possibility, we shall employ a dummy variable[51] to control for the party of the president in the theoretically significant relationships between presidential popularity among Democratic and Republican party identifiers and the presidential support given by Democratic and Republican members of Congress, respectively. The results are shown in Tables 4.5 and 4.6.

Comparing Tables 4.2 and 4.5, we find that, with the exception of Senate foreign policy support, the correlations among Democrats are reduced when we control for the influence of the president's party. Nevertheless, the correlations for overall and foreign policy support are strong and those for domestic policy, while weaker, still indicate some influence of presidential prestige on presidential support. Also worth noting is that the correlations for each chamber are remarkably similar, possibly indicating the consistency of presidential popularity as a source of presidential influence.

The figures for the Republicans (Tables 4.3 and 4.6) tell a different story. The correlations are all reduced by controlling for the president's party, and four are negative. Our theory is not supported here. However, some Republicans in Con-

Table 4.5

Correlations between Presidential Prestige among Democrats in the Public and Presidential Support among Democrats in Congress, Controlling for the President's Party

	OVERALL POLICY 1953–1976	DOMESTIC POLICY 1955–1970	FOREIGN POLICY 1955–1970
House	.57	.31	.54
Senate	.56	.29	.52

Table 4.6

Correlations between Presidential Prestige among Republicans in the Public and Presidential Support among Republicans in Congress, Controlling for the President's Party

	OVERALL POLICY 1953–1976	DOMESTIC POLICY 1955–1970	FOREIGN POLICY 1955–1970
House	−.03	−.30	.08
Senate	.19	−.15	−.54

gress could still be responding to presidential popularity among an exclusive group of fellow party members. This possibility is suggested in a study by Converse, Clausen, and Miller, which provides evidence that Republican elites may respond to the more "partisan" opinion within their party.[52] Furthermore, McClosky, Hoffman, and O'Hara have shown that the views of Republican party leaders are less congruent with those of the Republican rank and file than are the views of Democratic party leaders with the Democratic rank and file,[53] a finding that has been corroborated in a more recent study of mass and elite opinions.[54]

To varying degrees, each individual has a nonpartisan element in his or her response to individuals and events in the political arena. For some, notably Independents, this is the only element in their responses. Those with party identifications, however, also have a partisan element in their responses. As an individual's partisan identification increases, the magnitude of the partisan element increases; persons with extremely strong party identifications have nearly totally partisan responses to political persons and events.[55] We suspect that Republican members of Congress may be responding to just such a group of Republicans.

While ideally we could separate out this extreme group, we cannot do so here because we only have data on presidential popularity among all Republicans. Nevertheless, partisan modes of response *within* individuals can be isolated by controlling for presidential support among Independents (with nonpartisan responses). In this way we can isolate the more partisan responses of Republicans, which we can reasonably expect to be concentrated among highly partisan Republican identifiers.

However, as Table 4.7 clearly shows, the added control does not uncover any significant relationships. Thus, we cannot conclude that presidential prestige influences support for the president by Republicans in Congress.

Despite these findings, further examination is necessary because of the multicollinearity between presidential party and presidential prestige. Between 1953 and 1976, the two factors correlate at .83 for Democrats and −.86 for Republicans. (The figure for the Republicans is negative due to the scoring of the dummy variable for presidential party.) These figures make it difficult to assess the degree of influence of the two variables on presidential support.

Table 4.7

Correlations between Presidential Prestige among Republicans in the Public and Presidential Support among Republicans in Congress, Controlling for the President's Party and the Less Partisan Element of Presidential Popularity

	OVERALL POLICY 1953–1976	DOMESTIC POLICY 1955–1970	FOREIGN POLICY 1955–1970
House	.07	−.02	.19
Senate	−.08	.09	−.21

Much of the relationship between presidential prestige and presidential support has been found to be closely tied to partisanship. What is unclear, because of the multicollinearity, is whether presidential party links the two variables in whole or in part. In other words, all, none, or some of the inlfuence of presidential party on presidential support could work through presidential popularity. If none of this influence is through presidential prestige, then most of any relationship between presidential prestige and presidential support would be spurious. The relationships are illustrated in Figure 4.1.

One way to avoid this problem of multicollinearity is to remove the variable of the president's party from our computations. We can do this while still controlling for its influence by examining the relationship between presidential prestige among identifiers with each party in the public and the presidential support among the corresponding party members in the House and the Senate, separately in Democratic and Republican presidential years. The results of these calculations are shown in Tables 4.8 and 4.9.

In Democratic presidential years (Table 4.8) Democrats in both the House and the Senate appear to be very responsive to presidential prestige among Democrats. Republicans, however, generally react strongly negatively to presidential popularity among Republicans in Democratic presidential years. In Republican presidential years (Table 4.9) the figures for Democrats in overall and foreign

Table 4.8

Correlations between Presidential Prestige among Party Groups in the Public and Presidential Support among Party Groups in Congress in Democratic Presidential Years (1961–1968)

	OVERALL POLICY	DOMESTIC POLICY	FOREIGN POLICY
Democrats			
House	.84	.81	.71
Senate	.76	.75	.51
Republicans			
House	−.56	−.63	.02
Senate	−.57	−.41	−.70

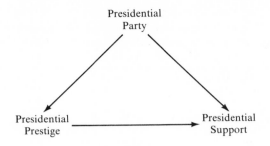

Figure 4.1

Paths of influence among presidential party, presidential prestige, and presidential support.

policy support are strong and positive, but those for domestic policy support are negative. However, the lower scores for domestic policy support may result from the fact that the period covered for these scores is only half as long as covered in the much higher and positive overall scores. With the exception of Senate foreign policy support, the figures for Republicans also support the hypothesized relationships.

The major exception to our hypothesis of congressional responsiveness to presidential popularity is Republican support for Democratic presidents. However, if we control for the less partisan element of presidential popularity (Table 4.10), we get results quite different from those in Table 4.8. All but one of the correlations are positive, indicating responsiveness to presidential prestige (to varying degrees). Apparently, when a Democratic president occupies the White House, Republicans in the House and Senate are more attuned to the more vocal elements in their party, who probably feel freer to speak out than when a Republican occupies the White House.

Republican Senate foreign policy support under Democratic presidents is negative because Kennedy and Johnson became increasingly less popular among

Table 4.9

Correlations between Presidential Prestige among Party Groups in the Public and Presidential Support among Party Groups in Congress in Republican Presidential Years

	OVERALL POLICY 1953–1960, 1969–1976	DOMESTIC POLICY 1955–1960, 1969–1970	FOREIGN POLICY 1955–1960, 1969–1970
Democrats			
House	.51	−.20	.54
Senate	.44	−.69	.60
Republicans			
House	.31	.51	.47
Senate	.76	.65	−.04

Table 4.10

Correlations between Presidential Prestige among Republicans in the Public and Presidential Support among Republicans in Congress, Controlling for the Less Partisan Element of Presidential Popularity in Democratic Presidential Years (1961–1968)

	OVERALL POLICY 1953–1960, 1969–1976	DOMESTIC POLICY 1955–1960, 1969–1970	FOREIGN POLICY 1955–1960, 1969–1970
House	.26	.18	.32
Senate	.41	.57	−.54

Republicans until the figure for Johnson leveled off at 27 percent approval in 1967 and 1968. However, Republican senators gave both presidents, especially Johnson, substantial support. The support for Johnson was probably due to the Republicans feeling that they should provide the president with bipartisan support during the war in Vietnam as well as to the Republicans favoring the continued escalation of the war. Republicans in the public could only voice their displeasure with the war through disapproval, while Republican senators could vote for ever stronger measures in order to reach their goal of an all-out effort.

The fact that Republican support for the president generally correlates with Republican public opinion more strongly when we separate the data for Democratic and Republican presidential years and the similar occurrence for Democratic domestic policy support indicate that opinion and support vary together in each time period but at different rates. Thus, by aggregating data into twenty-four- or sixteen-year periods we mask some relationships. This also explains why the figures for Democratic support are generally higher for Democratic than for Republican presidential years.

Together, Tables 4.5 through 4.10 indicate that presidential prestige does serve as a source of presidential influence in Congress. To illustrate this point further, let us turn to a case study.

Nixon's 1973 Decline

In 1973 President Nixon won only 51 percent of the votes in Congress on which he took a stand—the lowest percentage of any president in our study, and 15 percent lower than his next lowest percentage of 66 percent, earned the previous year. Moreover, his record for 1973 would have been even lower without the many routine votes that took place at the end of the year. Measured by Presidential Support Scores, his support decreased among all members of Congress, especially Democrats, as shown in Table 4.11.

Why did this happen? Nixon had just won one of the greatest landslide victories in history, carrying every state except Massachusetts (and the District of Columbia). There were twelve more Republicans in the House and two more in the Senate in 1973 than in 1972, when he received considerably more support.

Table 4.11

Percentages of Congressional Support of the President, 1972–1973

	1972	1973
House Democrats	47	35
Republicans	64	62
Senate Democrats	44	37
Republicans	66	61

Moreover, American military involvement in Vietnam ended at the time of his second inauguration and therefore should have been less of an irritation to Congress. Nixon had also made changes to improve his personal relations with Congress. Bob Haldeman and John Ehrlichman, who were disliked for their arrogance and formed the cornerstone of the so-called Berlin Wall around the president, were early victims of Watergate. The ineffective Vice President Spiro Agnew fell to his own tragedy, and the president brought Bryce Harlow and Melvin Laird into the White House and nominated Gerald Ford as vice president. These three men were experienced in dealing with Congress, which liked and respected them. Chief congressional liaison aide William Timmons reported that the president held more bipartisan leadership meetings, more meetings with the Republican leadership, and more meetings with the Republican rank and file and had more social contact with members of Congress than ever before.[56] All of these actions should have increased rather than lowered Nixon's support in Congress. What, then, explains the decline in support for the president?

One might argue that Congress was angered by Nixon's arrogant approach toward it and his unique conception of the separation of powers, which involved massive impoundments, waging an undeclared war, and an extensive claim of executive privilege. However, just because members of Congress were alienated by one or more actions by the president, they would not necessarily oppose him on pieces of legislation that were unrelated to those actions (as almost all legislation was). In addition, the three types of acts noted above were prevalent well before 1973. In view of our findings in this chapter, the most reasonable explanation for Richard Nixon's substantial decline in support among members of Congress in 1973 is his equally substantial decline in popularity, primarily because of Watergate. In December 1972 his overall popularity stood at 62 percent; one year later his popularity had plummeted 33 points to 29 percent. Without public support his legislative program languished.

Presidential Electoral Performance

The Variable

The second of our indicators of the president's standing in the public is his electoral performance. Unfortunately, there has not been a full constituency-by-constituency survey of public opinion about the president. That is why we had to aggregate constituency opinion to the national level in the previous section. The one indicator of constituency opinion about the president that is available over several years is voting behavior in presidential elections.

Most studies focusing on presidential election results have tried to explain those results rather than examining their implications. Here we shall study the influence of the presidential vote in a congressional district on the support given by that constituency's representative for the president's policies. (For reasons that will become obvious, we will not be examining the Senate.)

Presidential electoral performance is a good indicator for the study of the influence of the president's popular support on representatives' presidential support for several reasons. First, both public opinion and representatives are responding to the same object: the president. Second, voting for the president occurs in all congressional districts. Third, votes in presidential elections represent, at least in part, the public's evaluation of the president. Finally, the sample of public opinion (voters) is larger in presidential elections than in other elections or in other common means of individual expression of opinion such as writing letters to political leaders or signing petitions because participation is generally higher.

Despite its potential utility, only a few studies have employed congressional district voting patterns in presidential elections as an independent variable to explain presidential influence in Congress.Those studies that have been done extend over only a few years, do not include all mebers of the House, fail to differentiate between domestic and foreign policy presidential support, aggregate representatives from widely varying electoral circumstances, or do not use analytical techniques that allow conclusions to be confidently drawn about the influence of presidential electoral performance on presidential support.[57]

In this study, presidential electoral performance is operationalized as the percentage of the vote that the president received in each congressional district in his most recent election. This figure should be a readily available and easily interpretable indicator for representatives of the support for the president in their constituencies.[58] The main hypothesis is that the better a president runs in a representative's district, the more support he should receive for his policies from that representative. Conversely, the more poorly a president runs in a representative's district, the less support he should receive from that representative. The period covered runs between 1953 and 1973 (it was necessary to stop at 1973 since President Nixon resigned in the middle of 1974, and his successor, Gerald Ford, did not run for office until 1976).

The Model

Presidential electoral performance may influence presidential support indirectly as well as directly by determining which party holds the district's seat. Since representatives of the president's party generally give the president more support than members of the opposition party, the influence of presidential coattails, if they exist, on which party wins the seat in a congressional district and the influence of the winning representative's party affiliation on presidential support are relationships that must be examined. To do this the party affiliation of a representative will be operationalized as a dummy variable with "1" representing the Democratic party and "0" the Republican party. Figure 4.2 shows both the direct and indirect paths of influence of presidential electoral performance on presidential support.

At first glance it may not seem reasonable to look at coattail effects in the last two years of a presidential term, but there are several reasons for examining their persistence. First, once they obtain office, incumbents have numerous, well-known advantages over challengers in an election. Second, some of the voters who voted for representatives on the basis of the president's coattails in the previous election may continue to be loyal to these representatives. Finally, if the president remains popular with those who voted for a representative as a result of a coattails effect, they may continue to identify the representative with the president in the midterm election.

Any apparent influence of presidential electoral performance on presidential support (whether direct or indirect) may be spurious, resulting from a third variable that is related to them both. The level of support for a political party in a congressional district undoubtedly influences the presidential vote as well as the congressional vote in that constituency.[59] The variable of constituency party strength will be measured as it was in the previous chapter.[60] These relationships, along with the possible paths of influence of presidential electoral performance on presidential support, are shown in Figure 4.3.

Analysis

The first step in the data analysis is to calculate the influences of constituency party strength (CPS) on presidential electoral performance (PEP) through the use of equation (1).[61]

$$PEP = \beta CPS + e \qquad (1)$$

The second step is to estimate the influence of presidential electoral performance and constituency party strength on representative's party affiliation (RPA) through the use of equation (2).

$$RPA = \beta_1 CPS + \beta_2 PEP + e \qquad (2)$$

The results of these calculations are shown in Table 4.12.[62]

The last steps in testing the relationships predicted in the model involve estimating the influence of representative's party affiliation and presidential electoral performance on each of the three measures of presidential support (PS) by the use of equation (3).

$$PS = \beta_1 RPA + \beta_2 PEP + e \qquad (3)$$

The results are presented in Table 4.13.

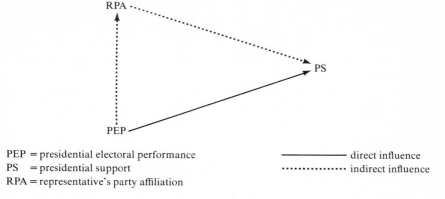

PEP = presidential electoral performance   ——————— direct influence
PS   = presidential support   ·············· indirect influence
RPA = representative's party affiliation

Figure 4.2
Direct and indirect paths of influence of presidential electoral performance on presidential support.

The final phase of the analysis entails calculating the combined direct and indirect influence of presidential electoral performance on presidential support by using path analysis. The direct influence of presidential electoral performance on presidential support is added to its indirect influence. The indirect influence travels along the path from presidential electoral performance through representative's party affiliation to presidential support and is the product of the two relationships.

The results of these calculations, shown in Table 4.14, generally support the hypothesis that presidential electoral performance has a significant influence on presidential support. This is particularly true in each of the eight Democratic

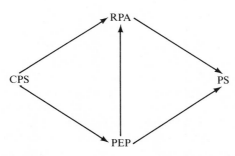

CPS = constituency party strength   PS   = presidential support
PEP = presidential electoral performance   RPA = representative's party affiliation

Figure 4.3
Possible relationships in the model of the influence of presidential electoral performance on presidential support.

Table 4.12

Estimated Impact of Constituency Party Strength on Presidential Electoral Performance and Representative's Party Affiliation and of Presidential Electoral Performance on Representative's Party Affiliation

YEARS	N	PEP on CPS	RPA on CPS	RPA on PEP
1953–54	410	−.72	.53	−.32
1955–56	429	−.72	.41	−.41
1957–58	413	−.79	.59	−.19
1959–60	420	−.84	.52	−.13
1961–62	420	.56	.63	.17
1963–64	390	.50	.45	.29
1965–66	415	.11	.53	.17
1967–68	411	.26	.63	.04
1969–70	398	−.69	.61	−.16
1971–72	419	−.74	.64	−.08
1973–74	391	−.45	.67	.03

NOTE: All decimal figures are standardized regression coefficients. CPS = Constituency party strength; PEP = presidential electoral performance; RPA = representative's party affiliation.

presidential years. As Table 4.15 shows, the median beta coefficients for overall, domestic, and foreign policy support are .41, .42, and .38, respectively. The strength of the influence of presidential electoral performance is consistent not only between measures of presidential support but also over time, as indicated by the modest size of the average deviations of the coefficients (also shown in Table 4.15).

The pattern for Republican presidential years is mixed. The figures in Table 4.14 are considerably lower in these years than in Democratic presidential years (1961 through 1968) for all three measures of presidential support. The summary figures in Table 4.15 indicate that the influence of presidential electoral performance on presidential support was about half as great in Republican presidential years as in Democratic presidential years. In some years (as shown in Table 4.14) there seems to have been almost no influence at all. Moreover, in 1955 and 1956 the coefficients are negative for foreign policy support.

There are several possible reasons for the variability in the coefficients under administrations of the two parties. For instance, one might argue that Republicans tend to be less responsive to public opinion than Democrats[63] and that the coefficients are higher in Democratic presidential years because there are more Democratic representatives in these years. However, there actually were more Democrats in the House in 1959–1960 under President Eisenhower than in

Table 4.13

*Estimated Direct Influence of Representative's Party Affiliation and Presidential
Electoral Performance on Presidential Support*

YEAR	OVERALL POLICY SUPPORT		DOMESTIC POLICY SUPPORT		FOREIGN POLICY SUPPORT	
	On RPA	On PEP	On RPA	On PEP	On RPA	On PEP
1953*	−.67	.02	——	——	——	——
1954*	−.65	.11	——	——	——	——
1955	−.20	.07	−.55	.08	.33	−.02
1956	−.56	.11	−.58	.15	.01	−.12
1957	−.04	.14	.04	.10	−.17	.17
1958	.02	.19	−.06	.18	.24	.13
1959	−.67	.23	−.79	.15	.32	.27
1960	−.38	.17	−.56	.15	.02	.14
1961	.62	.18	.69	.18	.28	.17
1962	.49	.29	.54	.26	.37	.26
1963	.69	.18	.70	.18	.63	.16
1964	.59	.22	.55	.25	.61	.15
1965	.57	.43	.58	.42	.53	.42
1966	.45	.46	.47	.44	.37	.47
1967	.54	.41	.55	.40	.46	.40
1968	.31	.45	.31	.42	.25	.46
1969	−.32	.17	−.44	.14	.32	.16
1970	−.37	.21	−.43	.19	.13	.27
1971*	−.61	.02	——	——	——	——
1972*	−.36	.10	——	——	——	——
1973*	−.66	.38	——	——	——	——

NOTE: All figures are standardized regression coefficients. RPA = representative's party affiliation;
PEP = presidential electoral performance.

*Domestic and foreign policy support scores not available.

1961–1964 under Presidents Kennedy and Johnson, and the coefficients are
higher for the latter period.

Another possibility is that the coattail effect was stronger for Democratic
presidents, providing a stronger indirect influence of presidential electoral performance on presidential support. Yet an examination of the last column in Table
4.12 shows that this is not so. Regarding the other half of the indirect path of
influence, although the relationships between a congressperson's party affiliation
and presidential support are sometimes lower in Republican presidential years,
as shown in Table 4.13, they are not consistently so. Moreover, the indirect path
of influence usually represents only a minor portion of the total influence.

Table 4.14

*Combined Direct and Indirect Influence of Presidential Electoral Performance on
Presidential Support*

YEAR	OVERALL POLICY SUPPORT	DOMESTIC POLICY SUPPORT	FOREIGN POLICY SUPPORT
1953*	.23	——	——
1954*	.32	——	——
1955	.15	.31	−.16
1956	.34	.39	−.12
1957	.15	.09	.20
1958	.19	.19	.08
1959	.32	.25	.23
1960	.22	.22	.14
1961	.29	.30	.22
1962	.37	.35	.32
1963	.38	.38	.34
1964	.39	.41	.33
1965	.53	.52	.51
1966	.54	.52	.53
1967	.43	.42	.42
1968	.46	.43	.47
1969	.22	.21	.11
1970	.27	.26	.25
1971*	.07	——	——
1972*	.13	——	——
1973*	.36	——	——

NOTE: All figures are standardized regression coefficients.

*Domestic and foreign policy support scores not available.

The reason why the coefficients vary with the party occupying the White House is probably a combination of two factors. First, congressional Democrats in each of the two years under study here represented the majority party in the electorate. Thus, they may have felt more freedom than their Republican colleagues to oppose a president of the opposite party, reasoning that the favorable party bias in the electorate insulated them from more issue-oriented elements of public opinion. This makes considerable sense, given the important role of voter party identification in voting for Congress.[64]

At the same time, presidential support in the electorate should have a greater impact on representatives when a Democratic president is proposing liberal programs. In this case the influences of ideology, party, and presidential electoral performance overlap for most Democratic representatives (who were always the majority in the two Democratic administrations). In addition, the influences of

Table 4.15

Median and Average Deviation of Beta Coefficients for Democratic and Republican Presidential Years

POLICY	DEMOCRATIC		REPUBLICAN	
	MEDIAN	AVERAGE DEVIATION	MEDIAN	AVERAGE DEVIATION
Overall	.41	.07	.23	.07
Domestic	.42	.06	.24	.06
Foreign	.38	.09	.13	.11

ideology and presidential electoral performance flow in the same direction for liberal Republican representatives (in whose districts the president probably ran well). Conversely, when a Republican president proposed more conservative programs, the influences of ideology, party, and presidential electoral performance run together only for conservative Republican representatives (always a minority in the years under study).

This argument helps to explain the very high coefficients in Table 4.13 for the relationships between presidential electoral performance and presidential support between 1965 and 1968. Lyndon Johnson ran very well in the congressional districts that elected liberal Democrats and Republicans, who were disposed to support his Great Society legislation on the basis of party and ideology (Democrats) or just ideology (Republicans). He ran unusually poorly for a Democrat in the South, particularly the Deep South, which generally elected conservative representatives, who were most likely to oppose his policies. Thus, Johnson ran well in districts where his evident popularity with the voters reinforced congressional predispositions to support his programs.

There are also variations in the size of the coefficients within the terms of presidents, as shown in Table 4.14. A number of plausible hypotheses may explain this variance. First, the psychological impact of a landslide election on representatives may strengten the relationship between presidential electoral performance and presidential support. To test this possibility, we can look at the 1956, 1964, and 1972 presidential elections, which were all landslides, and compare the coefficients for the years following these elections with those for the years preceding them and with those for years following closely contested elections. The coefficients for 1965 and 1966 are the highest figures in Table 4.14, exceeding those for 1964 (preceding the election) and for 1961 and 1962 (following a close Democratic victory). However, with regard to the 1956 presidential election, the coefficients for 1957 and 1958 are not higher than those for 1956, 1953 and 1954, or 1969 and 1970. The coefficient for 1973 is less than all but one of the coefficients for overall policy support in Democratic years but is the highest of all those for Republican years, substantially exceeding the figures for the other Nixon years. In sum, although the findings are suggestive, they are too mixed to verify the hypothesis that the psychological impact of landslide presidential elections strengthens the relationship between presidential electoral performance and presidential support.

A second possible explanation for the variability in the influence of presidential electoral performance on presidential support is that the impact of a president's electoral performance may be greater in the years immediately following his election; after that time other factors may intervene and obscure his electoral success. However, in Table 4.14 the coefficients are higher in the years immediately following presidential elections only for the full Johnson and Nixon terms, which are only two of the five presidential terms studied. Thus, nearness of election does not appear to be a significant factor.

A third possible explanation is that representatives of the president's party may be most sensitive to his electoral success. Therefore, the larger the number of members of the president's party in the House, the higher the coefficients in Table 4.14 should be. Since the 1958, 1964, and 1966 elections resulted in large party turnovers in the House, an examination of the coefficients before and after these elections should provide a reasonable test of this hypothesis. The coefficients are actually lower before than after the 1958 election, despite the Republican losses. On the other hand, the coefficients rise after the Democratic gains in the 1964 election and decrease after the Democratic losses in the 1966 election. Thus, the evidence for this hypothesis is mixed. The applicability of the hypothesis is also limited to years when there is substantial party turnover in the House, because there is variance in the coefficients for years when the party composition of the House changed very little (i.e., 1955–58, 1961–64, 1969–73). Nevertheless, this hypothesis is consistent with the argument made earlier about the overlapping of influences on congressional voting.

A hypothesis of very limited applicability is that presidents at the end of their tenures are "lame ducks"; representatives therefore no longer perceive presidential electoral performance as relevant to their decision making. There are three lame duck presidents in this study—Eisenhower, Johnson, and Nixon. The coefficients for Eisenhower's second term and his last year in office are not unrepresentative of his tenure as a whole, while Johnson's 1968 figures are higher than those for 1967, when no one knew that he would not seek reelection. Nixon's 1973 figure is his highest. Therefore, the "lame duck" hypothesis does not seem to be very useful.

Overall, the proposed hypotheses are not very successful in explaining the variance in the impact of presidential electoral performance on presidential support within Democratic and Republican presidential years. Apparently nonsystematic factors are responsible for this variance, which could be anything from changes in presidential skills in using popularity, to changes in their desire to do so, to changes in broader political, social, or economic factors.

The Findings in Perspective

The central findings here have their most direct implications for presidential-congressional relations and the separation of powers. "What the Constitution separates," writes Neustadt, "political parties do not combine."[65] Since the president is the primary initiating force in national politics, he must solve this problem if his programs are to be enacted into law.

Thus, a president interested in increasing his congressional support should not overlook the influence potential of his popularity. In other words, he should attempt to influence members of Congress indirectly by strengthening his support among the American people. Moreover, he should be concerned with his prestige among members of both parties, because all members of Congress respond to his prestige, particularly his popularity among their electoral supporters.

Presidential prestige, however, is not solely determined by the president himself. Such diverse factors as political scandals in the executive branch, the extent of the president's personal and media charisma, international events, and the state of the private sector of the economy can also affect a president's prestige[66]—factors that may be largely beyond his control.[67]

Although the image of a president is fairly stable, "the values men assign to what they see can alter rather quickly." A president's prestige is threatened when people become frustrated about their own situations.[68] Thus, although presidential popularity appears to be an effective tool of presidential influence, it is not one that he can easily manipulate.

While a discussion of the president's ability to manipulate public opinion is beyond the scope of this study,[69] it seems reasonable that if presidents could achieve consistently high popularity, they would. Yet despite the increasing sophistication of the White House in public relations, recent presidents have not been overly popular. Johnson and Ford ended their presidencies with about 50 percent approval, Nixon had only half that, and Carter ran into problems with his standing in the public early in his administration. Kennedy was perhaps saved from a similar fate of unpopularity by his untimely death.

Moreover, nothing inherent in presidential prestige makes it useful only as an instrument of presidential influence. It may also restrain the president. Presidential policies that require positive congressional action, such as providing the necessary authorization or resources, may be constrained by a lack of presidential support in the public. Therefore, opponents of presidential policies should emphasize the meaning that the public places on presidential actions (which in turn affect presidential prestige) in addition to attempting to persuade members of Congress to oppose the president.

The argument regarding presidential electoral performance is similar to that presented in the preceding paragraphs. Presidential candidates, particularly Democrats, have an incentive to win office by as large a margin as possible, since high percentages of the vote in congressional districts provide them with future policy support. Conversely, the supporters of a candidate who appears certain to lose, such as George McGovern in 1972, have an incentive to keep campaigning in order to keep the opposition candidate's percentage as low as possible. Again, all of this is much easier said than done.

If we integrate these findings into larger theories of congressional voting, presidential prestige and presidential electoral performance must be added to the list of variables that have been found useful in explaining roll call behavior.

Moreover, they are more purely political variables than many variables that have been used as indicators of public opinion, such as various demographic characteristics of constituencies, states, and regions. Thus, they have greater value in explaining relationships between citizens and their elected representatives.[70]

A second important finding concerning legislative voting behavior relates to constituency influence. When making decisions on whether to support the president, members of Congress seem to respond not to presidential prestige among the public or their district as a whole but to presidential prestige among their own electoral supporters. This finding is consistent with Kingdon's discovery of closer relationships between the attitudes of the majority element in a congressional district and the voting of that district's representative than between such voting and constituency attitudes as a whole.[71]

Finally, this research provides evidence that members of Congress *do* respond to public opinion. Presidential elections do make a difference; they are important not only in determining who will hold the office of the presidency but also in influencing the president's chances of having his policy proposals enacted. Members of Congress also respond to the president's current popularity among their supporters, and people from both ends of the socioeconomic scale are included in winning electoral coalitions in different constituencies. Thus, presidential popularity provides a vehicle by which the public can express its general views to its congressional representatives and affect congressional behavior without having detailed views on specific policies.

Notes

1. Richard E. Neustadt, *Presidential Power* (New York: New American Library, 1964), chap. 5, especially pp. 89, 91. For an interesting approach, see Stuart Gerry Brown, *The American Presidency* (New York: Macmillan, 1966), pp. 3–4, 182–183, 259. Brown differentiates between types of presidential popularity, concluding that the "partisan" type is more useful than the "unpartisan" type in passing controversial legislation. Unfortunately, however, he fails to describe the distinction between the two.

2. Emmet John Hughes, *The Living Presidency* (Baltimore: Penguin, 1974), p. 68.

3. See, for example, Richard Rovere, *Affairs of State: The Eisenhower Years* (New York: Farrar, Straus, 1956), pp. 261–262; Harry McPherson, *A Political Education* (Boston: Little, Brown, 1972), pp. 105–106.

4. Neil MacNeil, *Dirksen: Portrait of a Public Man* (New York: World, 1970), pp. 138, 142.

5. Robert Donovan, *Eisenhower: The Inside Story* (New York: Harper & Row, 1956), p. 279.

6. Lyndon B. Johnson, *The Vantage Point: Perspectives of the Presidency, 1963–1969* (New York: Popular Library, 1971), p. 443.

7. Jack Valenti, *A Very Human President* (New York: Norton, 1975), p. 144. See also Doris Kearns, *Lyndon Johnson and the American Dream* (New York: Harper & Row, 1976), pp. 216–217; Eric F. Goldman, *The Tragedy of Lyndon Johnson* (New York: Dell, 1974), pp. 306–307; McPherson, *Political Education,* pp. 268, 428.

8. Johnson, *Vantage Point,* p. 323. See also Goldman, *Tragedy of Lyndon Johnson,* pp. 306–307.

9. McPherson, *Political Education,* pp. 267–268.

10. William Safire, *Before the Fall: An Inside View of the Pre-Watergate White House* (New York: Doubleday, 1975), p. 284.

11. "Run, Run, Run," *Newsweek,* May 2, 1977, p. 38. See also the statement of Hamilton Jordan in the same article.

12. "Carter Seeks More Effective Use of Departmental Lobbyists' Skills," *Congressional Quarterly Weekly Report,* March 4, 1978, p. 585.

13. "Slings and Arrows," *Newsweek,* July 31, 1978, p. 20.

14. "O'Neill on Carter," *New Orleans Times-Picayune,* June 6, 1977, sec. 1, p. 2.

15. "Carter's Courtship of Congress," *Houston Chronicle,* August 13, 1978, sec. 1, p. 12.

16. Roger H. Davidson, *The Role of the Congressman* (New York: Pegasus, 1968), pp. 79–80, 117.

17. Roger H. Davidson, David M. Kovenock, and Michael K. O'Leary, *Congress in Crisis: Politics and Congressional Reform* (New York: Wadsworth, 1966), p. 64.

18. Neustadt, *Presidential Power,* p. 53.

19. Joseph Schlesinger, *Ambition and Politics* (Chicago: Rand McNally, 1966), pp. 90–99. See also Neustadt, *Presidential Power,* p. 54.

20. Neustadt, *Presidential Power,* p. 88.

21. Lewis A. Dexter, "The Representative and His District," in *New Perspectives on the House of Representatives,* 2nd ed., ed. Robert L. Peabody and Nelson W. Polsby (Chicago: Rand McNally, 1969); Raymond A. Bauer, Ithiel de Sola Pool, and Lewis A. Dexter, *American Business and Public Policy: The Politics of Foreign Trade* (New York: Atherton, 1963), pp. 419–420; Lewis A. Dexter, "What Do Congressmen Hear: The Mail," *Public Opinion Quarterly* 20 (Spring 1956): 16–27; Lewis A. Dexter, "Candidates Make the Issues and Give Them Meaning," *Public Opinion Quarterly* 19 (Winter 1955–56): 408–414; Donald G. Tacheron and Morris K. Udall, *The Job of a Congressman* (Indianapolis, Ind.: Bobbs-Merrill, 1966), pp. 282–283; Leroy N. Rieselbach, *Congressional Politics* (New York: McGraw-Hill, 1973), p. 216; John W. Kingdon, *Congressmen's Voting Decisions* (New York: Harper & Row, 1973), pp. 56–57.

22. Rieselbach, *Congressional Politics,* p. 218.

23. Neustadt, *Presidential Power,* p. 88.

24. Davidson, *Role of the Congressman,* p. 121.

25. Richard F. Fenno, Jr., "U.S. House Members in Their Constituencies: An Exploration," *American Political Science Review* 71 (September 1977): 886–887.

26. Donald E. Stokes and Warren E. Miller, "Party Government and the Saliency of Congress," *Public Opinion Quarterly* 26 (Winter 1962): 531–546; Warren E. Miller and Donald E. Stokes, "Constituency Influences on Congresss," *American Political Science Review* 57 (March 1963): 45–56; Charles F. Cnudde and Donald J. McCrone, "Linkage between Constituency Attitudes and Congressional Voting Behavior: A Causal Model," *American Political Science Review* 60 (March 1966): 66–72.

27. John W. Kingdon, *Candidates for Office* (New York: Random House, 1968), p. 145. See also Kingdon, *Congressmen's Voting Decisions,* pp. 59–61.

28. Miller and Stokes, "Constituency Influence," p. 55.

29. Walter D. Burnham, "Insulation and Responsiveness in Congressional Elections," *Political Science Quarterly* 90 (Fall 1975): 418; "1974 Support in Congress: Ford

Low, Nixon Up," *Congressional Quarterly Weekly Report,* January 18, 1975, p. 148.

30. Davidson, Kovenock, and O'Leary, *Congress in Crisis,* pp. 59–63; Robert B. Arsenau and Raymond E. Wolfinger, "Voting Behavior in Congressional Elections," paper presented at the annual meeting of the American Political Science Association, New Orleans, September 1973, pp. 3–4, 16.

31. Edward R. Tufte, "Determinants of the Outcomes of Midterm Congressional Elections," *American Political Science Review* 69 (September 1975): 812–826; James E. Piereson, "Presidential Popularity and Midterm Voting at Different Electoral Levels," *American Journal of Political Science* 19 (November 1975): 683–694; Samuel Kernell, "Presidential Popularity and Negative Voting: An Alternative Explanation of the Midterm Congressional Decline of the President's Party," *American Political Science Review* 71 (March 1977): 44–66.

32. McPherson, *Political Education,* p. 246–247; James L. Sundquist, *Politics and Policy: The Eisenhower, Kennedy, and Johnson Years* (Washington, D.C.: Brookings Institution, 1968), p. 213, and the sources cited therein.

33. Richard M. Nixon, *RN: The Memoirs of Richard M. Nixon* (New York: Grosset and Dunlap, 1977), p. 753.

34. For a brief effort to use empirical data, see "House Freshman Democrats Giving LBJ Less Support," *Congressional Quarterly Weekly Report,* September 16, 1966, p. 2173. My own earlier efforts can be found in George C. Edwards III, "Presidential Influence in the House: Presidential Prestige as a Source of Presidential Power," *American Political Science Review* 70 (March 1976): 101–113; George C. Edwards III, "Presidential Influence in the Senate: Presidential Prestige as a Source of Presidential Power," *American Politics Quarterly* 5 (October 1977): 481–500.

35. The Gallup Poll data used here comes from the Roper Public Opinion Research Center at Yale University.

36. As Mueller points out, because the percentage of "no opinion" answers varies only slightly over time, the trend in the "approval" rating of the president largely indicates the trend in his "disapproval" rating. See John Mueller, *Wars, Presidents, and Public Opinion* (New York: Wiley, 1973), p. 203.

37. Neustadt, *Presidential Power,* pp. 88–89.

38. We can use 369 polls in the period because for these polls the responses can be cross-tabulated with the respondents' party affiliation.

39. Neustadt, *Presidential Power,* p. 91.

40. See, for example, Malcolm E. Jewell and Samuel C. Patterson, *The Legislative Process in the United States,* 3rd ed. (New York: Random House, 1977), p. 259; Brown, *American Presidency,* p. 7; the authors cited in Elmer Cromwell, *Presidential Leadership of Public Opinion* (Bloomington: Indiana University Press, 1965), p. 309; Arthur M. Schlesinger, Jr., *A Thousand Days: John F. Kennedy in the White House* (Boston: Houghton Mifflin, 1965), p. 714.

41. Richard A. Brody and Benjamin I. Page, "The Impact of Events on Presidential Popularity: The Johnson and Nixon Administrations," paper presented at the annual meeting of the American Political Science Association, Los Angeles, September 1972; Mueller, *Public Opinion,* chaps. 9–10; Sundquist, *Politics and Policy,* pp. 496–497; Neustadt, *Presidential Power,* p. 96; Samuel Kernell, "Explaining Presidential Popularity," *American Political Science Review* 72 (June 1978): 506–522.

42. Neustadt, *Presidential Power,* pp. 94, 98.

43. Schlesinger, *Thousand Days,* p. 726.

44. Donald E. Stokes, "Some Dynamic Elements of Contests for the Presidency," *American Political Science Review* 60 (March 1966): 26.

45. Significance tests are not appropriate here because we are not dealing with a sample of members of the House or Senate. Thus, sampling error is impossible. Also, neither the dependent (presidential support) nor independent (presidential prestige) variables take on extreme values that would bias the findings.

46. See note 4 in Chapter 2.

47. Edwards, "Presidential Influence in the House," p. 107.

48. Frank J. Sorauf, *Party Politics in America,* 2nd ed. (Boston: Little, Brown, 1972), p. 173.

49. Stokes and Miller, "Saliency of Congress"; George C. Edwards III and Ira Sharkansky, *The Policy Predicament* (San Francisco: W. H. Freeman and Company, 1978), pp. 24–25.

50. See, for example, Chapter 3.

51. Presidential party is operationalized here with "1" representing Democratic and "0" representing Republican.

52. Philip E. Converse, Aage R. Clausen, and Warren E. Miller, "Electoral Myth and Reality: The 1964 Election," *American Political Science Review* 59 (June 1965): 321–336.

53. Herbert McClosky, Paul J. Hoffman, and Rosemary O'Hara, "Issue Conflict and Consensus among Party Leaders and Followers," *American Political Science Review* 54 (June 1960): 406–427.

54. William Shaffer, Ronald E. Weber, and Robert Montjoy, "Mass and Political Elite Beliefs about the Policies of the Regime," paper presented at the annual meeting of the American Political Science Association, New Orleans, September 1973, pp. 14–16. See also Rowland Evans and Robert Novak, "'Potentially Disastrous' Republican Syndrome," *Washington Post,* May 19, 1974, p. 7, which discusses "a potentially disastrous Republican syndrome of mistaking the blind pro-Nixon loyalty of precinct workers for popular opinion. What's more, they press this misconception on congressmen." Yet further support for this argument is found in Christopher H. Achen, "Measuring Representation," *American Journal of Political Science* 22 (August 1978): 486.

55. Philip E. Converse, "The Concept of a Normal Vote," in *Elections and the Political Order,* ed. Angus Campbell, Philip E. Converse, Warren E. Miller, and Donald E. Stokes (New York: Wiley, 1966); Angus Campbell, Philip E. Converse, Warren E. Miller, and Donald E. Stokes, *The American Voter* (New York: Wiley, 1960), pp. 128–136.

56. "White House Study of Nixon Support in 93rd Congress . . . Finds Only 100 Votes at Present for Impeachment," *Congressional Quarterly Weekly Report,* January 19, 1974, p. 81.

57. Loren K. Waldman, "Liberalism of Congressmen and the Presidential Vote in Their Districts," *Midwest Journal of Political Science* 11 (February 1967): 73–85; Marvin G. Weinbaum and Dennis R. Judd, "In Search of a Mandated Congress," *Midwest Journal of Political Science* 14 (May 1970): 276–302; Milton Cummings, *Congressmen and the Electorate* (New York: Free Press, 1966); J. Vincent Buck, "Presidential Coattails and Congressional Loyalty," *Midwest Journal of Political Science* 16 (August 1972): 460–472; Jeanne Martin, "Presidential Elections and Administration Support among Congressmen," *American Journal of Political Science* 20 (August 1976): 483–490.

58. A second way to measure presidential electoral performance is by the difference

between the president's percentage of the presidential vote and a representative's percentage of the congressional vote in their most recent election. The difference demonstrates the relative popularity of the two and may indicate to the representative his constituency's desires. This point should be true regardless of the party of the representative and regardless of whether the figure for the representative is from a presidential or midterm election year.

This formulation of presidential electoral performance was substituted for the percentage of the president's vote in each district in an analysis that parallels that following analysis in the text. The results for both variables were similar, and therefore the findings reported here are those using the original operationalization of the variable.

59. It is not likely that constituency party strength would directly influence presidential support because each representative has more recent indicators of public opinion: his own vote percentage and that of the president.

60. In the last two years of each presidential term, the variables measuring presidential electoral performance and constituency party strength contain data from the same election (though *not* the same office). Thus, when a presidential coattails effect is present, there can be an element of reciprocal causation between the presidential vote and the congressional vote. The general effect of this is to increase the strength of the estimated relationships between constituency party strength and presidential electoral performance and between constituency party strength and representative's party affiliation. This in turn decreases the estimated relationship between presidential electoral performance and constituency party affiliation.

The question is whether including the coattail effect is likely to have a strong or a weak influence. The answer has several aspects. First, the constituency party strength variable is only partially composed of data from elections that took place simultaneously with the presidential election measured in the presidential electoral performance variable. Second, presidential coattails only explain a small part of the vote of representatives or senators. Third, because we have one coefficient esimating both aspects of the relationship between constituency party strength and presidential electoral performance, the bias of presidential coattails reflected in the estimated coefficient will be less than the full impact of whatever reciprocal causation exists. Fourth, the type of coattail effect measured in constituency party affiliation (seats) is different from the type of coattail effect measured in constituency party strength (votes), and the two relationships are different enough that controlling for one is not equivalent to controlling for the other. Therefore, the estimated relationship between presidential electoral performance and constituency party affiliation is unlikely to be significantly decreased. Finally, whatever bias does occur works against the hypothesis of presidential electoral performance influencing presidential support by decreasing the strength of part of its path of indirect influence (through representative's party affiliation).

61. All of the figures in the following tables and in the text are standardized regression coefficients (beta weights). Using them allows us to assess the relative impacts of two or more variables on another variable and to take advantage of the technique of path analysis. The beta coefficients are symbolized as "β" in the equations that follow.

62. As discussed earlier, the variables of constituency party strength and representative's party affiliation have been operationalized as percentage of the constituency that is Democratic for the former variable and "1" for a Democratic affiliation and "0" for a Republican affiliation for the latter. Thus, in Republican presidential years, the relationships between these variables and presidential electoral performance and between repre-

sentative's party affiliation and presidential support are generally negative. This has no special significance, since the negative direction of the relationships is a result of scoring Democratic districts or Democratic congresspersons "higher" than their Republican counterparts. Only when the beta coefficients are positive are the relationships in a direction other than that which is expected under Republican presidents.

63. See the sources cited in notes 52 through 54.

64. Arsenau and Wolfinger, "Voting Behavior"; Barbara Hinckley, "Issues, Information Costs, and Congressional Elections," *American Politics Quarterly* 4 (April 1976): 131–152; Barbara Hinckley, Richard Hofstetter, and John Kessel, "Information and the Vote: A Comparative Election Study," *American Politics Quarterly* 2 (April 1974): 131–158.

65. Neustadt, *Presidential Power,* p. 33.

66. See, for example, the sources cited in note 41.

67. For an argument that the president can manipulate the economy to his benefit, see Edward R. Tufte, *Political Control of the Economy* (Princeton, N.J.: Princeton University Press, 1978).

68. Neustadt, *Presidential Power,* pp. 95–96.

69. For such a discussion, see Edwards and Sharkansky, *Policy Predicament,* chap. 3.

70. See James H. Kuklinski, "District Competitiveness and Legislative Roll-Call Behavior: A Reassessment of the Marginality Hypothesis," *American Journal of Political Science* 21 (August 1977): 627–638, for a discussion of the problems of using demographic data to measure public opinion.

71. John W. Kingdon, "Politicians' Beliefs and Voters," *American Political Science Review* 61 (March 1967): 137–145. See also Miller and Stokes, "Constituency Influence," pp. 49–50.

5 | *Presidential Legislative Skills: I*

The next three chapters should be viewed as parts of a whole. In these chapters we will investigate the more personal and manipulatable potential sources of presidential influence in Congress, to which we assign the general label "presidential legislative skills." These skills range from direct appeals for support to the bestowal of amenities.

Not only is the range of potential presidential legislative skills great, but so is the range of situations in which they may be needed. The words of one presidential aide illustrate this complexity:

> Senator A might come with us if Senator B, an admired friend, could be persuaded to talk to him. Senator C wanted a major project out of Chairman D's committee; maybe D, a supporter of our bill, would release it in exchange for C's commitment. Senator E might be reached through people in his home state. If Senator F could not vote with us on final passage, could he vote with us on key amendments? Could G take a trip? Would the President call Senator H?[1]

We have several goals in these chapters. First, we want to categorize and describe the degree of legislative skills exercised by recent presidents. Second, we want to analyze these skills to see if they could logically serve as broad sources of influence in Congress. This discussion extends across this chapter and the next.

This chapter focuses on presidential involvement in the legislative process, bargaining, professional reputation, and arm-twisting. In Chapter 6 we will examine the services and amenities provided by the White House to members of Congress, generally to create long-term goodwill. We will also investigate White House efforts to mobilize public opinion and interest groups on behalf of the president's proposals. In addition, we will briefly discuss presidents using their vice presidents in legislative relations and the need for presidents to be detached, that is, not to take opposition personally, and to compromise. The chapter ends with an examination of President Carter's legislative skills. Rather than integrate this discussion into our earlier analysis, we have chosen to apply all the categories to Carter at once in order to have a coherent picture of his performance.

Our final goal, addressed in Chapter 7, is to determine empirically whether presidential legislative skills function as an important source of presidential influence in Congress.

Presidential Involvement in the Legislative Process

According to Lyndon Johnson, "There is only one way for a President to deal with the Congress, and that is continuously, incessantly, and without interruption."[2] He believed that "merely placing a program before Congress is not enough. Without constant attention from the administration most legislation moves through the congressional process at the speed of a glacier." Thus, one of a president's most important jobs is to keep Congress concentrated on his legislative program.[3] "The thing that counts," Johnson remarked, "is getting those bills through."[4] Following his own advice, Johnson got to know members of Congress well and developed a legislative system that involved activities from drafting bills to pushing them through Congress. We shall focus on Johnson's involvement with Congress first because of its intensity before considering the involvement of other presidents.

Lyndon Johnson

Intimate knowledge. The foundation of Johnson's involvement was intimate knowledge of Congress, knowledge that came from beyond even his own vast experience.[5] At least in the Eighty-ninth Congress (1965–1966), his favorite reading was the *Congressional Record*. A White House messenger picked up the newest issue at the Government Printing Office every morning, and an aide then read it before dawn, clipping each page on which a member of Congress praised or criticized Johnson and summarizing and marking up other important parts for Johnson's breakfast reading. When he read criticism, Johnson often asked his chief legislative aide, Lawrence O'Brien, to find out the cause of the problem.[6]

Before retiring at night, Johnson read detailed memos from his staff on their legislative contacts of the day, special problems that arose, and noteworthy conversations, all of which he absorbed rapidly and thoroughly.[7] When Congress was in session, he received continuous status reports. The White House staff had a standing order to put through calls from O'Brien to Johnson at any hour. O'Brien's office phone was directly connected to the phone on the president's desk. Johnson also developed a system (rarely used) whereby any memo with a red tag would be brought to his attention immediately.[8] "No detail of the legislative program was too minute to involve him." While Kennedy gave congressional affairs the time that O'Brien requested, Congress was for Johnson "a twenty-four-hour-a-day obsession."[9]

Johnson was disturbed if his staff was not on top of every detail of government, particularly legislation, and he expected them to work as hard as he did. He arranged for all of them to have radios in their offices so they could catch the news, and he even had a hot line put into Joseph Califano's bathroom so that Califano would not miss presidential calls.[10]

Johnson also kept in touch with Congress by spending time with its members. He liked to spend free time with them and was more approachable than Kennedy—more "one of the boys." Thus, early in his tenure, he might be found lunching with some senators in a Capitol hideaway, dining with the Texas delegation, or spending an evening with the House Rules Committee.[11]

All of this time and effort spent on congressional relations helped Johnson to maintain an intimate knowledge of Congress and its personnel, which he felt was essential in order to get his legislation passed. He sometimes viewed Congress as a sensitive animal. If pushed gently, it would go his way. If pushed too hard, it would balk. Thus, he had to be constantly aware of how much pressure Congress would take and what its mood was.[12]

This detailed knowledge helped Johnson to know which people should or could be approached and how to approach them. He felt that knowing members of Congress was important so that he could interpret their reactions, their "tone, nuance, and spirit," to presidential requests for support. He also found it useful to know who faced a tough election and who had higher ambitions, who had power and who was gaining and losing it, what the rules and habits of committees were, what skeletons were in whose closets, what issues were critical to whom and why, and what organizational needs leaders had.[13]

Before calling members of Congress who opposed legislation that he supported, Johnson would study detailed staff memos on the bill in question that indicated the reason for the members' opposition, what was necessary to change their minds, and their vulnerabilities. He also knew the politics of their states and of many of their districts. He knew he could not just call and compliment them and expect their votes. He needed to know them and to have a sympathetic understanding of their situations.[14]

Doris Kearns argues that Johnson's achievements in civil rights were made possible by his intimate knowledge of Southerners in Congress, upon which he could base his efforts to influence or manipulate. When he spoke with them privately, his accent deepened, his manner suggested that although he understood and even shared their attitudes toward blacks, he was president and has to answer to the entire nation. Employing teasing humor that implied intimacy, he decreased the intensity of their opposition.[15]

On the 1968 income tax surcharge, Johnson had members asked not only how they would vote but also what criteria would determine whether they would vote for or against the bill (for example, their state delegation's vote breakdown or the closeness of the vote). On the basis of their answers, they were categorized in one of five ways: "with us," "probably with us," "uncommitted," "probably against," and "against." He and his aides then concentrated on the uncommitteds and those probably against the tax, with the approach to each member tailored to meet his or her needs. [16]

Timing.   Johnson also felt that sending his bills to Congress at the right moment was important, and he based his timing on the facts he learned and the moods he sensed. The right moment to him depended on momentum, the availability of sponsors in the right place at the right time, and the opportunities for neutralizing the opposition. The timing of legislation was also viewed as important in overcoming Congress's tendency to bog down. In 1965 he decided to push for Medicare and aid to education before pushing for housing and home rule for the District of Columbia on the basis of his estimates of the time needed for each to be considered in Congress and his estimates of which bills would provoke debate and controversy. [17]

He sent bills one by one rather than in a clump, which he felt would lead to automatic opposition. Also, he sent them when the agendas of the receiving committees were clear so that they could be considered right away, without time for opposition to develop and when the members most intensely concerned about the bills would be most likely to support them. Nor did he allow premature disclosure of the details of his bills, which would allow the opposition to coalesce. [18]

Consultation.   Johnson consulted with Congress at all stages of the legislative process, from what problems and issues his task forces should consider to the drafting of bills. He appointed members to secret task forces, thus implicating them in the resulting proposals. Sometimes legislators were intimately involved in the drafting of programs because Johnson felt that they would then give the programs more support. [19]

Before sending a bill to Congress, Johnson made special efforts to clear it in advance with key representatives and interest groups. He would not approve draft bills until the relevant department head had proved that he or she had consulted with Congress and had gauged the level of support for the legislation. Lining up support in advance helped a bill to move quickly and aided in strategic planning. [20]

To Johnson, legislative drafting was a "political art." He sought congressional advice on a bill's prospects and had his aides make their own estimates. These analyses gave him a sense of his likely supporters and opponents and an opportunity to redraft a bill so that it would be assigned to a more favorable committee. This was not always possible, but his staff tried through secret consultations with the official parliamentarian and discussions with himself. Along with these efforts, he sought congressional judgments on tactical decisions, such as whether a bill should be single purpose or omnibus in form, how it should be packaged, and when it should be sent. [21]

Advance Notice.   The evening before transmitting a bill to Congress, Johnson would hold a White House briefing with congressional leaders, during which cabinet members and the White House staff reviewed and explained the bill and answered questions. He felt that the risk of leaks was worth the goodwill gained from the leaders.[22] Once, when aide Joseph Califano wanted to brief the press ahead of time about the upcoming and complex Model Cities program, Johnson refused permission until Congress had been told first.[23]

Johnson found that giving important senators advance notice was useful in clearing controversial appointments. Thus, he called Senator John McClelland of Arkansas concerning the appointment of Carl Rowan to head the United States Information Agency, and he invited Senator Russell Long of Louisiana to the White House concerning the appointment of Andrew Brimmer to the Federal Reserve Board. Both appointees were black, and Johnson's show of respect and deference helped clear the path for their confirmations.[24]

Preemption of Problems.   Officials in both the Kennedy and Johnson administrations criticized Kennedy for coming too late to many of his problems in Congress, waiting for problems to develop and then intervening at the height of crises, after positions had hardened. Johnson, more intimately involved with Congress and more knowledgeable about it, anticipated problems and, as shown above, acted to preempt them.[25]

Use of the Cabinet.   Before Vietnam dominated his time, Johnson made pending legislation a major item of every cabinet meeting. Each department secretary reported on the progress of legislation in his area, and the president used charts on the status of bills to put cabinet members on the spot and urge them to exert more effort. He also emphasized to the cabinet the importance of congressional liaison and liaison officials, and he gave its members responsibility for team efforts in congressional relations. He wanted to be able to use the secretary of agriculture on an education bill if he had friends on the Hill who could help.[26] Johnson also insisted that the appropriate executive branch officials be ready with strong testimony when congressional hearings began.[27]

On the weekends each department official gave status reports for each bill assigned to him or her. On Monday all legislative officers met with the White House staff. These meetings were frequently attended by ranking executive officers, who sometimes gave briefings on national problems. Johnson attended these meetings about once every six weeks, boosting morale. Occasionally legislative officers were allowed to bring a staff member to make a special report, a special treat to the staff member if the president was present. Agency legislative officers also had access, direct or indirect, through the White House staff to the president, giving them more respect in Congress.[28]

Demands on the President.   Johnson paid great attention to detail, controlling legislative strategy and organizing support for his legislation.[29] This put great demands on his time and energy. He alone knew the full implications of the many decisions that had to be made concerning congressional relations, and he alone was in contact with all the groups and subgroups in Congress and the administration. His personality and interests were complementary to his legislative activity, but because of the escalation of the war in Vietnam, he was not able to maintain this commitment to legislation.[30]

Other Presidents

The involvement of other recent presidents in the legislative process pales in comparison with Johnson's, at least at its peak. Other presidents lacked Johnson's compulsion for detail, his consuming interest in the legislative process and the passage of legislation, and his deep respect for and understanding of Congress, which led him to seek useful information, anticipate problems, devote his energies to Congress, and work closely with its members.

This is not to argue that efforts similar to Johnson's were not made. According to Lawrence O'Brien, President Kennedy believed that he would have to take an "active, aggressive role with Congress" if his programs were to pass, and the White House engaged in vigorous advocacy from the outset of his administration. Soon after the election, O'Brien met with three leading Democratic members of the House and they reviewed every member in regard to the prospects of supporting Kennedy. Occasionally, leading members of Congress were also consulted on legislation in advance.[31] Kennedy aide Arthur Schlesinger felt that Kennedy spent more time working with Congress than people realized.[32]

Nevertheless, Johnson's actions were on another plane. One political scientist reports that at first Kennedy felt that once he made proposals, it was up to Congress to decide details without him continuously intervening. (Having learned from experience, he changed this view during his first year in office.)[33] President Johnson felt that Kennedy had less interest than he did in dealing with Congress and that Kennedy often appeared to look upon congressional liaison with contempt.[34]

According to columnists Evans and Novak, President Nixon knew little of the workings of Congress and cared less.[35] His top aide, H. R. Haldeman, was quoted by other journalists as saying, "I don't think Congress is supposed to work with the White House."[36] The 1970 Senate vote on the confirmation of G. Harrold Carswell as Supreme Court justice is an example of problems that arise when the White House lacks intimate knowledge of Congress. The White House mistakenly thought that Senator Margaret Chase Smith would vote yes and told other senators this. However, she had not made up her mind, was angered by the White House's actions, and eventually cast a crucial no vote. The president's staff wasted its time trying to influence Senator William Fulbright, who had already decided to oppose Carswell. Similarly, the White House focused on the vote to recommit the nomination to committee while the opposition focused on the final vote, which turned out to be the wiser action. Meanwhile, the White House was wasting further efforts searching for a paired vote for Senator Carl Mundt, a Nixon supporter who was in the hospital, totally incapacitated. No one was going to waste a no vote unnecessarily, and the Senate was unlikely to believe that Mundt could decide how to vote, given his state of health. Finally, the White House was clearly off on both the final vote count and its confidence that almost anyone would be confirmed following the rejection of Haynsworth.[37]

President Dwight Eisenhower also had problems due to inadequate involvement in Congress. Senator William Knowland, the Senate Republican leader, was irritated when he read in the newspapers about the Eisenhower Doctrine on the Middle East before he was told about it by the president; by proposing a school construction bill in 1955 without consulting educators and members of Congress who favored federal aid to education, Eisenhower angered those whose support he needed to pass the bill; members of the cabinet provided conflicting testimony to Congress on submerged lands and reciprocal trade because of the president's failure to coordinate the testimony; and the president failed to consult the Republican Senate Foreign Relations Committee chairperson, Alexander Wiley, on a strategy regarding the Bricker amendment.[38]

Next to Johnson, Gerald Ford was probably the most intimately involved in Congress of the recent presidents. He worked hard at his congressional relations, had a detailed knowledge of Congress and its members, and was sensitive to their needs and desires. He spent time with them and gave them access, and he frequently participated in "head count" sessions.[39]

Working with Congressional Leaders

Johnson's consultation with Congress did not end with the introduction of a bill or nomination. When Congress was in session, he met with the Democratic leaders at Tuesday breakfasts. Here he spoke frankly and traced the course of each bill on a huge chart.[40] He often called leaders on the Hill,[41] and we saw in Chapter 3 that Johnson worked closely with Republicans like Senator Dirksen as well. Naturally, he worked with the leaders on more than just the short-run attainment of votes.[42]

Johnson's staff also worked closely with Democratic leaders. They attended strategy sessions in the leaders' Capitol offices and were present at the president's weekly meetings. At these meetings strategy, tactics, and the substance of legislation was discussed; the participants felt that the meetings were valuable. The congressional leadership and the White House formed an effective team, not only in planning but also in operations such as head counts.[43]

Kennedy also had Tuesday breakfasts with the Democratic leadership, but Theodore Sorenson, one of the president's closest aides, reports that these meetings merely maintained morale and kept channels of communication with Congress open; little was learned.[44] It does not appear as though Kennedy sought to "guide" the leaders as Johnson was to do, but he did receive solid support from them, and they worked closely with the White House.[45]

Nixon met with congressional leaders of both parties before many of his major national addresses, but these speeches usually dealt with foreign policy and required little, if any, direct legislative support. Moreover, the meetings tended to be *pro forma* and did not entail consultation.[46] Following one of these sessions in mid-1972, House Minority Whip Leslie Arends said he had yet to sit in conference with Nixon and have him ask, "What should we do?"[47]

Nixon's scheduled meetings with congressional leaders were not very useful. He only had two sessions with Republican leaders per month during his second term, with less frequent bipartisan meetings.[48] Although the president was in frequent contact with Senate Minority Leader Everett Dirksen, their relationship lacked the rapport, confidence, and easy access that characterized the senator's relationship with Johnson.[49] The president's meetings with Majority Leader Mike Mansfield were unproductive, and Mansfield could or would do little for him.[50]

Eisenhower held many bipartisan meetings with congressional floor and committee leaders on foreign policy and defense issues, especially during his second term, and he sought cooperation across the center aisles in Congress. Sometimes these leaders met as a group, and at other times the president saw individuals. Aside from foreign aid and his defense reorganization proposal, most of these meetings did not deal with issues calling for immediate legislation but with crises such as Vietnam, Germany, Lebanon, or the Suez Canal. In these meetings he often sought congressional views and did not just inform the leaders of his decisions.[51]

Eisenhower got along well with Democratic leaders Lyndon Johnson and Sam Rayburn and had many sessions with them.[52] Nevertheless, he did not feel broader bipartisan meetings would be useful in domestic policy areas.[53] From the beginning he regularly saw Republican floor leaders and Republican committee leaders and was open to requests from congressional leaders for meetings. The meetings appear to have been informal with a free exchange of views, and the president did not pressure the legislators, thereby avoiding the risk of a breakdown in relations. He did, however, give his views on issues of importance to him.[54] From 1956 to the end of Eisenhower's tenure, all Republican senators were invited to hear reports on these meetings, and House Minority Leader Charles Halleck reported on them to all House Republicans in 1959 and 1960.[55]

How should we evaluate these meetings with congressional leaders, meetings that Eisenhower felt were his most effective mechanism for coordinating relations with Congress? Even he admitted that the meetings "were sometimes tiresome,"[57] and one can readily imagine this to be true, with, for example, Senate Republican leader William Knowland spending hours advocating to the president.[58] House Republican leader Joseph Martin termed them generally "empty affairs" that accomplished little.[59] Inspiration and not the development of strategy or the application of pressure seems to have been the main goal, and the results appear to have been mixed at best.[60] Perhaps by being so low-keyed and by relying so heavily on institutionalized means such as leadership meetings for carrying out relations with Congress, Eisenhower lost opportunities to influence its members.

Personal Appeals and Access

A special aspect of presidential involvement in the legislative process is the personal appeal for votes and giving members of Congress access to the president. According to Richard Neustadt, "when the chips are down, there is no substitute for the President's own footwork, his personal negotiation, his direct appeal, his voice and no other's on the telephone."[61] This view is seconded by Johnson aide Harry McPherson, who "had an almost mystical faith in Presidential intervention."[62] The distinguished correspondent Neil McNeil, writing of Kennedy's personal lobbying, adds that "direct lobbying by the President with individual Representatives had a profound effect on how they voted."[63]

One reason that phone calls from the president are often effective is human nature. Lyndon Johnson understood that representatives were human beings who liked to feel important and that they were impressed when he called.[64] He knew that, in the words of aide Jack Valenti, "most congressmen can go through a lifetime without ever having talked to the President over the phone in a conversation not initiated by the congressmen."[65] (President Kennedy once remarked that he didn't recall Truman, Eisenhower, or any of their staff ever talking to him about legislation during his fourteen years in Congress.)[66]

Calls from the president must be relatively rare to maintain their usefulness. If the president calls too often, his calls will have less impact. Moreover, members might begin to expect calls, for which the president has limited time, or they may resent high-level pressure being applied on them. On the other hand, they may exploit a call and say that they are uncertain about an issue in order to extract a favor from the president. In addition, the president does not want to commit his prestige to a bill by personal lobbying and then lose. Also, his staff's credibility when speaking for him will decrease the more he speaks for himself.[67]

Johnson became intensely involved only after the long winnowing process of lining up votes was almost done and his calls were needed to win on an important issue, a situation that arose only a few times a year.[68] Other presidents have followed similar patterns.[69] When Johnson did call about a vote, he, like other presidents, focused on key members of Congress, whose votes served as cues for other members,[70] and other members who were uncommitted or weakly committed in either direction. He learned the latter by studying the head counts prepared by the White House staff, which provided detailed information on each member's position.[71]

When Johnson decided to intervene, his actions were intensive. One White House aide has said that the president never let Senate Republican leader Everett Dirksen alone for thirty minutes during Senate consideration of the 1964 Civil Rights Act.[72] On the 1965 Voting Rights Act he even had one senator's mistress contacted.[73] That same year several education bills were in the House Education and Labor Committee, and its mercurial chairperson, Adam Clayton Powell, was nowhere to be found. Johnson had aide Jack Valenti scour Washington to find Powell and then bawled out Powell for holding up legislation; Powell returned to work the next day (without anger). On the 1963 foreign aid bill, his calling in key representatives for private chats was described by one aide as "endless talking, ceaseless importuning, torrential laying on of the facts, [and] it went on for several days."[74]

Johnson's persistence in searching for votes was extraordinary. He had a dogged reluctance to accept no and went to great lengths to gain a yes or bring a supporter to the floor. His actions on the 1963 foreign aid bill illustrate this last point. He called Congress back into session near Christmas but delayed the vote until his supporters were all back to cast their ayes. House Majority Leader Carl Albert was found fishing in Canada by a Mountie pushing his horse upstream. Representative J. J. Picket, newly elected in a special election in Texas, could not be certified until December 24, seven days after his election. So Johnson had the governor and the secretary of state of Texas swear Picket in at 12 midnight, and he arrived in Washington at 3:30 a.m., in time for the vote taken that day. The president also had the Georgia State Patrol track down Representative Elijah Forrester, who was driving home for the holidays, and bring him back to Washington by helicopter. Historian Eric Goldman attributes Johnson's victory on the final vote to his recall of favorable votes.[75]

The president personally rounded up votes on a number of other issues, including the poverty program, food stamps, farm bills, a federal pay increase, rent supplements, and the vote to discharge the District of Columbia home rule bill from the District of Columbia Committee.[76] On the latter issue a discharge petition was also needed to release the bill from the House Rules Committee and get it on the floor for a vote. The petition required 218 signatures, and Johnson had a list of twenty-two representatives who should have signed but had not. He called each one and "persuaded, cajoled, and pleaded" with them to sign, speaking movingly of the inequity of denying the city democratic government; he got the required signatures.[77]

On the 1964 tax cut, Johnson, after intensive personal lobbying within the Senate Finance Committee to reverse a vote on one of Senator Dirksen's amendments, sent word that he wanted no amendments on the Senate floor. Meanwhile, Senator Hubert Humphrey (soon to be vice president) was urging a change in the bill. Nevertheless, after a call from the White House, he voted against his own amendment.[78]

Johnson's telephone technique varied from person to person. He might begin, "What's this I read about your opposing my bill?" or "What do you think of this bill?" or "Say, Congressman, I haven't seen you around in a while, just wondering how you've been?"[79] His style always reflected a personal, reasonable approach: "Man to man. Phone to ear. Come let us reason together. This is Lyndon Johnson talking. Now, we don't have to be at each other's throat, do we? Your country needs your help and so do I."[80] The approach would vary with the party and ideology of the member of Congress. He was a master of role manipulation. On a tax question he might emphasize budget balancing with Republicans and personal loyalty with Democrats. On a rat extermination bill, he argued politics with Republicans, morality with moderates, and economics with conservatives.[81] He felt that members of Congress needed to feel like people of principle. Therefore, he sought to say whatever called up the best in each person. Emotional patriotism played a role here, since it was easier for a member to say yes to the "country's good" than to a politician in the White House.[82]

If the president could not obtain a favorable vote, he might ask, in effect, for an abstention. For example, he once called some Southern Democrats and asked them to stay away from a committee markup session on foreign aid,[83] knowing that if they attended they would vote against his program.

President Eisenhower's personal efforts at gathering votes are not as well understood as President Johnson's. On the one hand, we hear that he was accessible and a good listener who spent many hours listening to members of Congress in the hope of getting them to support his policies. Moreover, he sometimes "argued himself hoarse," especially on foreign aid, employing the rhetoric of self-interest, the economy, or national security, according to his needs. Much of this arguing, according to aide Bryce Harlow, was off-the-record.[84] Eisenhower himself wrote in his memoirs that he had to change congressional votes and ceaselessly explain, persuade, cajole, and cultivate the understanding and confidence of members of Congress through countless meetings and phone calls. He felt that his personal involvement in vote gathering was successful more often than not, and there is evidence that on several issues he was successful in switching a few votes.[85]

On the other hand, we learn that Eisenhower rarely made calls himself, not liking to use the telephone for public business. His order that calls to him from members of Congress be put through as soon as was convenient does not seem to have pleased even his own party members in Congress. His staff reviewed requests to see him, and a member of the congressional liaison staff sat in on any meetings with the president that were requested by a member.[86] House Republican leader Joseph Martin complained that the rank and file in Congress "found it extremely difficult, if not impossible, to see the President, and hard enough to get an appointment with his top assistants." Eisenhower, he said, worked too much through subordinates in dealing with Congress, and members resented this. They liked to hear from the president personally and felt that they were entitled to such communication.[87]

Eisenhower was not anxious to jump into the political fray. One of his aides later said Eisenhower did not understand that he had to fight for his programs and that he showed a lack of drive and leadership on the Hill. For instance, he was particularly interested in the 1954 trade bill. However, it was not enthusiastically supported by the conservative Republican congressional leaders and was held up in the House Ways and Means Committee without hearings or action. Nevertheless, the president refused to prod the committee.[88]

There is no lack of commentators to point out that President Kennedy felt personal contacts with Congress were important and that he spent considerable time with members, much of it off-the-record, and did not deny access to anyone in Congress who insisted on seeing him. Yet it appears that his staff tried to conserve his efforts in personal relations and his involvement in details, knowing that he was impatient with such activities, that he felt uncomfortable with many members of Congress (who had previously outranked him), and that he had limited time for and interest in domestic legislation. He was less likely than Johnson to call legislators and ask for their votes.[89]

When Kennedy did personally seek support, he sometimes had unexpected success. On one occasion Kennedy, during a walk in the White House gardens, convinced House Armed Services Committee chairperson Carl Vinson to cut language forcing him to spend money on the RS-70 bomber, which the president opposed.[90] In 1963 he found to his surprise in a talk with House Republican leader Charles Halleck that the latter supported his civil rights bill. After their talk, Halleck helped get the bill out of the House Judiciary Committee.[91] His willingness to talk to certain conservative members of Congress may have helped to gain their votes for liberal legislation that they had previously opposed.[92]

President Nixon reportedly did not feel that he should have to lobby for his programs. He saw himself more as an administrator and executive decision maker and not as a power broker pushing to get his bills through Congress. He usually called only members of Congress whom he knew and then mainly for small talk. Moreover, his interchange with Congress became more formal and less frequent, and he became less accessible to nonfriends and rank and file members. Calls to the president from members of Congress were carefully screened, and 90 percent never got through to Nixon. Nixon was briefed if he needed to call back. Occasionally the White House asked a department or agency to call a legislator concerning some specific legislation. The president rarely made such requests himself.[93]

While every president has to have his calls screened, the Nixon administration seemed to overuse the policy, or at least Capitol Hill thought so. There was also a widespread feeling among members of Congress from both parties that Nixon would not be informed of their calls or letters, and there were doubts about whether he could be spoken to at all.[94] During the Senate debate on Nixon's nomination of G. Harrold Carswell to the Supreme Court, Republican senator Charles Mathias asked to interview the nominee. His request received no response until right before the vote, when he was told that he could see Carswell in a motel room after midnight. By then it was too late.[95]

Gerald Ford was much less hesitant to use the phone to ask for votes than his predecessor, and he kept notes of his calls for follow-up action by his staff.[96] Once in 1975 he took three Republican representatives on a trip on Air Force One and lectured each on how strongly he felt about the House sustaining his veto of a jobs bill. On the trip back he called member after member from the presidential plane. In all, eighteen members switched their votes from the vote on the bill's passage, and the president's veto was sustained.[97] Ford was personally involved in his legislative battles and was willing to call, see, and keep in contact with many members of Congress.[98]

Failure of Personal Appeals

Despite the prestige of their office, their invocations of national interest, and their persuasiveness, presidents have often failed in their personal appeals. President Eisenhower liked to depend heavily on charm and reason, but in 1953 he tried to persuade Republican chairperson Daniel Reed of the House Ways and Means Committee to support the continuance of the excess profits tax and to oppose a tax cut. "I used every possible reason, argument, and device, and every kind of personal and indirect contact," he wrote, "to bring Chairman Reed to my way of thinking." But he failed.[99]

At the same time, Eisenhower frequently failed to bring around Republican Styles Bridges, the chairperson of the Senate Foreign Relations Committee (ranking minority member after 1954). He had similar disappointments in his personal appeals to members of Congress concerning the St. Lawrence Seaway, the nomination of Chip Bohlen as ambassador to the Soviet Union, the 1953 immigration bill, his defense department reorganization bill, and foreign policy in general.[100] As he noted in his memoirs, while his exhortations seemed to be effective at the time, they were often forgotten later as other pressures, such as the next congressional election, were brought to bear.[101]

Eisenhower, Kennedy, and Johnson all failed, despite considerable personal effort, to convince Representative Otto Passman, chairperson of the House Appropriations Committee's Subcommittee on Foreign Aid, to support foreign aid.[102] To beat Passman, Johnson finally had to stack the subcommittee with members who would vote against the chairperson.

Johnson, renowned for his persuasiveness, nevertheless failed on many issues, ranging from civil rights and education to Medicare and the Panama uprising. "No matter how many times I told Congress to do something," he wrote, "I could never force it to act."[103] If Eisenhower and Johnson often failed in their efforts at persuasion, we should not be surprised that other presidents did also.[104]

Bargaining

The authors of *Who Runs Congress?*, which was commissioned by Ralph Nader, argue that the president can buy votes in Congress with a pen at a bill-signing ceremony, by attending a local school dedication, with a government favor, or with confidential information.[105] Conversely, Kennedy-Johnson legislative liaison chief Lawrence O'Brien said near the end of his government service, "This suggestion that you trade the bridge or the dam or some project for a vote, . . . it's just not the case."[106] Similarly, William Timmons, O'Brien's counterpart in the Nixon administration, maintains that there were no blatant trades for votes in his experience.[107] Which view is correct? Are trades—that is, bargains—made, and are these bargains as easy to strike and as fundamental to presidential influence in Congress as the Nader researchers seem to believe?

Examples of Bargains

There is considerable evidence that bargaining does take place, as the examples below illustrate. John Kennedy was trying to make a case to Senator Robert Kerr for an investment credit tax bill that was bottled up in the Senate Finance Committee, of which Kerr was an influential member. Kerr responded by asking why the administration opposed his Arkansas River project and by demanding a trade. Kennedy smiled and replied, "You know, Bob, I never really understood that Arkansas River bill before today." Kerr got his project as well as several other benefits. In return, he provided Kennedy with important support and managed the president's high-priority Trade Expansion Act in the Senate.[108]

President Johnson wanted a tax cut in 1964, while Senate Finance Committee chairperson Harry Byrd wanted a decrease in spending. Byrd promised to get a tax cut out of his committee if the president pared the 1965 budget below $100 billion. Both men got what they wanted. To get Senator Russell Long to sponsor the tax cut, Johnson agreed to several tax provisions that Long desired.[109] That same year he directly offered Democrats everything from personal notes and photos to projects and judgeships to aid passage of the Civil Rights Act, and he gave Republican leaders an important role in the act's language to gain their support for ending the Senate's filibuster.[110] He reluctantly acceded to the demands of the North Carolina congressional delegation that in return for their support of the War on Poverty legislation, Adam Yarmolinsky, a leading figure in the development of the bill, would not be associated with the Office of Economic Opportunity. Johnson also increased the Farmer's Home Administration loan authorization and rural water supply and waste disposal system grants to gain support from Southern Democrats on the House Agriculture Committee.[111]

The next year, concerned about Senate amendments to the Medicare bill, Johnson began talking to individual senators. He made a campaign appearance for one and offered the possibility of "other things," too. To another senator Johnson mused out loud, "It seems that your state may not be getting its fair share of conservation projects here of late." Johnson got what he wanted. He also persuaded the House leadership to give Education and Labor Committee chairperson Adam Clayton Powell more committee expense funds so that Powell would get to work on the education bill.[112]

Johnson at times was quite overt in his trading. He once called Representative Porter Hardy of Virginia to seek his vote and said, in effect, "You may need me some time, and I'll remember this if you'll do it." (Hardy had decided to vote for Johnson's bill but pretended to be doing the president a favor. He later called on Johnson to return the favor and Johnson did.)[113] He regularly traded favors with Senate Republican leader Everett Dirksen, such as when he supported the Kaskaskia River navigation project in return for Dirksen's support on excise taxes. According to Johnson biographer Doris Kearns, their "brazen exchange of memos" occupies a file six inches thick in the LBJ library. When Dirksen was sick, a messenger brought his week's requests on jobs, tariff rulings, Illinois projects, complaints, and so on, to the White House.[114]

In 1971 Representative Chet Holifield, the chairperson of the House Government Operations Committee, opposed President Nixon's proposal to consolidate several cabinet departments into four new departments—until he went on a jet ride with President Nixon. Subsequently the president came out in support of the breeder reactor Holifield wanted for his district. North American Rockwell, a contractor for the reactor, was also in his district. On his part, the representative found new virtues in the president's reorganization plan.[115]

Just before the Senate voted on the appointment of Judge Clement Haynsworth to the Supreme Court, the White House announced through the office of Senator William Jennings Randolph the awarding of a $3 million grant for urban renewal in Randolph's state of West Virginia. Representative Ken Hechler, in whose district the grant was to be used, was not mentioned; Hechler was Randolph's potential primary opponent, and Randolph had been the center of lobbying efforts on the confirmation vote. The senator voted for Haynsworth.[116]

Representative F. Edward Hebert, chairperson of the House Armed Services Committee, told Defense Secretary Elliot Richardson in 1973 that he would not introduce a multi-billion-dollar military spending bill if Richardson did not appoint a board of regents (including an Hebert constituent) for the new military medical school (which the secretary opposed). Hebert eventually went to President Nixon and told him the same thing. Then the board was appointed and the spending bill was introduced.[117] Nixon also forced the Department of Health, Education and Welfare to make concessions on school desegregation to Senator John Stennis of Mississippi, chairperson of the Senate Armed Services Committee, in return for the senator's support of the ABM (antiballistic missile).[118]

President Ford was involved in bargaining, also. In 1975 Representative Donald Mitchell of New York switched his vote on an emergency jobs bill, voting to sustain President Ford's veto. Three weeks later the Air Force reversed its decision to close the Rome Air Development Center in his district.[119]

Presidents also sometimes facilitate bargaining between groups in Congress—or force them to bargain to achieve their own goals. President Kennedy included a wide range of educational programs in his 1963 omnibus education bill to encourage education groups to work for each other's programs. The bill also carried as hostage the renewal of aid to federally impacted areas, a program strongly supported by school officials all across the country.[120] In 1964 President Johnson conceived the idea of trading the food stamps program for his farm bill. Thus, he called members supporting each and told them to support each other's bills.[121] Both Kennedy's and Johnson's strategies worked.

Sometimes the bargaining becomes quite involved and a bit abused. During Kennedy's tenure, Representative Mike Kirwan of Ohio wanted to build an aquarium in Washington, D.C. Senator Wayne Morse made a speech in his home state of Oregon criticizing the idea. Irritated by this, Kirwan used his position as a subcommittee chairperson on the House Appropriations Committee to cut out a major public works project in Oregon. Morse then appealed to the president, who supported the aquarium in return for Kirwan's support of the Oregon project. (Kennedy held a one-person bill signing ceremony in the White House for the aquarium bill.)[122]

Limits of Bargaining

Hindering direct and open deals is the scarcity of resources to deal with and the desire of members of Congress for these resources. If many direct bargains are struck, word will rapidly spread, everyone will want to trade, and persuasive efforts will fail. Thus, most of the bargains that are reached are implicit.[123] The lack of respectability surrounding bargaining also encourages implicitness. This, however, has drawbacks. The terms of an implicit bargain are likely to be less clear than those of an explicit one, increasing the likelihood for misunderstanding and subsequent ill will when the member of Congress wishes to reap his or her reward for supporting the president.[124]

The president cannot bargain with Congress as a whole because it is too large and decentralized for one bargain to satisfy everyone. Also, the president's time is limited, as are his resources—only so many appointive jobs are available and the federal budget is limited. Moreover, funding for public works projects is in the hands of Congress.[125]

Fortunately for the president, bargaining with everyone in Congress is not necessary. Except on vetoes and treaties, he only needs a simple majority of those voting. A large part of Congress can be "written off" on any given vote. Moreover, we have already seen that the president generally starts with a substantial core of party support and then adds to this number those of the other party who agree with his views on ideological or policy grounds. Others may support him on the basis of goodwill that he has generated through his services or because of public support for him or his policies. Thus, the president only needs to bargain if all these groups do not provide a majority for crucial votes, and he need only bargain with enough people to provide him with that majority. As Vice President Lyndon Johnson said in 1963, "Not many votes are converted in the corridors."[126]

Since resources are scarce, the president will usually try to use them for bargaining with powerful members of Congress, such as committee chairpersons or those whose votes are crucial on an issue, as the above examples of bargaining illustrate. However, there is no guarantee that a tendered bargain will be accepted. The members may not desire what the president offers, or they may be able to obtain what they want on their own. This is, of course, particularly true of the most powerful members, whose support the president needs most.

Sometimes members of Congress do not want to trade at all. This may be due to either constraints such as constituency opinion or personal views. In 1961 Representative Jim Delaney cast the vote responsible for holding the federal aid-to-education bill in the House Rules Committee. He wanted to include aid to parochial schools, which Kennedy opposed. The president desperately needed his vote, but Delaney was not interested in bargaining on other subjects. As legislative liaison chief Lawrence O'Brien exclaimed, "He didn't want a thing. I wish he had." [127]

At other times the president is unwilling to bargain. In 1961 Representative D. B. Saund of California was angered by President Kennedy's closing of a veteran's hospital in his district, and in retaliation he opposed an important provision of the president's foreign aid bill. Nevertheless, Kennedy refused to reopen the inadequate and unsafe hospital in return for Saund's support on foreign aid (his opposition was ultimately successful.)[128]

At yet other times the president is simply unable to bargain. A representative told one high White House official that he would vote to sustain an important presidential veto "if, and only if, we would get a CAB route into his town." The official responded, "Congressman, that is impossible. We can't touch regulatory agencies." Thus, the member voted against the president. [129]

Richard Neustadt argues in *Presidential Power* that the president must bargain even with those who agree with him in order to insure their support because most people in government have interests of their own beyond the realm of policy objectives. [130] Yet the importance of other explanations of presidential support in Congress discussed in earlier chapters and the limitations on bargaining mentioned above indicate that Neustadt's view needs to be revised. The president does not have to bargain with everyone to receive his or her support, and he cannot bargain with very many members of Congress at any one time.

However, we have also seen that some bargains are struck. It is important to distinguish between a president's usual supporters and opponents. All bargains are not equal. Rewarding one's opponents for short-term support is much costlier than rewarding supporters, since the former action may not only alienate supporters who did not receive benefits but also give opponents greater strength in the future. Rewarding supporters, on the other hand, may make them more effective in advancing the president's policies, thus multiplying the positive effect of bargains. Thus, people who recommend that presidents rely upon bargaining, such as Neustadt, should specify with whom bargains should be made and what their long-run consequences are.

Much of what the president offers in bargaining is ultimately in the hands of the bureaucracy or other members of Congress. Consequently, he must often bargain within the executive branch or within Congress before he can bargain with a particular member of Congress whose vote he needs. This uses the president's time, energy, and bargaining resources. In addition, once credit is built up between a department (which has done a favor) and a member of Congress, it may be drawn upon by the department without the president's approval.

According to the *Congressional Quarterly,* most of the pressure for bargaining actually comes from the Hill. When the White House calls and asks for support, representatives and senators frequently raise a question regarding some request that they have made.[131] In the words of an Eisenhower aide, "Every time we make a special appeal to a Congressman to change his position, he eventually comes back with a request for a favor ranging in importance from one of the President's packages of matches to a judgeship or cabinet appointment for a 'worthy constituent.'"[132]

Another frustrated presidential aide spoke of his experience with one representative as follows:

> Every time you wanted a vote from him he wanted something for the walnut growers in his district or something else. Finally, I sat him down and said "Look, I can't bargain for every vote. Why don't you draw up a shopping list of things that would be really helpful to you and we'll do our best to help. In turn, how about giving us a little more support?"[133]

We have already seen other examples of members of Congress responding to White House requests for support with a request of their own. Sometimes members of Congress try to initiate bargains as well. Senator Carl Curtis of Nebraska wanted to cut his staff in 1975 and told Commerce Secretary Rogers Morton that he would aid President Ford in his fight with Congress over energy legislation if the Commerce Department hired one of his aides.[134]

More general bargains also take place. In the words of Nixon's chief congressional aide, William Timmons, "I think they [members of Congress] knew that we would try our best to help them on all kinds of requests if they supported the President, and we did. It kind of goes without saying." His successor, Max Friedersdorf, added his assurance that people who want things want to be in the position of supporting the president. This implicit trading on "accounts" is more common than explicit bargaining.[135]

The Kennedy, Johnson, and Nixon administrations kept a record of presidential support given by each member of Congress. The Ford administration kept a less formal tally. Each president checked the record before granting requests.[136] Although the White House generally tries to be helpful to everyone, it is likely to be most helpful to those members providing the most support.[137]

In interviews with members of the congressional liaison staffs in the Kennedy, Johnson, Nixon, and Ford administrations, Joe Pika found near unanimity on the view that the relationships between the White House and members of Congress were reciprocal: Voting support by members was exchanged for administrative responsiveness to their requests for assistance.[138] The White House tried to get members of Congress in its debt by providing favors and sympathetic hearings. Many members, in turn, tried to create favorable impressions in the White House of their support for the president, sometimes writing to the president and reminding him of their votes.[139]

For the White House, a member of Congress indebted to the president is easier to approach and ask for a vote. For the member, previous support increases the chances of a request being honored. Thus, office holders at both ends of Pennsylvania Avenue want to be in the other's favor. The degree of debt determines the strategy used in presidential requests for support. While services and favors increase the president's chances of obtaining support, they are not usually exchanged for votes directly. They are strategic and not tactical weapons.[140]

This point is illustrated in the following statement by Lawrence O'Brien, discussing various White House services for Congress:

> [There is] no single element of [them] that is overridingly important, but [in] the over-all activity . . . in putting the package together over a period of years [we] can only hope the Member up there has the view that the White House is interested in him and his problems . . . and therefore when we have our problems—we will get favorable reaction at least from the sense of giving us a hearing, seriously considering our viewpoint, if he feels that we in turn understand his problem.[141]

Professional Reputation

In *Presidential Power* Richard Neustadt coined the phrase "professional reputation" to label the concept of a president using his bargaining advantages to aid his supporters and not his opponents. Because public officials base their expectations on what they see the president do (and they always watch), his policy views must be consistent and he must clearly indicate his personal concern for the outcomes of congressional actions. Neustadt argues that professional reputation is a fundamental source of presidential power.[142]

We have seen that the president's ability to bargain is very limited. Although maximizing the probabilities that supportive members of Congress will receive presidentially endowed benefits may be helpful to the president in some cases, it is unlikely to influence many votes. Probably the more important aspect of professional reputation is providing members of Congress consistent cues about the president's position and his concern for their votes.

Lawrence O'Brien argues that it is important for the president not only to advocate his programs initially but also to remind everyone constantly of the programs and their meaning. These actions show that the president is vitally concerned about his programs.[143] Since members of the president's party and all members who respect him personally or whose constituents approve of him are often open to taking cues from the president, these cues must be clear, and those who are vacillating in their decisions must know that the president really desires their support.

President Johnson believed that it was important for his congressional opponents to understand his concern for the passage of his policies. He wrote that during the battle for the 1964 Civil Rights Act, he took special care that leaders of the opposition understood his uncompromising attitude and commitment to the passage of a strong bill. He felt that the slightest wavering on his part would give hope to their strategy of amending the bill to uselessness. He also made it clear that he was willing to take strong steps to defeat a filibuster and that he would keep the Senate in session, suspend all other activities, and concentrate on this matter alone or call a special session of Congress if necessary to pass the bill.[144]

Johnson believed that all legislators were influenced by the desire for recognition and the fear of losing. Thus, the president tried to satisfy their desires and decrease their fears by establishing close ties to Congress. He increased congressional recognition by having Congress participate in the initiation of programs. Therefore, legislators would risk allying themselves with him in order to receive recognition for developing new programs. By taking an active role in pushing legislation through Congress, he decreased the risks of those who supported him.[145] On the 1964 antipoverty bill, he phoned representatives to tell them that he would have "gold stars" for those who supported him and who got others to support him.[146]

Johnson also felt that the first impression of his presidency would be crucial and therefore went to great lengths to win the vote on the 1963 foreign aid bill, as we have seen. He felt that a loss at the beginning of his tenure would have been a serious blow; after winning the vote, he sensed the power of government moving back to the White House. He felt similarly about the tax cut and civil rights bills of 1964, that is, that winning them would help to reestablish presidential leadership in Congress. He had to demonstrate that he was committed to winning votes, that he could do so successfully, and that Congress should therefore follow him.[147]

President Eisenhower was in many ways the opposite of President Johnson in professional reputation. He was notable for his seeming lack of concern for or involvement in getting many of his programs passed. He failed to give priority to programs,[148] thus losing the opportunity to communicate his special interests in and desires for programs and his willingness to aid their enactment into law. He also frequently wavered in his support, providing potential supporters with inconsistent cues. He was no better in aiding his supporters. The White House did little or nothing to succor the original Eisenhower supporters in the Senate, for example, and made no protests when Senator Taft, his chief rival for the Republican nomination, pushed them into the background.[149] The Republican floor leaders opposed Eisenhower's 1953 public housing bill and told their colleagues that the president would not be upset if authority for new public housing was cut, which the president himself later acknowledged. Needless to say, the authority was cut.[150]

During his first term, one of the most controversial issues facing Eisenhower was the Bricker amendment, which would have constrained the president's ability to make executive agreements with other nations. Eisenhower opposed it but was anxious to conciliate Bricker and gave him a friendly hearing in the White House. This created the impression of a greater willingness to compromise than was the case. Moreover, Eisenhower told Bricker that he would accept the amendment if a key clause was deleted, while Secretary of State John Foster Dulles was telling Republican senators that no part of the amendment was acceptable. At a cabinet meeting, Eisenhower responded to Dulles's criticism of his fuzziness on the amendment by saying that he told Bricker to go only so far and no further. Dulles retorted, "I know, Sir, but you haven't told anyone else."

This discussion, it should be added, did not occur until July, although Bricker had called on Eisenhower in early January to solicit his support, and the original amendment had sixty-four cosponsors.[151]

There are many other instances of Eisenhower's seeming lack of personal concern for his legislative program and for legislation initiated in Congress that was contrary to his views. At one point during consideration of a labor bill, Senator H. Alexander Smith, the chairperson of the Labor and Public Welfare Committee, heard Eisenhower's response to objections to his bill by Republican senators and said that the president did not "know quite what it [was] all about!"[152]

In his first State of the Union message, Eisenhower asked for prompt help for schools but never mentioned the subject again that year and sent no legislation on it to Congress. During the debate on the 1956 school construction bill, he did not send a single word to Congress (the bill failed). The 1957 school construction bill failed by three votes as the secretary of Health, Education and Welfare (HEW) waited for Eisenhower to make calls on its behalf. Republican forces tried to reach him to elicit a statement of his support after his support became the central issue of debate. On several occasions the president had spoken the correct words in support of the school aid program advocated by HEW Secretary Marion Folsom but then withdrew from the political fray. Thus, his handling of the matter indicated a lack of conviction and earnestness and left a strong suspicion that he was really doubtful about the bill's necessity or desirability. When the president heard of complaints about his lack of action and accessibility six days later at a press conference, he replied that he had been unaware of them.[153] In his memoirs Eisenhower blames the death of the bill on an antisegregation rider, says he sent a Republican representative from Ohio a letter citing the support of former senator Robert Taft of Ohio for federal school construction aid, and then drops the subject completely.[154]

Eisenhower was less than wholeheartedly behind his 1956 program to decrease unemployment, omitting it from a "must" list of legislation and giving it only lukewarm support at a news conference. Congressional relations on the bill were left to unenthusiastic, business-oriented Department of Commerce officials, some of whom, including Assistant Secretary Mueller, told Republicans in Congress to oppose the administration's bill. The president and the bill's advocates within the administration did not communicate with the bill's Republican supporters on the Hill. At a news conference after the bill failed to pass, Eisenhower once again seemed to have little grasp of the reasons for its failure or even of the behavior of his own officials at the Commerce Department.[155]

The Eisenhower administration also vacillated on civil rights legislation. In 1956 Eisenhower gave restrained support to his four civil rights proposals; however, he did not place them among his "must" legislation, nor did he make pleas for their passage during a period of hospitalization as he did for foreign affairs bills. (The White House staff actually put more pressure on Republicans when Eisenhower was in the hospital than when he was out.) The congressional debate on the bills was punctuated by questions of the president's support for them. And

Representative William Miller, who had sponsored the president's bills earlier, attacked them in the debates. Only after the programs failed to pass, the session was over, and the presidential campaign had concluded did Eisenhower endorse all four bills.[156]

During the 1957 Senate debate on his civil rights bill, Eisenhower revealed at a news conference that he did not understand certain phrases in it. At his next press conference, he reported that he did not agree with a portion of the bill that he had earlier accepted. These statements, quite naturally, surprised some Republicans.[157]

Eisenhower's 1955 legislative program asked for both decreased expenditures and increased program responsibilities.[158] The 1958 State of the Union message was strong, but his budget message four days later seemed to ignore or refute it. On foreign trade even Secretary of State Dulles privately lamented the contradictions between Eisenhower's proclaimed intent and his practical action.[159]

In 1958 the president presented a plan for reorganizing the Defense Department. He felt strongly about this issue, but at a press conference he said that the language of the bill was not sacrosanct. He added that since he would be commander in chief for only three more years, his personal view could not be the final answer. Moreover, Secretary of Defense Neil McElroy admitted to a congressional committee that some of the provisions of the bill were unnecessary. Thus, the bill was altered in Congress in a way contrary to the thrust of the president's proposal.[160]

Early in Eisenhower's first term in office, the Hoover Commission recommended that the validity of appropriations be limited to one year. The president supported this idea and proposed it to Congress, where it passed the Senate. But in the House Appropriations Committee, Representatives Clarence Cannon and John Taber, two senior members, opposed it, arguing that it was a wasteful idea. Eisenhower responded that theirs was a "new point of view" and seemed to waver in his support for the measure. This caused former President Hoover to pressure Eisenhower to issue a letter of support for the bill. Yet before the letter was signed, Cannon and Taber mobilized Secretary of Defense Charles Wilson to say that the bill might endanger national security. Hoover then called the White House and got a news release out, which was followed by the release of Wilson's testimony and, finally, by the death of the bill. The administration's position was simply unclear.[161]

At the time of the presentation of the final 1958 budget, Secretary of the Treasury George Humphrey released a letter to the president that warned of a "depression that will curl your hair" if the budget were not brought under control. Eisenhower had agreed to the release of this letter because he felt that it would discourage congressional increases in the budget, but the statement was viewed as Humphrey criticizing the budget as being too extravagant. Shortly thereafter, the president told a press conference that it was Congress's responsibility to cut the budget if it found places where it could do so. In the words of White House chief of staff Sherman Adams, this "gummed up the sapworks." While Eisenhower was just referring to the normal, marginal cuts made by Congress, his statement sounded more extreme; the Democrats had a heyday in criticizing a presidential budget that even the president did not support. The House ended up asking the president for a list of items that it should cut. Eisenhower tried to defend his budget, but the effort was too late and the budget was cut substantially. Once again we see an insensitivity concerning congressional reaction to administration statements and the president looking on hopelessly and feeling that his statements were being exploited.[162]

Eisenhower did not appear to hold strong policy views. "His support of his own legislative program was sporadic and by failing to lift a hand at critical moments he would let down his moderate Republicans in Congress even on items of his own program."[163] He was weak in situations where he was pulled in several directions, trying to please too many people and allowing his irresolution to weaken his public posture. He reacted to fast-moving, unstructured situations slowly and lacked a sense of personal power.[164]

One Eisenhower aide has suggested that the president's lack of commitment on many of his programs may have been due to his being unsure about what he wanted in domestic policy. He was skeptical of the objectives of his civil rights proposals and of using legislation to accomplish these objectives.[165] In his memoirs Eisenhower indicates strong support for his 1957 civil rights proposals, but his actions were not consistent with this view. For example, his aides, but not he, called members on the crucial conference committee. The leader of the Democrats in the Senate, Lyndon Johnson, and not he, came up with a critical compromise.[166]

In foreign affairs, which Eisenhower cared more about and felt he more fully understood, he did often show firm leadership. In the last two years of his second term he became more resolute on his domestic programs and used the veto more effectively. For example, in 1959 he twice vetoed Democratic housing bills; finally, the Democrats capitulated by passing a scaled-down third. On the fiscal 1960 budget, he proposed a balanced budget and threatened to veto even moderate additions. If the veto was overridden, he threatened to ask for a tax increase, calling a special session if necessary.[167]

Early in his tenure, President Kennedy developed a problem with his professional reputation. During the 1961 congressional consideration of his aid-to-education bll, he softened his opposition to aid Roman Catholic schools by stating in a press conference that special purpose loans might be acceptable to him. Some members of Congress viewed this as abandoning under pressure a principle that he had previously insisted upon and not as merely retreating or compromising on details.[168]

Examining his handling of the Family Assistance Plan (FAP) gives some insight into President Nixon's professional reputation. FAP was his program for reforming the welfare system and was presented to the nation in a nationally televised speech in August 1969. In the words of Daniel P. Moynihan, his chief adviser on welfare matters, "initial thrusts were rarely followed up with a sustained . . . second and third order of advocacy. . . . The impression was allowed to arise . . . [that] the President wasn't really behind them."[169] In addition, several White House aides wanted FAP defeated and falsely intimated that the president's support was wavering. This, Moynihan argues, provided liberals of both parties an excuse not to support FAP.[170]

Other observers have also noted Nixon's indecision and lack of follow-through on FAP, giving congressional Republicans the feeling that they could oppose the plan without incurring presidential displeasure. Two authors even speculate that the president may have been working both sides: If the bill passed, fine; if it failed, he could claim that he tried, blame Congress for the welfare mess, and not antagonize his conservative supporters by trying too hard.[171]

In 1970 Senator Stennis of Mississippi introduced an amendment requiring an end to the legal distinction between *de facto* and *de jure* segregation and the creation of a common policy for school desegregation in the North and the South. This amendment was designed to halt school desegregation, not to equalize it. The president wavered in his responses to the amendment. On the final vote, Senate Republican leader Hugh Scott had plans to add language that would have made the amendment meaningless and thought he had Nixon's support. Yet on the floor he faced the humiliation of having his statement of the administration's position openly contradicted by another Republican senator who had information from a high White House aide that the president really favored the amendment. The amendment passed in the Senate. It was thrown out of the conference committee bill only after Nixon finally stated his support for maintaining the legal distinction between the two types of segregation.[172]

Nixon also seemed to lose interest in programs quickly and was frequently upbraided in Congress for not trying to get his programs passed. Those who opposed him met little resistance. Perhaps this attitude reflected his attempts to bring change without the participation of Congress.[173]

Gerald Ford's professional reputation was mixed. He probably hurt himself with Congress when he promised national health insurance in 1974 but failed to deliver on it.[174] On the other hand, in 1976 he threatened to hold two bills appropriating funds for jobs, which the Democrats badly desired, until revenue sharing was passed. His threat worked; the revenue sharing bill passed and he signed all three bills.[175]

The threat of a veto played an important role in Ford's (and Nixon's) legislative strategy. To make the threat credible, vetoes had to be sustainable. This became the major strategic objective in Ford's relationship with Congress, and the efforts paid off; a good many bills were altered to satisfy Ford.[176] Still, Ford did veto sixty-six bills in two-and-a-half years in office and had twelve overridden, evidence that the threat was not completely effective.

Arm-Twisting

One special variant of presidential involvement in seeking support from Congress is arm-twisting. This term has no precise definition. We may define arm-twisting as the use of coercive techniques like pressure and threats to gain support from members of Congress.

Lawrence O'Brien once claimed that "arm twisting . . . does not exist."[177] In discussing President Johnson's treatment of Congress, former aide Jack Valenti argued that a president really cannot twist the arms of powerful, influential members lest they become "sullen, intractable and vengeful." Thus, a president must be more sophisticated.[178] In his memoirs Johnson comments on arm-twisting, arguing that he could not rely on threats. "It is daydreaming," he wrote, "to assume that any experienced Congressman would ignore his basic instincts or his constitutents' deepest concerns in quaking fear of the White House. My best hope was to make him a good, solid, convincing case for the administration's position."[179] O'Brien supports this view in his comments that the Johnson White House was not going to ask anyone to commit political suicide. Rather, it had to rely on the soft sell, looking to develop long-run influence.[180]

One Southern Democrat agreed with this in his description of Johnson's efforts to influence him. "What he really twists," the representative said, "is your heart. He says he's got to have your help, and the tears are practically coming out of the telephone receiver."[181] Barefoot Sanders, chief of the Office of Congressional Relations at the end of Johnson's presidency, said that his office generally tried to be helpful to everyone and took no revenge on opponents.[182]

Nevertheless, Johnson's behavior was not always so gentle. One aide recalls his systematic use of "sheer force—embarrassing, bullying, and threatening." If these tactics failed, he used reprisals to make the members more amenable to his desires in the future. During the debate on Medicare, Johnson told one senator that he understood the senator's problems, but worse ones would occur if he did not see the light.[183]

Johnson often had Senate Republican leader Everett Dirksen sit at the head table at state dinners as a reward for the senator's support of Johnson's Vietnam policy and other policies. Conversely, after their opposition to the war was clear, Senate Foreign Relations Committee chairperson William Fulbright frequently was not invited to state dinners, and Senate Majority Leader Mike Mansfield was seated at a side table. Johnson also exhorted, "The next time [Senator] Frank Church [who opposed his policies in Vietnam] wants a dam, let him build it," and reviewed the Army Corps of Engineers budget to hurt those who opposed him. His aides also could be "pretty insistent."[184]

One interesting bit of Johnsonian high-handedness occurred when he was trying to get Senate Finance Committee chairperson Harry Byrd to hold hearings on Johnson's Medicare bill. Unknown to Byrd, television cameras awaited him after a meeting between the president and congressional leaders. As the president and the senator faced the cameras, Johnson was able to extract publicly a promise from Byrd for quick hearings.[185]

President Eisenhower relied very little on arm-twisting. It was contrary to his style of leadership, which developed over the four decades of his successful military career. He said of himself, "I am not the desk-pounding type that likes to stick out his jaw and look like he is bossing the show." He preferred to persuade members of Congress into giving him their support rather than scare them with "noisy, strong-armed tactics." It was his belief as well as his inclination that persuasion would be more successful with Republicans, who had grown accustomed to opposing the president through the Roosevelt-Truman years and who might be alienated by pressure. He also believed members would stick by him more if they were persuaded as to the correctness of their actions. Thus, his leadership style emphasized persuasion, conciliation, education, and patience.[186] He courted rather than challenged Congress.

Several months after leaving office, Eisenhower was asked if he ever "turned the screw on Congress to get something done . . . saying you'll withhold an appointment or something like that." He responded, "No, never. . . . I never thought that any of these appointments should be used for bringing pressure on the Congress." In the opinion of one of his aides, this reluctance to pressure Congress contributed to the floundering of his legislative program and a blurring of his party's image.[187]

About the closest Eisenhower came to arm-twisting were occasional threats to withhold campaign support from unresponsive Republicans and telling Republican leaders in 1957 that if members of Congress failed to support his national security proposals, "I would not be able to understand them should they ever request my help in the future." His postmaster general, Arthur Summerfield, sometimes threatened to cut off patronage to Republicans who broke party ranks.[188]

In a January 1954 cabinet meeting, Vice President Nixon suggested that administration officials accept or reject speaking engagements in Republican congressional districts and states depending upon the support that those members of Congress had given to the administration's programs. But the president said that Republicans in Congress should know that this policy *might* be implemented, hoping that the administration would never have to resort to such a course later.[189]

Senator Joseph McCarthy regularly attacked the president and at one point even publicly apologized for supporting him in 1952. Yet Eisenhower levied no sanctions against him beyond ignoring him. (On the Senate's censure vote on the senator, most of the Republican leadership in the Senate voted for McCarthy.)[190] At an April 1953 cabinet meeting, Eisenhower said that anyone who wanted to support the Bricker amendment (which he strongly opposed) could do so. In 1958 Senator Andrew Schoeppel, chairperson of the Republican Senatorial Campaign Committee, announced that candidates could ignore reciprocal trade and foreign aid (two of the issues closest to Eisenhower's heart) if they found it convenient during the campaign.[191]

On his desk the president had a small block of wood bearing the inscription "Gentle in manner, strong in deed." This reflects the fact that he was temperamentally unable to impose sanctions to enforce discipline on recalcitrant Republicans. He also refused to criticize Republicans publicly because he felt to do so would do more harm than good. At a news conference he once said that he did not think it was the function of a president to punish anyone for not voting right.

These words were undoubtedly not lost upon Congress. Even on issues about which he was deeply concerned, such as mutual security legislation, and on which he received little support from Republican leaders, he did not try to punish them.[192]

Lawrence O'Brien, who headed the White House Office of Congressional Relations under both Kennedy and Johnson, has contrasted the former's "more restrained approach" with the latter's "hard-sell, arm-twisting style of operation."[193] Generally, the Kennedy White House employed a positive rather than a negative approach to congressional relations.[194] Nevertheless, there are examples of arm-twisting in the Kennedy years. In the midst of the 1962 fight over raising the ceiling on the national debt, then representative Gerald Ford, among others, accused the Kennedy administration of threatening to cancel military contracts in his Michigan district if he did not support the bill. At other times during the Kennedy era, there were threats to cancel National Guard and reserve armories.[195]

After he lost the Senate vote on Medicare in 1962 by a vote of 52 to 48, Kennedy had Senator Jennings Randolph of West Virginia (who voted against the bill) notified that his controversial $11 million grant, which the president had promised to support before the vote, was being dropped from the budget. Other Kennedy opponents had federal buildings for their constituencies dropped from the budget. Kennedy once excluded a local representative from the platform on a California trip because of his consistent desertion on foreign aid votes.[196]

In the 1961 battle over expanding the House Rules Committee, the president's supporters in the House threatened freshmen with poor committee assignments (his opponents did the same), and Secretary of Interior Stewart Udall called four Republicans and suggested that their projects might have problems with the pro-Kennedy forces if they voted against expansion of the committee.[197]

Thus, although Kennedy rarely asked a member of Congress for a specific vote, his aides did at times apply pressure. Even when members of Congress complained that their constituents were opposed to an item high on the president's priority list, they were sometimes told that they had "to take the heat."[198]

The Nixon administration also employed arm-twisting. During the legislative fight over the ABM in 1969, which Nixon favored, heavy pressure was applied. Senator James Pearson of Kansas, a Republican, was opposed to the ABM. At a crucial point in the debate, he was told by a Kansas plane manufacturer that an army general had informed him that Pentagon contracts might not be forthcoming to Kansas if the ABM failed in the Senate. The senator was also told by the Department of Agriculture that the rural job development bill that he and the department had backed would not now receive the latter's support. Besides threatening him with the loss of benefits, the White House did not tell him that it was moving a regional federal office from Denver to Kansas City, thus denying him the opportunity to take credit for the move.[199]

In that same year there was a major fight, which the president eventually lost, over the confirmation of Clement Haynsworth to the Supreme Court. During the consideration of the nomination, the White House attempted to generate mail supporting Haynsworth to senators and threatened Republicans with strong primary opponents, cutoffs or slowdowns of public works funds, withdrawing personal and monetary campaign support, reviews of income tax returns, the loss of agricultural subsidies, and the loss of access to the White House. When G. Harrold Carswell was nominated to fill the same seat, the White House relied on polite inquiries and quiet persuasion until the end of the fight, when it once again began its high-pressure campaign. Two Democratic senators (Howard Cannon and Quentin Burdick) were told that they would face weak Republican opposition in their reelection campaigns that year if they supported the president and that Nixon and Vice President Agnew would personally campaign against them if they voted against confirmation. (Following Cannon's vote against Carswell, the White House did make special efforts, in vain, to defeat him in the fall election.) The White House also released to *Newsweek* a list of all the people that it had called in Pennsylvania and asked to support the president in order to pressure Senator Richard Schweiker;[200] thus, Schweiker was placed in the position of publicly opposing these people if he voted against confirmation.

Despite the fact that the Nixon administration sometimes applied heavy pressure on Congress,[201] the president did not apply it himself. Nixon could not bring himself to ask for a vote and would frequently end meetings with representatives with "I know you're going to do what you have to do and that's fine. Whatever you do is OK with me." He hated face-to-face confrontations and did not demand or plead for votes, even on a matter as important to him as the Carswell nomination. The hard sell came from the White House staff.[202]

Congress was not immune to White House arm-twisting when Gerald Ford, a "man of Congress," occupied the presidency, either. Again, this came from the staff rather than the president. In 1975, White House aide Douglas Bennett threatened to block an appointment in which two Republican representatives from Maine were interested if they failed to support President Ford on a veto override attempt. The following year Representative Larry Pressler of South Dakota complained of a threat from one of President Ford's lobbyists that he would have "political trouble" in his district if he failed to support the president on a natural gas deregulation bill. He was also warned after the vote that he could be cut off from White House favors.[203] Other complaints of arm-twisting by White House aide Vernon Loen came from Senator James Abourezk, who was threatened with "We're going to get you in '78," and Representative Berkley Bedell, a religious freshman, who was told by a White House aide, "I don't have to take any ——— from a freshman."[204]

At the beginning of this section we heard disclaimers about both the existence and effectiveness of arm-twisting. We have since seen that presidents have occasionally used high-pressure tactics on members of Congress, often unsuccessfully. None of the four Republicans threatened with the loss of public works projects in their districts voted for Kennedy in the 1961 House Rules Committee fight,[205] and Nixon's staff's actions in the Haynsworth and Carswell episodes either were ineffective or backfired.[206]

Members of Congress do not like arm-twisting. As one prominent student of Congress put it, "The rule here is to forgive and remember."[207] Given the limited success and the possibility of backfiring, it is not surprising that arm-twisting is generally relied upon only as a last resort and then only on particularly important votes.[208]

Notes

1. Harry McPherson, *A Political Education* (Boston: Little, Brown, 1972), p. 192.

2. Doris Kearns, *Lyndon Johnson and the American Dream* (New York: Harper & Row, 1976), p. 226.

3. Lyndon B. Johnson, *The Vantage Point: Perspectives on the Presidency 1963–1969* (New York: Popular Library, 1971), p. 448.

4. Eric F. Goldman, *The Tragedy of Lyndon Johnson* (New York: Dell, 1974), p. 68.

5. Joseph A. Califano, Jr., *A Presidential Nation* (New York: Norton, 1975), p. 217. The author suggests this attention to detail was in part due to Johnson's natural skepticism.

6. Lawrence F. O'Brien, *No Final Victories* (Garden City, N.Y.: Doubleday, 1974), p. 194; George Christian, *The President Steps Down: A Personal Memoir of the Transfer of Power* (New York: Macmillan, 1970), p. 6. See also Goldman, *Tragedy of Lyndon Johnson,* p. 72.

7. Kearns, *Lyndon Johnson,* p. 233; Stephen J. Wayne, *The Legislative Presidency* (New York: Harper & Row, 1978), p. 151.

8. O'Brien, *No Final Victories,* p. 172; Wayne, *Legislative Presidency,* p. 148.

9. O'Brien, *No Final Victories,* pp. 171–172. See also Johnson, *Vantage Point,* pp. 159, 211; Goldman, *Tragedy of Lyndon Johnson,* pp. 340–341; Wayne, *Legislative Presidency,* p. 151; Kearns, *Lyndon Johnson,* p. 233; Califano, *Presidential Nation,* p. 215; Jack Valenti, *A Very Human President* (New York: Norton, 1975), p. 189.

10. O'Brien, *No Final Victories,* p. 184.

11. Goldman, *Tragedy of Lyndon Johnson,* p. 71; Jack Bell, *The Johnson Treatment* (New York: Harper & Row, 1965), p. 178.

12. Johnson, *Vantage Point,* p. 451. See also Goldman, *Tragedy of Lyndon Johnson,* p. 70.

13. Kearns, *Lyndon Johnson,* pp. 186, 225; Johnson, *Vantage Point,* p. 447; Goldman, *Tragedy of Lyndon Johnson,* p. 70; "Carter Seeks More Effective Use of Departmental Lobbyists' Skills," *Congressional Quarterly Weekly Report,* March 4, 1978, p. 581; Joseph A. Pika, "White House Office of Congressional Relations: A Longitudinal Analysis," paper presented at the annual meeting of the Midwest Political Science Association, Chicago, April 1978, p. 13. See also Rowland Evans and Robert Novak, *Nixon in the White House: The Frustration of Power* (New York: Vintage, 1972), p. 109, for Bryce Harlow's argument for this need for intimate knowledge.

14. Kearns, *Lyndon Johnson,* p. 236; Wayne, *Legislative Presidency,* p. 151; Goldman, *Tragedy of Lyndon Johnson,* pp. 73–74; Valenti, *Very Human President,* p. 304.

15. Kearns, *Lyndon Johnson,* p. 185.

16. Johnson, *Vantage Point,* p. 457. For another example, see Wayne, *Legislative Presidency,* p. 147.

17. Goldman, *Tragedy of Lyndon Johnson,* pp. 70, 227; Kearns, *Lyndon Johnson,* pp. 226, 337.

18. Goldman, *Tragedy of Lyndon Johnson,* p. 308.

19. Kearns, *Lyndon Johnson,* p. 222; Johnson, *Vantage Point,* p. 446; Goldman, *Tragedy of Lyndon Johnson,* p. 382; Neil MacNeil, *Dirksen: Portrait of a Public Man* (New York: World, 1970), pp. 252–254.

20. Johnson, *Vantage Point,* pp. 209–210, 447; Goldman, *Tragedy of Lyndon Johnson,* p. 74; Kearns, *Lyndon Johnson,* p. 223; Alan L. Otten, "By Courting Congress Assiduously Johnson Furthers His Program," *Wall Street Journal,* April 9, 1965, p. 1.

21. Kearns, *Lyndon Johnson,* pp. 222–223.

22. Ibid., pp. 222–224.

23. Califano, *Presidential Nation,* p. 222. See also Johnson, *Vantage Point,* pp. 447–448, 456, on briefing Congress ahead of time.

24. Kearns, *Lyndon Johnson,* pp. 184–186.

25. Tom Wicker, "The Johnson Way with Congress," *New York Times Magazine,* March 8, 1964, p. 103.

26. O'Brien, *No Final Victories,* pp. 183–184; Wayne, *Legislative Presidency,* p. 150; Kearns, *Lyndon Johnson,* pp. 233–234; "Carter Seeks More Effective Use," p. 581; "Larry O'Brien Discusses White House Contacts with Capitol Hill," in *The Presidency,* ed. Aaron Wildavsky (Boston: Little, Brown, 1969), p. 480.

27. For example, see Johnson, *Vantage Point,* p. 448.

28. Ralph K. Huitt, "White House Channels to the Hill," in *Congress against the President,* ed. Harvey C. Mansfield, Sr. (New York: Praeger, 1975), p. 75; "Carter Seeks More Effective Use," pp. 581, 586.

29. Goldman, *Tragedy of Lyndon Johnson,* pp. 81–82.

30. Kearns, *Lyndon Johnson,* p. 225.

31. O'Brien, *No Final Victories,* pp. 111–112; MacNeil, *Dirksen,* p. 225; Neil MacNeil, *Forge of Democracy* (New York: McKay, 1963), p. 258. See Donald C. Lord, "JFK and Civil Rights," *Presidential Studies Quarterly* 8 (Spring 1978): 151–163; for a very positive view of Kennedy's legislative skills regarding his civil rights bill.

32. Arthur M. Schlesinger, Jr., *A Thousand Days: John F. Kennedy in the White House* (New York: Houghton Mifflin, 1965), p. 711.

33. Randall B. Ripley, *Majority Party Leadership in Congress* (Boston: Little, Brown, 1969), p. 37.

34. Valenti, *Very Human President,* p. 304.

35. Evans and Novak, *Nixon in the White House,* p. 106.

36. Dan Rather and Gary P. Gates, *The Palace Guard* (New York: Warner, 1975), p. 279.

37. Evans and Novak, *Nixon in the White House,* p. 168; Richard Harris, *Decision* (New York: Dutton, 1971), pp. 29, 32, 176–177, 179, 185–186, 189–190, 197–199. See pages 100, 129–132, 139, for other examples of the Nixon White House's lack of knowledge of Congress on this issue. For another example, see William Safire, *Before the Fall: An Inside View of the Pre-Watergate White House* (New York: Doubleday, 1975), pp. 487–490.

38. Sherman Adams, *Firsthand Report* (New York: Popular Library, 1962), p. 269; James L. Sundquist, *Politics and Policy: The Eisenhower, Kennedy, and Johnson Years*

(Washington, D.C.: Brookings Institution, 1968), pp. 161–162; Gary W. Reichard, *The Reaffirmation of Republicanism: Eisenhower and the Eighty-third Congress* (Knoxville: University of Tennessee Press, 1975), p. 225; Malcolm E. Jewell, *Senatorial Politics and Foreign Policy* (Lexington: University of Kentucky Press, 1962), pp. 117–118; Ripley, *Majority Party Leadership,* p. 121.

39. "Carter Seeks More Effective Use," p. 586; "House GOP: Its Survival May Be at Stake," *Congressional Quarterly Weekly Report,* June 26, 1976, p. 1634.

40. Johnson, *Vantage Point,* p. 456; Kearns, *Lyndon Johnson,* p. 233; Wayne, *Legislative Presidency,* p. 151.

41. For example, see Bell, *Johnson Treatment,* p. 40.

42. For example, see Johnson, *Vantage Point,* p. 214.

43. Wayne, *Legislative Presidency,* pp. 152–153; John F. Manley, "White House Lobbying and the Problem of Presidential Power," paper presented at the annual meeting of the American Political Science Association, Washington, D.C., September 1977, pp. 27–28.

44. Theodore C. Sorensen, *Kennedy* (New York: Bantam, 1966), p. 398.

45. Abraham Holtzman, *Legislative Liaison: Executive Leadership in Congress* (Chicago: Rand McNally, 1970), pp. 223–229, 249; Benjamin Bradlee, *Conversations with Kennedy* (New York: Norton, 1975), p. 65; O'Brien, *No Final Victories,* pp. 111–113, 117–119, 127, 134.

46. Safire, *Before the Fall,* pp. 375–376, 422, 676. Sometimes his staff briefed congressional leaders. See, for example, pp. 172–173.

47. Emmet J. Hughes, *The Living Presidency* (Baltimore: Penguin, 1974), p. 258.

48. Stephen J. Wayne, personal communication, January 9, 1979.

49. MacNeil, *Dirksen,* pp. 343–344, 346, 358.

50. Evans and Novak, *Nixon in the White House,* p. 107.

51. Adams, *Firsthand Report,* pp. 284, 288, 359–360, 372; Dwight D. Eisenhower, *Waging Peace: 1956–1961* (Garden City, N.Y.: Doubleday, 1965), pp. 44–46, 246–249, 252, 271–272; Jewell, *Senatorial Politics,* pp. 128, 156, 158; Robert J. Donovan, *Eisenhower: The Inside Story* (New York: Harper & Row, 1956), pp. 226–227, 311.

52. Wayne, *Legislative Presidency,* p. 145; Donovan, *Eisenhower,* p. 312.

53. See, for example, Eisenhower, *Waging Peace,* p. 642. See also Merlo J. Pusey, *Eisenhower the President* (New York: Macmillan, 1956), p. 206. For an exception, see Richard E. Neustadt, "Presidency and Legislation: Planning the President's Program," in *The Presidency,* ed. Aaron Wildavsky (Boston: Little, Brown), p. 571.

54. Reichard, *Reaffirmation of Republicanism,* pp. 219, 290–291; William S. White, *The Taft Story* (New York: Harper & Row, 1954), p. 213; Wayne, *Legislative Presidency,* pp. 144–145; Pusey, *Eisenhower the President,* pp. 206–207; Adams, *Firsthand Report,* pp. 214–215.

55. Jewell, *Senatorial Politics,* p. 92; MacNeil, *Dirksen,* p. 168; "The Congress: The Gut Fighter," *Time,* June 8, 1959, p. 18.

56. Dwight D. Eisenhower, *Mandate for Change, 1953–1956* (New York: Signet, 1963), p. 349; Donovan, *Eisenhower,* pp. 314, 323; Adams, *Firsthand Report,* p. 379; Neustadt, "Presidency and Legislation," pp. 569–571; Reichard, *Reaffirmation of Republicanism,* p. 220.

57. Eisenhower, *Mandate for Change,* pp. 245, 365. See also Donovan, *Eisenhower,* p. 235.

58. Emmet J. Hughes, *The Ordeal of Power: A Political Memoir of the Eisenhower Years* (New York: Atheneum, 1975), p. 123; "The Gut Fighter," pp. 15, 18.

59. Joe Martin, *My First Fifty Years in Politics* (New York: McGraw-Hill, 1960), p. 13. Nevertheless, Martin drew upon his personal goodwill with Republicans to help the president (p. 230). See also Neustadt, "Presidency and Legislation," p. 596.

60. See Eisenhower, *Mandate for Change,* p. 349; Eisenhower, *Waging Peace,* pp. 146, 151–152; Reichard, *Reaffirmation of Republicanism,* pp. 91–92, 197–199, 220–221; Neustadt, "Presidency and Legislation," pp. 569–570; Adams, *Firsthand Report,* p. 372, 379–380; Donovan, *Eisenhower,* p. 323; Jewell, *Senatorial Politics,* pp. 95–96, 158.

61. Neustadt, "Presidency and Legislation," p. 596.

62. McPherson, *Political Education,* p. 192.

63. MacNeil, *Forge of Democracy,* p. 265. See also Stephen Horn, *Unused Power: The Work of the Senate Committee on Appropriations* (Washington, D.C.: Brookings Institution, 1970), p. 195.

64. Goldman, *Tragedy of Lyndon Johnson,* p. 71; Bell, *Johnson Treatment,* p. 37; "Turning Screws: Winning Votes in Congress," *Congressional Quarterly Weekly Report,* April 24, 1976, p. 954.

65. Valenti, *Very Human President,* p. 178.

66. O'Brien, *No Final Victories,* p. 111.

67. Otten, "By Courting Congress," p. 1; Wayne, *Legislative Presidency,* p. 151; Horn, *Unused Power,* p. 195; John W. Kingdon, *Congressmen's Voting Decisions* (New York: Harper & Row, 1973), pp. 184, 187; McPherson, *Political Education,* p. 192; Jewell, *Senatorial Politics,* pp. 160–161; Holtzman, *Legislative Liaison,* p. 247.

68. Kearns, *Lyndon Johnson,* p. 235; William Chapman, "LBJ's Way: Tears, Not Arm-Twists," *Washington Post,* October 17, 1965, p. E-1.

69. Pusey, *Eisenhower the President,* p. 212; Horn, *Unused Power,* p. 195; "White House Report: Ford's Lobbyists Expect Democrats to Revise Tactics," *National Journal,* June 21, 1975, p. 926.

70. Johnson, *Vantage Point,* p. 459; Wayne, *Legislative Presidency,* p. 151; Kearns, *Lyndon Johnson,* p. 236; "Ford's Lobbyists," p. 926.

71. Kearns, *Lyndon Johnson,* pp. 234–236.

72. Sundquist, *Politics and Policy,* p. 268.

73. Califano, *Presidential Nation,* p. 215.

74. Valenti, *Very Human President,* pp. 187, 192–193. See also pp. 302–303 for Johnson discussing his toughness.

75. Goldman, *Tragedy of Lyndon Johnson,* pp. 35–38, 75.

76. Sundquist, *Politics and Policy,* p. 146; Bell, *Johnson Treatment,* pp. 187, 189; Chapman, "LBJ's Way," p. 1.

77. O'Brien, *No Final Victories,* p. 175.

78. Goldman, *Tragedy of Lyndon Johnson,* pp. 77–78. See also MacNeil, *Dirksen,* p. 228; Bell, *Johnson Treatment,* pp. 93–94.

79. Johnson, *Vantage Point,* p. 459.

80. Valenti, *Very Human President,* p. 194.

81. Bell, *Johnson Treatment,* pp. 93–94, 181; Johnson, *Vantage Point,* p. 85.

82. Goldman, *Tragedy of Lyndon Johnson,* pp. 72–73, 75–76.

83. Horn, *Unused Power,* p. 200.

84. Wayne, *Legislative Presidency,* pp. 144–145; Hughes, *Ordeal of Power,* p. 125; Adams, *Firsthand Report,* pp. 369, 373; Holtzman, *Legislative Liaison,* p. 246; Eisenhower, *Waging Peace,* p. 642; Reichard, *Reaffirmation of Republicanism,* pp. 71, 77, 170.

85. Eisenhower, *Mandate for Change,* pp. 347, 364; Reichard, *Reaffirmation of Republicanism,* pp. 67–68, 151–152, 169–171. See also Donovan, *Eisenhower,* pp. 84–86, 284, 313, for his urging the cabinet to cooperate with Congress and his discussing ways to improve relations with it.

86. Wayne, *Legislative Presidency,* p. 145; Reichard, *Reaffirmation of Republicanism,* p. 221.

87. Martin, *My First Fifty Years,* pp. 226–227; Reichard, *Reaffirmation of Republicanism,* pp. 92, 224. Martin did not think Eisenhower's aides were skillful in solving this problem.

88. Wayne, *Legislative Presidency,* p. 144; Ripley, *Majority Party Leadership,* pp. 126–127.

89. Sorensen, *Kennedy,* pp. 386, 391–392, 399–400; O'Brien, *No Final Victories,* pp. 113–114; MacNeil, *Forge of Democracy,* pp. 256–257, 264–265; McPherson, *Political Education,* pp. 192–193; Wayne, *Legislative Presidency,* p. 151. Even in the extremely close and important fight over expanding the House Rules Committee in 1961, he hardly made personal contact at all (partly to maintain the symbol of presidential non-involvement in internal congressional affairs). See also O'Brien, *No Final Victories,* p. 109.

90. Sorensen, *Kennedy,* p. 389; O'Brien, *No Final Victories,* pp. 119–120.

91. O'Brien, *No Final Victories,* pp. 147–148.

92. MacNeil, *Forge of Democracy,* pp. 26, 266.

93. "Ford's Lobbyists," p. 925; Wayne, *Legislative Presidency,* pp. 160–161. Nixon reports that he made several calls to members of Congress and had meetings with others on the ABM issue in 1969 but then stopped because he felt he was squandering his prestige; Richard M. Nixon, *RN: The Memoirs of Richard Nixon* (New York: Grosset and Dunlap, 1978), p. 417.

94. Wayne, *Legislative Presidency,* p. 161.

95. Evans and Novak, *Nixon in the White House,* p. 168. Administration officials conceded after the vote that they were not anxious for wavering senators to see Carswell.

96. Wayne, *Legislative Presidency,* p. 161.

97. "Ford's Lobbyists," p. 923; "The Veto Sticks," *Time,* June 16, 1975, p. 12.

98. "Ford's Lobbyists," p. 923; "House GOP," p. 1634.

99. Eisenhower, *Mandate for Change,* pp. 254–255. See also Reichard, *Reaffirmation of Republicanism,* p. 104; Donovan, *Eisenhower,* p. 60.

100. Horn, *Unused Power,* p. 196; Reichard, *Reaffirmation of Republicanism,* p. 169; Martin, *My First Fifty Years,* p. 234; Jewell, *Senatorial Politics,* p. 163; Eisenhower, *Mandate for Change,* pp. 267, 273; Eisenhower, *Waging Peace,* p. 162.

101. Eisenhower, *Mandate for Change,* p. 365.

102. MacNeil, *Dirksen,* pp. 171–172; O'Brien, *No Final Victories,* pp. 122–123; Adams, *Firsthand Report,* p. 370; Bell, *Johnson Treatment,* pp. 176, 178.

103. Johnson, *Vantage Point,* p. 40. See also Bell, *Johnson Treatment,* pp. 103–105; MacNeil, *Dirksen,* p. 287; O'Brien, *No Final Victories,* p. 188; Otten, "By Courting Congress," p. 1.

104. For example, see Harris, *Decision,* p. 183; Tom Wicker, *JFK and LBJ: The Influence of Personality upon Politics* (Baltimore: Penguin, 1968), pp. 79–80; MacNeil, *Forge of Democracy,* p. 264.

105. Mark J. Green, James M. Fallows, and David R. Zwick, *Who Runs Congress?* (New York: Bantam, 1972), pp. 95–97.

106. "Larry O'Brien Discusses," p. 481.

107. "Turning Screws," p. 952.

108. McPherson, *Political Education,* p. 197; Russell D. Renka, "Legislative Leadership and Marginal Vote-Gaining Strategies in the Kennedy and Johnson Presidencies," paper presented at the annual meeting of the Southwestern Political Science Association, Houston, April 1978, pp. 26–27.

109. Valenti, *Very Human President,* pp. 196–197; Renka, "Legislative Leadership," p. 37. Hubert Humphrey reports that Johnson extracted the same promise from Byrd after a late-night session at the White House, during which he employed the charms of Mrs. Johnson, liquor, and his famous "treatment" to persuade the senator; Hubert H. Humphrey, *The Education of a Public Man: My Life and Politics* (Garden City, N.Y.: Doubleday, 1976), pp. 290–293.

110. Kearns, *Lyndon Johnson,* pp. 191–192; Renka, "Legislative Leadership," p. 38.

111. Sundquist, *Politics and Policy,* p. 149; Bell, *Johnson Treatment,* pp. 98–99; Rowland Evans and Robert Novak, *Lyndon B. Johnson: The Exercise of Power* (New York: Signet, 1966), p. 455; Renka, "Legislative Leadership," pp. 40–41.

112. Goldman, *Tragedy of Lyndon Johnson,* pp. 348–349, 357–358.

113. "Turning Screws," p. 954. For a view of the opposite technique of making necessary choices appear as discretionary favors, see Kearns, *Lyndon Johnson,* p. 186.

114. Kearns, *Lyndon Johnson,* pp. 182–183; Valenti, *Very Human President,* pp. 182–183; Renka, "Legislative Leadership," pp. 28–30. Johnson's bargaining is also discussed in Goldman, *Tragedy of Lyndon Johnson,* pp. 74–75.

115. Green, Fallows, and Zwick, *Who Runs Congress?,* p. 97.

116. Harris, *Decision,* pp. 147–148.

117. *Weekend,* National Broadcasting Company, televised February 5, 1977; "Turning Screws," p. 949.

118. Evans and Novak, *Nixon in the White House,* pp. 152–153.

119. "Turning Screws," pp. 948, 953. See also Wayne, *Legislative Presidency,* p. 160.

120. Sundquist, *Politics and Policy,* pp. 206, 210.

121. Bell, *Johnson Treatment,* p. 189.

122. O'Brien, *No Final Victories,* pp. 123–124.

123. Johnson, *Vantage Point,* p. 457; Kearns, *Lyndon Johnson,* p. 236; "Turning Screws," pp. 947, 949.

124. Stanley Kelly, Jr., "Patronage and Presidential Legislative Leadership," in *Presidency,* Wildavsky, p. 273.

125. O'Brien, *No Final Victories,* p. 121.

126. Schlesinger, *Thousand Days,* p. 970.

127. Sorensen, *Kennedy,* pp. 404–405; O'Brien, *No Final Victories,* pp. 129–130, 136–137.

128. O'Brien, *No Final Victories,* p. 122.

129. Wayne, *Legislative Presidency,* p. 160. However, some congressional liaison officers suggest that delivery on congressional requests is less important than members of Congress perceiving that the White House tried its best. See Pika, "White House Office of Congressional Relations," p. 16.

130. Richard E. Neustadt, *Presidential Power* (New York: Mentor, 1964), pp. 54–61.

131. "Turning Screws," pp. 947, 949, 954.

132. Reichard, *Reaffirmation of Republicanism*, p. 173.

133. Pika, "White House Office of Congressional Relations," p. 15.

134. "Turning Screws," p. 951.

135. Ibid., pp. 952–953. Also see Holtzman, *Legislative Liaison,* p. 252; Johnson, *Vantage Point,* pp. 457–458; Kearns, *Lyndon Johnson,* pp. 236–237; Pika, "White House Office of Congressional Relations," p. 15.

136. Pika, "White House Office of Congressional Relations," p. 16.

137. Wayne, *Legislative Presidency,* pp. 154–155.

138. Pika, "White House Office of Congressional Relations," p. 6.

139. Manley, "White House Lobbying," pp. 12–13, 15–16.

140. Ibid., p. 13.

141. "Larry O'Brien Discusses," p. 485.

142. Neustadt, *Presidential Power,* chap. 4.

143. "Larry O'Brien Discusses," p. 484.

144. Johnson, *Vantage Point,* p. 157; Goldman, *Tragedy of Lyndon Johnson,* pp. 80–81; Sundquist, *Politics and Policy,* pp. 267–268.

145. Kearns, *Lyndon Johnson,* pp. 221–222.

146. Bell, *Johnson Treatment,* p. 96.

147. Kearns, *Lyndon Johnson,* p. 180; Johnson, *Vantage Point,* pp. 35, 40. See Wicker, *JFK and LBJ,* p. 146, for the view that Kennedy's record in Congress in 1961 set the stage for relations with Congress during the rest of his term.

148. Ripley, *Majority Party Leadership,* pp. 119, 121, 159.

149. White, *Taft Story,* p. 226. See also Reichard, *Reaffirmation of Republicanism,* pp. 200–202; Richard H. Rovere, *Affairs of State: The Eisenhower Years* (New York: Farrar, Straus, 1956), pp. 103–104.

150. Reichard, *Reaffirmation of Republicanism*, p. 121. It was cut again in 1954.

151. Hughes, *Ordeal of Power,* p. 144; Adams, *Firsthand Report,* pp. 111–112; Donovan, *Eisenhower,* pp. 232, 237, 239. See also Jewell, *Senatorial Politics,* p. 117.

152. Reichard, *Reaffirmation of Republicanism,* pp. 145–146.

153. Sundquist, *Politics and Policy,* pp. 156–157, 168, 171–173; Wilfred E. Binkley, *President and Congress* (New York: Vintage, 1962), p. 355; Marquis Childs, *Eisenhower: Captive Hero* (New York: Harcourt Brace, 1958), p. 248; James C. Duram, " 'A Good Growl': The Eisenhower Cabinet's January 16, 1959 Discussion of Federal Aid to Education," *Presidential Studies Quarterly* 8 (Fall 1978): 434–443.

154. Eisenhower, *Waging Peace,* pp. 139–140.

155. Sundquist, *Politics and Policy,* pp. 65–66; Arthur Larson, *Eisenhower: The President Nobody Knew* (New York: Scribner's, 1968), pp. 24–25.

156. John W. Anderson, *Eisenhower, Brownell, and the Congress* (University: University of Alabama Press, 1964).

157. Sundquist, *Politics and Policy,* p. 238 (see p. 243 for the 1959 civil rights efforts); Adams, *Firsthand Report,* pp. 336–337.

158. Neustadt, "Presidency and Legislation," p. 572.

159. Hughes, *Ordeal of Power,* pp. 258–260.

160. Ibid., pp. 260–261. For a different evaluation, see Eisenhower, *Waging Peace,* pp. 252–253.

161. Binkley, *President and Congress,* pp. 355–356.

162. Adams, *Firsthand Report,* pp. 360–374; Eisenhower, *Waging Peace,* p. 127; Larson, *Eisenhower,* pp. 25–26; Neustadt, *Presidential Power,* pp. 70–78. For other examples of Eisenhower wavering on policy stances, see Binkley, *President and Congress,* p. 357; Reichard, *Reaffirmation of Republicanism,* p. 83.

163. Binkley, *President and Congress,* p. 355.

164. Erwin C. Hargrove, *Presidential Leadership: Personality and Political Style* (New York: Macmillan, 1966), p. 132.

165. Larson, *Eisenhower,* pp. 26–27, chap. 8. See also Sundquist, *Politics and Policy,* p. 421; Reichard, *Reaffirmation of Republicanism,* pp. 120, 147; Hargrove, *Presidential Leadership,* p. 134; Earl Warren, *The Memoirs of Chief Justice Earl Warren* (Garden City, N.Y.: Doubleday, 1977), pp. 291–292. It should be noted that part of Eisenhower's hesitancy on the 1965 civil rights bills was due to Attorney General Brownell's "bootlegging" two of the four bills to Congress. These had previously been rejected by the president, but the White House could not denounce them in an election year. Nevertheless, many members of Congress guessed that Brownell went farther than Eisenhower had desired. See Anderson, *Eisenhower, Brownell, and the Congress,* pp. 28–29, 39–41, 43, 45.

166. Eisenhower, *Waging Peace,* pp. 156–161.

167. See Reichard, *Reaffirmation of Republicanism,* p. 56; Sundquist, *Politics and Policy,* pp. 198–199; Jong R. Lee, "Presidential Vetoes from Washington to Nixon," *Journal of Politics* 37 (May 1975): 524; MacNeil, *Forge of Democracy,* pp. 244–245; Eisenhower, *Waging Peace,* pp. 385, 642.

168. Wicker, *JFK and LBJ,* pp. 138, 145. See also p. 146 for Kennedy's actions on the 1961 minimum wage bill.

169. Theodore C. Sorensen, *Watchmen in the Night* (Cambridge, Mass.: M.I.T. Press, 1975), pp. 57–58.

170. Daniel P. Moynihan, *The Politics of a Guaranteed Income: The Nixon Administration and the Family Assistance Plan* (New York: Vintage, 1973), pp. 373–374.

171. Rather and Gates, *Palace Guard,* pp. 114–115, 121; Evans and Novak, *Nixon in the White House,* p. 231.

172. Gary Orfield, *Congressional Power: Congress and Social Change* (New York: Harcourt Brace Jovanovich, 1975), pp. 76–77.

173. Huitt, "White House Channels," p. 76.

174. Califano, *Presidential Nation,* p. 228.

175. "Congress Clears Revenue Sharing Extension," *Congressional Quarterly Weekly Report,* October 2, 1976, p. 2680.

176. Wayne, *Legislative Presidency,* p. 159.

177. "Larry O'Brien Discusses," p. 480.

178. Valenti, *Very Human President,* pp. 188–189.

179. Johnson, *Vantage Point,* p. 458. See also Wayne, *Legislative Presidency,* p. 155.

180. O'Brien, *No Final Victories,* p. 120; MacNeil, *Forge of Democracy,* p. 267.

181. Chapman, "LBJ's Way," p. E-1.

182. Wayne, *Legislative Presidency,* pp. 154–155.

183. Goldman, *Tragedy of Lyndon Johnson,* pp. 74–75, 348.

184. McNeil, *Dirksen,* p. 275; John A. Ferejohn, *Pork Barrel Politics: Rivers and Harbors Legislation, 1947–1968* (Stanford, Calif.: Stanford University Press, 1974), p.

72; Pika, "White House Office of Congressional Relations," p. 17; Manley, "White House Lobbying," p. 31. See also Bell, *Johnson Treatment,* pp. 159, 165; Sundquist, *Politics and Policy,* p. 266, for another example of Johnson's toughness.

185. Johnson, *Vantage Point,* pp. 216–217; Goldman, *Tragedy of Lyndon Johnson,* pp. 344–345; O'Brien, *No Final Victories,* pp. 189–190.

186. Sundquist, *Politics and Policy,* pp. 173, 421; Eisenhower, *Mandate for Change,* pp. 243–244; Hughes, *Ordeal of Power,* pp. 124–125, 347; Wayne, *Legislative Presidency,* p. 144; Ripley, *Majority Party Leadership,* p. 124.

187. Hughes, *Ordeal of Power,* pp. 334–335.

188. Eisenhower, *Waging Peace,* pp. 145–146, 642; Eisenhower, *Mandate for Change,* p. 366; Adams, *Firsthand Report,* p. 374; Reichard, *Reaffirmation of Republicanism,* p. 226; MacNeil, *Forge of Democracy,* p. 255.

189. Donovan, *Eisenhower,* p. 229.

190. Hughes, *Ordeal of Power,* p. 132.

191. Donovan, *Eisenhower,* p. 234; Childs, *Eisenhower: Captive Hero,* p. 282.

192. Hughes, *Ordeal of Power,* pp. 124, 132–133; Adams, *Firsthand Report,* pp. 36, 373–374; Donovan, *Eisenhower,* p. 224; Ripley, *Majority Party Leadership,* pp. 121, 124; Larson, *Eisenhower,* p. 25.

193. O'Brien, *No Final Victories,* p. 171.

194. Holtzman, *Legislative Liaison,* p. 252.

195. "Turning Screws," p. 950.

196. Sorensen, *Kennedy,* pp. 384–385, 392; MacNeil, *Forge of Democracy,* pp. 251–252.

197. Wicker, *JFK and LBJ,* pp. 34, 76–77.

198. O'Brien, *No Final Victories,* p. 114; Holtzman, *Legislative Liaison,* pp. 239, 252.

199. Evans and Novak, *Nixon in the White House,* pp. 113–114; Congressional Quarterly, *Guide to Current American Government: Fall 1969* (Washington, D.C.: Congressional Quarterly, 1969), pp. 99–104.

200. Harris, *Decision,* pp. 99, 176, 184, 191, 205–206.

201. For another example, see Green, Fallows, and Zwick, *Who Runs Congress?,* p. 99.

202. Wayne, *Legislative Presidency,* p. 160; Evans and Novak, *Nixon in the White House,* pp. 107–108. See also H. R. Haldeman, *The Ends of Power* (New York: Times Books, 1978), p. 71, on Nixon's lack of ability in arm-twisting.

203. "Turning Screws," pp. 947–948.

204. Jack Anderson and Les Whitten, "Ford Lobbyist Losing Friends on Hill," *Washington Post,* May 8, 1975, p. G-13.

205. Wicker, *JFK and LBJ,* p. 77.

206. Harris, *Decision,* pp. 99, 192.

207. Huitt, "White House Channels," p. 83.

208. Holtzman, *Legislative Liaison,* p. 252. See also Kingdon, *Congressmen's Voting Decisions,* pp. 156–157, 186–187; Pika, "White House Office of Congressional Relations," pp. 16–17.

Presidential Legislative Skills: II 6

In this chapter we continue our examination of presidential legislative skills. We will focus on services and amenities provided by the White House to members of Congress, presidents' use of their vice presidents in congressional relations, some important aspects of presidents' dispositions toward Congress, and White House efforts to mobilize public opinion and interest groups. We end the chapter by taking a comprehensive look at President Carter's legislative skills.

Services

White House aides of both parties believe that servicing the requests of members of Congress is important for building goodwill toward and support for the president.[1] Although most requests come from members of the president's party, members of the opposition party, especially senior members and leaders, also request White House favors.[2] In addition, not providing favors may antagonize those people who expect them.[3]

At the beginning of the Kennedy administration, the president and his aides, especially Lawrence O'Brien, made clear their interest in helping individual members of Congress who supported the president's policies. They promised presidential visits to constituencies, help with pet projects, and other benefits.[4] President Johnson asked the legislative liaison officials in each department to submit to him five names of members of Congress whom they knew best. The White House then gave each official the names of five members who were to be contacted and asked, "What can I do for you?"[5] In contrast, Bryce Harlow, Richard Nixon's chief of congressional relations, took the attitude that services for members of Congress were "terrible" and tried to cut them back. (Ultimately he was unable to do so because of the demand for services from members of Congress.)[6]

The Kennedy and Johnson administrations centralized the services that were offered. The departments were alerted to keep the White House informed about important patronage opportunities and to furnish data on major contracts, projects, and services. The departments were also to alert the White House when members of Congress requested favors so that it could create a sense of obligation to the president. Moreover, all favors by the Post Office Department (the center of federal patronage at the time) were to be recorded and forwarded to the White House. Routine congressional inquiries could go to the departments through the department liaison offices. This allowed the White House to act selectively as a court of appeals for rejected requests and, of course, to harvest credit for the president. [7]

While the departments administered minor appointments and contract announcements under Nixon and Ford, in contrast to the centralization of favors in the White House under the previous Democratic presidents, the White House still interceded on providing important services such as major public works projects and political appointments. [8]

Federal projects in local constituencies, sometimes termed "pork barrel projects," are commonly viewed as a source of presidential influence in Congress. Undoubtedly, the president has discretion in choosing where billions of dollars of expenditures will be spent. The White House Advisory Commission on Intergovernmental Relations estimated that in fiscal 1977 the administration would award about $15 billion for federal projects, which ranged from Department of Health, Education and Welfare (HEW) research projects and Department of Housing and Urban Development (HUD) demonstration programs to small military construction projects. The administration has wide latitude in choosing contractors, researchers, and the governmental units to carry out these projects. This latitude especially applies to small projects with low visibility in which few people are interested. [9]

Members of Congress are interested not only in gaining new projects for their constituencies but also in preserving old ones. While some projects are clearly designed only to last for a year or two, others have no time limit, especially military installations, which bring a substantial amount of money and jobs into congressional districts. Members of Congress are very reluctant to allow a military base, hospital, or administrative headquarters to close in their district without a fight. According to William Timmons, White House legislative liaison chief from 1970 to 1974, "Members become violent almost on these sorts of things." Many such decisions are reversed. In 1976 the *Congressional Quarterly* reported that the Pentagon had so many of its plans for closings, reductions, and realignments stymied by Congress that it had given up keeping track. Nevertheless, presidents attempt to use what discretion they have. A high-ranking Defense Department official in the Kennedy administration was "sure the list of base closings was scrutinized quite carefully for political purposes at the White House" and that this activity "didn't start with the Kennedy administration either." Timmons seconded this, commenting that the Nixon White House was quite anxious not to close some bases if the decisions were close. [10]

Under Eisenhower, Republicans were provided information on government contracts in their districts. This system was expanded and systematized during the Kennedy administration (continued under Johnson), when Lawrence O'Brien's office enforced a rule to ensure that Democrats who supported the president could make the first public announcement of federal grants and programs in their states and constituencies to help them gain favor with their constituents. To accomplish this, the White House centralized information on grants and projects. For example, each morning a military officer came to the White House with a briefcase full of the day's Defense Department announcements. Also necessary, of course, was centralizing the distribution of this information, with Democratic supporters of the president receiving it first.[11]

Naturally Republicans were not pleased by this, but O'Brien stuck to his guns, sometimes ingeniously. When Senator Margaret Chase Smith, a Republican, complained about not getting to make announcements about defense grants in her state of Maine and her Democratic colleague Senator Edmund Muskie getting all the credit, O'Brien had Muskie complain that he was not getting to make enough announcements himself. O'Brien felt so strongly about the importance of this system that it was not changed, even though Senator Smith could hurt the administration in her position as the ranking Republican on the Armed Services Committee.[12]

Nixon and Ford ended the preferential handling of impending government contracts. Because Republicans were a minority in Congress, the White House could not afford to irritate Democrats. At first the White House alerted Democrats and Republicans in order of seniority;[13] then, under Ford, the practice was eliminated altogether. Not only did the Ford administration not want to alienate members of the majority party, but it also found that little was gained with Republicans through this service because they expected it as a matter of course since a Republican occupied the White House.[14]

Presidents have more trouble with *initiating* projects in a specific constituency, especially if their party is in the minority in Congress.[15] While the executive branch usually has discretion in executing projects and programs, Congress must authorize them and appropriate funds. Thus, the first decisions are dependent upon Congress, especially if it is controlled by the opposition.

Also, the White House (and the Democratic National Committee under Kennedy and Johnson) has often helped members of Congress with their constituents. A wide range of services is offered, including greetings to elderly and other "worthy" constituents, signed presidential photographs, presidential tie clasps and other White House memorabilia, reprints of speeches, information about government programs, White House pressure on agencies in favor of constituents, passing the nominations of constituents on to agencies, influence on local editorial writers, ceremonial appointments to commissions, meetings with the president, and arguments to be used to explain votes to constituents.[16]

The president's role as national party leader can also provide service opportunities. When the districts of Democratic Representatives Victor Anfuso and John Rooney were merged following a reapportionment, the Kennedy White

House arranged a municipal judgeship for Anfuso. Similarly, when the district of Representative Alfred Santagelo of New York was eliminated by reapportionment, the White House aided his nomination to a new district.[17]

Ralph Huitt, a noted observer of Congress and sometime participant in congressional politics, argues that the most effective service that the White House can provide a member of Congress is knowledge and expertise. By helping a member of Congress be more effective, such as by aiding him or her in offering a "little language" in a bill, a president, Huitt claims, can gain access and a sympathetic hearing on Capitol Hill.[18] The White House legislative liaison office in various administrations has helped members of Congress to draft speeches and has even given help in answering hostile mail. It has also provided each member with short summaries of administration proposals, detailed data on a bill's effects, and a departmental representative to provide information and advice on relevant legislation.[19]

Campaign aid is yet another service that the White House can provide members of Congress. This aid may come in various forms, including campaign speeches by the president and executive officials for congressional candidates, funds and advice from the party national committees, presidential endorsements, pictures with the president, and letters of appreciation from the president. Sometimes campaign aid is more ingenious, as when Lawrence O'Brien, then postmaster general, held a stamp dedication ceremony, complete with parade and associated festivities, in Representative Stan Greigg's hometown in 1966.[20] Presidents sometimes dangle campaign aid before members of Congress as a reward for support.[21]

The utility of campaign aid is limited, however. It is of no help to members of the opposition party, who will receive no aid. If the president is unpopular, members of his own party will not want his aid; even if he is popular, he may have to concentrate on his own campaign. And in any election year, only one-third of the Senate seats are up for election. A Democratic president will find that elections in many southern districts are determined in the primaries, from which he will usually remain aloof, as discussed in Chapter 3. Moreover, since almost all incumbent members of Congress win reelection anyway, would-be beneficiaries have little reason for gratitude, and a threat to withhold campaign aid will cause little fear. Finally, campaign aid, unlike other services, is only useful at two-year intervals. Thus, promises are often for future aid and therefore must be somewhat vague; when election time comes, the aid may be unneeded or unwanted.

The utility of campaign aid can also be limited by the attitude of the president and the size of his party in Congress. Some presidents do not want to be involved in congressional elections. President Eisenhower did not like political campaigns and felt that he should be president of all the people and not intervene in congressional elections. He saw his role as helping to build a record of accomplishment on which his party could run. Moreover, he rarely received solid support from Republicans in Congress and he didn't want to alienate the Democrats, whose votes he regularly relied upon.[22]

Perhaps the oldest service that presidents have provided members of Congress is patronage, that is, jobs in the executive branch for the members' friends and supporters. Because patronage is used to varying degrees and with varying effectiveness, we examine it closely.

President Eisenhower continually showed his impatience with and even contempt for patronage, and he preferred not to use it to influence others or to build his party. He delegated primary responsibility for filling appointive positions to his cabinet, telling its members to fill jobs on the basis of merit first and party loyalty second. White House chief of staff Sherman Adams served as a buffer between the executive departments and congressional demands for patronage, thus helping to enforce the president's wishes. As a result of Eisenhower's policy, there were many holdover Democratic officials.[23] Also, department heads are usually more concerned with their administrative problems than with helping the president in Congress, especially if they must deal with committees chaired by members of the opposition party. Thus, Eisenhower's cabinet kept on Democratic officials who had the governmental expertise to run the departments.

In July 1953, six months after the first Republican administration in twenty years had taken office, Republican National Committee chairperson Leonard Hall complained that he could not find six members of Congress who were indebted to the administration because of member-sponsored appointments. A cabinet meeting six months later found Vice President Nixon suggesting that it might be time to use patronage to move Eisenhower's legislative program through Congress. About the same time House Rules Committee chairperson Leo Allen complained to the president that he, Allen, had not had one job filled, and Speaker William Martin asserted that he had had two more jobs at his disposal under a Democratic president than under Eisenhower. Nevertheless, nothing was done about the complaints and patronage remained, in Martin's word, "haphazard."[24]

Martin was also irritated when the White House failed to inform him that one of his constituents had been appointed assistant attorney general. Similarly, Eisenhower failed to check his appointment of Ohioan George Humphrey as secretary of the treasury with Senate Republican leader Robert Taft of Ohio. Even worse, he appointed Martin Durkin as secretary of labor, a Democrat who opposed the Taft-Hartley Act—the handiwork of Senator Taft.[25]

At the beginning of his tenure, Richard Nixon followed President Eisenhower's example in delegating responsibility for filling appointive positions, with similar results: a large number of Democratic officials. This upset Republicans in Congress as did Nixon's general failure to consult them about his appointments.[26]

In contrast was the Kennedy-Johnson patronage system. Lawrence O'Brien reports that the White House tried to help its friends with regards to appointments. In his first month in office, Kennedy notified heads of departments and agencies of White House procedures for clearing top-level appointments, attempting to insure that the recommendations of supporters in Congress and around the country received full consideration. Senior members of the president's staff met weekly at the White House to review openings and recommendations.

When appointments were made, O'Brien insured that the president got full credit.[27] President Johnson was willing to use patronage as a tool of influence, especially with powerful members of Congress. For example, he was engaged in a continuous patronage relationship with Senate Republican leader Everett Dirksen.[28]

How useful is patronage as a tool of presidential influence? Senator Dirksen argued that patronage is "a tremendous weapon. It develops a certain fidelity on the part of the recipient. He's going to be in that corner. When the chips are down, he's going to be there."[29] Perhaps President Kennedy's assessment that patronage is generally overrated but does give some leverage is more accurate.[30] Yet Dirksen's statement does imply an important point. Although there have been exceptions, most patronage has not involved an exchange for support on a bill. (Lawrence O'Brien termed "ridiculous" suggestions that patronage "bought" votes.)[31] Instead, patronage has generally been used to create goodwill and to reward general support.[32] To understand why, we must consider the limitations of patronage.

The first limitation of patronage is a lack of jobs. The president only has about 650 full-time jobs to fill since the removal of the post office from presidential politics (the cabinet and other agency heads fill another 2,000 full-time jobs with appointees), and most of these positions are filled early in a president's tenure, before he has sent much legislation to Congress. The natural turnover of jobs in the executive branch is insufficient to keep dangling patronage before members of Congress. Moreover, many of the jobs increasingly require special skills and cannot go to just any congressional favorite.

In addition, many presidential appointees must be confirmed by the Senate. An appointment made to please a member of Congress can be blocked by a senator of the president's party through the exercise of senatorial courtesy (discussed in Chapter 1) or by opposition from a majority of the Senate. President Eisenhower felt constrained in using patronage by the Democratic-controlled Congress[33] (although, as noted above, he still did not use it much when Republicans controlled Congress). Senate Republican leader Everett Dirksen took a great interest in President Nixon's appointments and employed his influence to block a number of them (as well as to get one or two of his own candidates nominated).[34] Powerful members of Congress may act to protect those already holding jobs; for instance, James Eastland, chairperson of the Senate Judiciary Committee, threatened to hold up Nixon's judicial appointments if a Democrat lost his job as U.S. attorney in Mississippi. Similarly, Wilbur Mills, chairperson of the House Ways and Means Committee, prevented Nixon's HEW Secretary Robert Finch from removing the Democratic head of the Social Security Administration.[35]

Certainly one of the biggest drawbacks to using patronage is that every appointment results in several disappointed members of Congress who desired the position for one of their favorites. Thus, presidents and presidential legislative liaison aides try to avoid direct responsibility for patronage. For example, John Bailey, Democratic National Committee chairperson under Kennedy, arranged with Office of Congressional Relations head Lawrence O'Brien that the latter would send approvals to congressional patronage requests while the former would issue the more numerous rejections so as not to bring congressional wrath upon the White House. President Johnson put off patronage requests and pressure by blaming Civil Service Commission head and chief White House talent scout John Macy for insisting on merit. The departments and the Bureau of the Budget/Office of Management and Budget have also played a role in saying no.[36]

A related difficulty is that the existence of patronage generates expectations of its use, independent of any *quid pro quo* arrangements. The first Kennedy administration bill to reach the House floor in 1961 was openly opposed by some Democrats, who were dissatisfied with the president's handling of patronage. New York Democrats were especially upset, as they were caught in a fight between Kennedy and local party leaders and had lost their patronage. Moreover, Italian Democratic House members wanted an Italo-American appointed as administrator of the State Department's Bureau of Security and Consular Affairs (which influenced immigration). Both groups finally voted for the Kennedy bill, but only after making it clear that they could have killed it (the bill passed 209–202). Kennedy got the message and each group received its patronage, as did Polish-American representatives when a Polish-American was named to the second spot in the Bureau of Security and Consular Affairs.[37]

Personal Amenities

Members of Congress are human beings, often with substantial egos, and therefore enjoy personal amenities as much as anyone. Recent presidents have usually been sensitive to this and have come a long way since a member of the cabinet told Henry Adams, "You can't use tact with a Congressman! A Congressman is a hog! You must take a stick and hit him on the snout!"[38] President Johnson's staff, in contrast, placed at least as much emphasis on personal niceties as it did on tangible rewards in its efforts to obtain votes.[39]

The range of personal amenities is great. President Eisenhower had Representative Charles Halleck renominate him in 1956,[40] President Kennedy invited influential legislators to Palm Beach to discuss pending legislation,[41] and President Johnson sent a bouquet to a representative who had broken his leg and invited a senator to his private living quarters in the White House.[42]

All recent presidents have used bill-signing ceremonies to reward members of Congress for their aid in passing legislation. Kennedy expanded the number of such ceremonies held,[43] and Johnson increased the number of people invited to them. He was also famous for using lots of pens at bill-signing ceremonies and then passing them out to favored members of Congress, once using 60 pens and twenty minutes to sign his name! Another time he signed three bills in one ceremony and used 169 pens.[44]

Kennedy sent Democratic members of Congress thank-you notes that could be used in their campaigns (Republicans were thanked with irreproducible phone calls). Eisenhower, naturally, did the opposite.[45] President Johnson also informed members of Congress that they were regarded as important by the White House. He called to thank members of Congress for their votes and their efforts to round up others' votes, often minutes after a bill's passage. For some senior members this may have been a welcomed pleasantry. For their less powerful colleagues, such a call may have prompted reactions similar to that of a Republican representative who said, "It's the only time since I have been in Congress that a president called me. I will never forget it." [46] Or that of a Southern Democrat who was impressed when, six days after Johnson had asked for his vote, the president singled him out of a White House reception line of 150 people, gripped his arm, and said, "I really thank you." [47]

Presidents have frequently attempted to see as many members of Congress as possible on a social basis, especially at the beginning of their tenures. Early in his first term Eisenhower had the entire Congress for luncheon in small groups. These were purely social occasions designed to give the members a feeling of Eisenhower's personal interest in them. He hoped that his emphasis on social relationships and developing personal acquaintances while discussing issues in a social atmosphere would help smooth out the difficulties of partisanship. In addition, Eisenhower also urged his cabinet to meet with relevant congressional committee members collectively and individually, off-the-record, to get to know them. [48]

In 1961 President Kennedy had almost all the members of Congress to the White House for a series of coffee hours, during which each member could chat with the president; he also included them in social evenings at the White House and held an annual congressional reception. [49] Nevertheless, Kennedy was not good at small talk, and he had "little taste for mundane courtship . . . for the attention to minutiae, the routine indulgences, the tolerance for banalities that pass for opinions." [50]

Others on Kennedy's staff moved to fill the social role. His congressional liaison chief, Lawrence O'Brien, asked Representative Edward Boland to give a series of parties in a House committee room so O'Brien could meet with House members on a purely social basis. He also held a series of brunches at his home on Sundays (and sometimes during the week) to which leading congressional figures were invited. In addition, O'Brien often used the presidential yacht for evening cruises with fifteen or twenty members of Congress and their wives, finding the cruises to be effective lobbying devices. He usually had two or three "targets" for the evening and reports to have sometimes obtained cooperation that he otherwise might not have received. [51]

In 1963, shortly after assuming the presidency, Lyndon Johnson was having problems getting the annual foreign aid bill passed in a suitable form. The vote was to be taken on Christmas Eve, and many members of Congress were disgruntled about still being in Washington. So the president invited the entire Congress to the White House for a party on December 23. At the party he made a speech, saying, "We can disagree without being disagreeable." According to his close aide, Jack Valenti, it was "pure undigested Texas corn," but it kept the Congress in town, decreased the bitterness, and helped soften the opposition. [52]

Johnson had frequent receptions for groups of members of Congress and their wives, often preceded by briefings on current issues by cabinet officials. Never one to pass up an opportunity to curry favor, he made it a point to dance with the wives of members.[53]

The Nixon and Ford staffs also used the presidential yacht as well as the press bar at the Kennedy Center for low-keyed discussions in social settings. Overall, however, the Nixon administration seemed to rely less on social activities for creating goodwill, using them more as rewards for supporters. When Gerald Ford became president, he increased presidential social contacts with members of Congress. There were more White House social events, and everyone in Congress received invitations. Ford mixed easily and informally with his old friends from the Hill, unlike Nixon, who even had receiving lines at White House prayer breakfasts.[54]

An amenity that the president can provide to many members of Congress at once and with little cost is credit. Lyndon Johnson was especially sensitive to this point and often went out of his way to give credit. He signed the 1965 Voting Rights Act at the Capitol to give "full measure" to Congress. No president had come there for a bill signing in over a quarter of a century. Although he was deeply involved in the fight to pass the 1964 Civil Rights Act, he toned down his personal involvement so that members of Congress, especially Senate Republican leader Everett Dirksen (whose support was essential to break the Senate filibuster on the bill), could receive more of the limelight.[55] He later gave Dirksen public praise and a prominent position at the bill-signing ceremony. After the 1964 tax cut (a milestone in fiscal policy) he praised Republicans as well as Democrats, and even Senate Finance Committee chairperson Harry Byrd, who voted against the bill.[56] The entire Eighty-ninth Congress, the "Great Society Congress," also received high praise.[57]

After the war in Vietnam began to erode his popularity, he began to violate his principle of sharing credit to create goodwill. Instead he created ill will with comments about "my Medicare bill," "my housing bill," and "my education bill." This attempt to take sole credit for congressional laws did little to improve his relationship with an increasingly hostile Congress.[58]

Johnson also did not neglect more general public praise and flattery, finding that it could be effective even on sophisticated men. He praised not only congressional leaders, as, for example, when he lunched with the Senate and praised Senator Dirksen in 1966, but also lesser figures, as when he called a gathering of a new representative's local Democratic party organization and told them that he regretted forcing the representative to miss the local session but that he was needed in Washington.[59]

Lyndon Johnson had great respect for Congress in general and for many individual members. This helped him get along with them and to be open to their advice and suggestions.[60] He once told aide Jack Valenti, "The most important people you will talk to are senators and congressmen. You treat them as if they were president. Answer their calls immediately. Give them respect. They deserve it. Remember senators and congressmen, they are your most important clients.

Be responsive to them." In Valenti's words, "LBJ would have flogged any of his assistants whom he found lording it over senators and congressmen."[61] The president's public rhetoric was usually equally respectful. In his 1965 State of the Union message, following his landslide victory the previous November, his tone was one of equality and not dominance, using phrases like "This Hill, which was my home."[62]

Gerald Ford was also a man of Congress who held the institution in high regard. Three days after becoming president, he went before a joint session of Congress and told it of his love for the House and his respect for the traditions of the Senate. His motto, he said, would be "communication, conciliation, compromise, and cooperation."[63] More dramatically, two months later (October 17, 1974), he appeared before a subcommittee of the House Judiciary Committee to explain publicly the reasons for his pardon of Richard Nixon.

At the opposite extreme was Ford's predecessor, Richard Nixon. Actions designed to bypass Congress, such as his extensive use of impoundments (discussed in Chapter 1), angered members. Sometimes he was overtly disrespectful. Perhaps his most famous swipe at Congress occurred after the Senate rejected his nomination of G. Harrold Carswell. He launched into a bitter tirade against the Senate in a televised press conference, declaring that the Senate's action had shown that no southern federal appellate judge who believed in a strict interpretation of the Constitution would be confirmed as a justice on the Supreme Court. The Senate was not pleased.

Even before the vote he sent Senator William Saxbe of Ohio a letter stating that the president had a right to *appoint* (not just nominate) anyone he wanted to the Supreme Court and the Senate should not substitute its judgment for his. By prearrangement, Saxbe released the letter to the press. Naturally, this misstating of constitutionally defined functions caused widespread indignation in the Senate (and also in the public). Nevertheless, this action was consistent with Nixon's tendency to use Congress as a whipping boy and to be derogatory toward many of its members in private.[64]

Nixon's aides frequently did not help matters. His top domestic aide, John Ehrlichman, has been described by observers as having "arrogant disdain" for Congress, feeling it was populated by a "bunch of clowns." He is also quoted as saying, "The President *is* the government."[65]

The administration of Presidents Eisenhower and Kennedy were inconsistent in displaying respect for Congress. Eisenhower did not publicly criticize congressional motives and made overtures to work together with Congress. He also took the trouble to personally sign letters in response to communications from members of Congress.[66] Other executive officials, however, were not always as attentive to congressional sensitivities. Secretary of Defense Charles Wilson was undiplomatic with Congress, and legislative liaison aide "Jerry" Persons had to "pick up" after him on the Hill. White House chief of staff Sherman Adams was curt on the phone to members of Congress, a manner that hardly endeared him to that branch. United States Information Agengy head Arthur Larson once made a partisan attack before bringing his budget to the opposition-controlled Congress.[67]

Kennedy was often respectful of congressional prerogatives as when he was careful to play no overt role in the 1961 fight to expand the House Rules Committee, ostensibly an internal congressional matter. However, the next year he tried to create a new Department of Housing and Urban Development and name a black, Robert Weaver, to head it. He chose to do these things by means of an executive reorganization plan because the legislation to establish the department was tied up in the House Rules Committee. The reorganization plan was defeated in both houses because, in the president's words, "I played it too cute. It was so obvious [the circumvention] it made them mad."[68]

President Johnson once claimed that it was not crises or assassinations that produce legislation but briefings. While a briefing may look like nothing, he claimed, "in fact, it was everything." He would use briefings to help legislators make a good impression on their constituents on the next day's news by helping them to organize their thoughts. He felt this made an important difference in attitudes toward the bills that he was proposing. He believed briefings flattered congressional egos and gave them useful information on bills, and he kept up the briefings after introducing legislation. On particularly sensitive matters he often conducted one-to-one briefings in person or on the phone.[69]

Other presidents have used briefings to a lesser extent. Eisenhower sent White House aides to brief the Senate Republican Policy Committee,[70] for example, and Kennedy sometimes sent members of Congress letters that announced major policy positions or contained arguments for those positions. The member could then make the letters public.[71] President Nixon probably used briefings least. For instance, in his important 1971 speech on wage and price controls, the devaluation of the dollar, and the removal of the United States from the gold standard, he ordered that briefings of members of Congress be minimal, on the phone, and only immediately before the speech. During the uproar following the Cambodian invasion, Nixon refused to meet alone with the Senate Foreign Relations Committee.[72]

Lyndon Johnson wrote in his memoirs, "If I were to name one factor above all others that helped me in dealing with Congress, I would say it was the genuine friendship and rapport I had with most Congressmen and Senators."[73] Similarly, Eisenhower wrote of his attempts to cultivate personal as well as political friendships and their importance in his efforts to persuade Congress.[74]

Representative Charles Mosher of Ohio, a liberal Republican, increased the regularity of his party voting after Gerald Ford succeeded Richard Nixon, despite Ford's greater conservatism. He supported the new president "because I like Jerry Ford so much." Interviews by the *Congressional Quarterly* found that Ford's personal popularity aided his efforts to obtain support from several members of Congress.[75]

Presidents may also benefit from the popularity of their subordinates. Senator B. Everett Jordan of North Carolina once supported a Kennedy-sponsored proposal because he liked Kennedy's secretary of commerce, Luther Hodges. Hodges was a North Carolinian, and Kennedy had charged him with the responsibility of getting the bill through Congress.[76]

A president can bestow on a member of Congress many other personal amenities, including a walk around the White House grounds (with a picture for the hometown newspaper), hints from White House sources of the value of the person's advice, designation as the sponsor of important legislation, appointment to a special presidential delegation or commission, a ride on Air Force One, baseball tickets in the presidential box seats, and recognition in speeches. President Kennedy sent congratulatory birthday notes to members of Congress, as did Johnson. Johnson also occasionally called to wish a member of Congress a happy birthday. He didn't just send staff-written notes like other presidents, and he was likely to add to his greeting that he had seen a recent speech by the member in the *Congressional Record.*[77]

When a member of Congress is particularly important, the amenities can be substantial. Senator Everett Dirksen was such a man. Eisenhower chose Dirksen to introduce him to the 1956 Republican national convention, went to Illinois on his behalf, publicly praised him, sent him thank-you letters, attended a fund-raising dinner for him, and passed the word that he depended on Dirksen. When President Kennedy returned from the Geneva summit conference, he had Dirksen meet him at the airport and ride to the White House in his helicopter. He also had private chats with Dirksen about once a month, called him about every two weeks, and asked him to tour the world's trouble spots in his plane. Johnson showered him with personal attention and praise, adding little touches such as unexpectedly dropping in on a dinner honoring the senator. Nixon went to a birthday party for Dirksen, gave him a special role in his first inauguration, went to the Capitol to lunch with him (and some other senators), had Dirksen escort him to the Senate floor, put him at the place of honor at his meetings with Republican congressional leaders, and invited him to accompany him to the Kentucky Derby.[78]

Each of these presidents was rewarded for their efforts. For example, Dirksen became increasingly supportive of Eisenhower, sometimes for association with the popular Eisenhower but at other times in spite of his constituents' views, especially on foreign policy. Dirksen also seemed to respond to the careful courting he received from the Kennedy administration, especially on foreign policy.[79]

Eisenhower's treatment of Senate Republican leader Robert Taft also illustrates this point. White House press secretary James Hagerty saw to it that after meeting with the president, the senator spoke to the press in Hagerty's office. This set him above the other Republican leaders, who talked to reporters in the corridor. In general, Eisenhower let Taft emerge into the limelight although he had been his principal rival for the Republican presidential nomination. Taft also got White House chief of staff Sherman Adams to accept in principle that if Republican senators' recommendations for appointments were rejected, they should be rejected gently.[80]

Personal amenities can also be used for conciliatory purposes. A number of House Republican Eisenhower supporters were upset about an administration attempt to bypass the Ways and Means Committee on a bill. The president moved to conciliate some of them by giving them places of honor at a White House luncheon.[81] When he gave the Christmas party described earlier, President Johnson privately apologized to House Minority Leader Charles Halleck for any nasty comments that may have been made about him.[82]

Of course, amenities do not always pay off. Once President Johnson sent a limousine to bring House Republican leader Charles Halleck to a breakfast at the White House, at which they discussed some pending legislation. Three weeks later, after casting his ballot against Johnson, Halleck responded to criticism of him for "selling out" by declaring, "I guess this shows it takes more than a thick piece of bacon to buy me."[83]

We should not presume that just because a president is able to provide members of Congress with a plethora of amenities that the latter will provide support. For example, in an effort to build goodwill, President Kennedy once unexpectedly flew by helicopter to a birthday party for Senate Finance Committee chairperson Harry Byrd and showered Byrd with praise. The next year Byrd, from the very same spot, decried the excessive number of planes and other costly means of transport (like helicopters) available to the president.[84] Similarly, writing about Eisenhower, one author concludes that "there are limits to what such amenities can accomplish," noting that the gap between the Republican president and the extreme right wing of his party "began to widen ominously."[85]

Additional Aspects of Presidential–Congressional Relations

Vice President's Role

It is interesting to note how presidents have used their vice presidents for congressional relations. Vice President Nixon advised President Eisenhower on congressional strategy and lobbying in Congress[86] but does not seem to have been a major figure in the president's congressional relations.

As vice president, Lyndon Johnson, the master of the Senate, had little to do with Congress. He made few suggestions at the president's weekly meetings with congressional leaders, keeping his criticisms of Kennedy's handling of congressional affairs private. His restraint may have stemmed from two factors. First, there was Johnson's pride. During the 1960 transition period, his successor as Senate majority leader, Mike Mansfield, proposed that Johnson chair the Senate Democratic Caucus. Seventeen senators opposed this innovation, and the new vice president was hurt personally as well as professionally. He never chaired the caucus. Moreover, within the White House he could not bear to be treated as just one of many advisers.[87]

A second factor seems to have been the fear that an active Johnson would dominate congressional relations, taking control from the president and possibly irritating congressional leaders. This fear was coupled with the concern that with Johnson as an active figure, those liberals who had attacked him in the late 1950s would turn their fire on Kennedy.[88]

Johnson employed his own vice president, Hubert Humphrey, quite differently. He used Humphrey as an active administration lobbyist, coordinating Humphrey's activities closely with the White House legislative liaison operation. The vice president was involved in head counts and soundings, strategy sessions, relaying information between Congress and the White House, and lobbying senators (especially liberal Democrats). His efforts seem to have increased support for Johnson's policies.[89]

Unlike Humphrey, Vice President Agnew was not experienced in dealing with Congress. Early in his tenure he adopted an active role in relations with the Senate, but Republican senators were angered by his heavy-handedness and his lobbying them in the Senate chamber. He soon abandoned this role.[90]

Gerald Ford's short tenure as vice president and the domination of the Watergate issue at that time did not give him much of an opportunity to function as an administration lobbyist. He kept a low profile on the Hill, and his impact was described by *Congressional Quarterly* as "minimal." Nevertheless, he spent a considerable amount of time in Congress and was open to its members. He was also warmly accepted by the Republicans there, attending the Senate Republican Policy Committee's weekly luncheon meeting as an insider.[91]

Compromise

Since presidents cannot influence every member of Congress or even a majority of members to agree with their policies, they must often compromise. President Johnson's favorite quote was from Isaiah 1:18: "Come and let us reason together." He assumed that he and a member of Congress had more in common on an issue than in conflict, and he recognized the necessity of compromise. He tried to avoid asking members to commit political suicide or to vote against their principles.[92] Thus, he regularly compromised on his programs to obtain support, generally from powerful members, sometimes thinking up amendments himself that would increase support for a bill.[93] He also attempted to tie leaders to his programs by getting them on so many committees and on delegations covering so many issues that no one wanted to be uncompromising on any one issue.[94]

Presidents Eisenhower, Kennedy, and Ford all compromised on many policies, although Eisenhower was less at home with negotiating than was an old Congress hand like Ford, who enjoyed bargaining and compromise. President Nixon of necessity engaged in compromise and political accommodation,[95] but seemed to find it difficult to adjust to this mode of relationship with Congress.

Detachment

Presidents also need a certain detachment so that they can battle for their programs without making personal enemies. Despite one aide's view that Johnson took votes against his bills personally, Johnson made sure that legislative fights did not lead to cutting off relations with members.[96] The president and Senate Republican leader Everett Dirksen remained close friends despite Dirksen's frequent public criticism of Johnson and Dirksen's nomination of Senator Barry Goldwater as Johnson's opponent in the 1964 presidential election. Dirksen would often call before making a critical speech, and the next evening he and Johnson would embrace as old friends.[97] Johnson also got along with other critics, such as Senator Wayne Morse.[98]

Kennedy was not embittered by defeat, accepting compromises and defeats fatalistically and without raging back at opponents. Thus, he could continue to work with them.[99] Eisenhower rarely took defeats personally,[100] nor did Ford. The exception seems to be Nixon, who often saw opponents as enemies.

The Outside Strategy

Presidents do not limit themselves to the direct methods of influencing members of Congress that we have discussed above. Since congressional representatives must run for election, they naturally want to please the public with their votes. Recognizing this, presidents try to show them that what the White House wants is also what voters desire.

Constituency Influence

Bryce Harlow has stressed the importance of working through the constituencies of members of Congress and emphasized the necessity of the difficult task of determining members' influential local supporters.[101] The White House has often called local supporters of members of Congress and contributors to their campaigns as well as state and local party leaders to have them influence the members. When issues affected states directly, as in the case of unemployment compensation, Lawrence O'Brien would often call governors, asking them to phone their states' senators and encourage them to support the president. Once Kennedy even tried to reach into the constituencies of opposition representatives. In the 1963 fight over permanent enlargement of the House Rules Committee, the White House contacted some of the financial backers of Republicans and told them an enlarged Rules Committee was necessary in order to pass a tax cut, which would stimulate the economy.[102]

In other instances local interests have been informed that they would be hurt if a presidentially supported bill failed to pass, hoping the interests would then phone their representatives. Such an instance seems to have occurred in 1962, when local defense contractors were told it was important that their representatives vote to raise the national debt lest defense contracts be cut.[103]

The Eisenhower White House efforts to have confirmed the nomination of Lewis Strauss as secretary of commerce did not ignore constituency influences. The South was provided the inducement of Strauss's future decision to restrict Japanese textile imports, and West Virginia was promised restrictions on Caribbean petroleum imports. The White House even had a Wyoming businessman call his senator and say that an anti-Strauss vote would be an anti-Semitic vote.[104]

Agencies frequently mobilize constituency support for their (and generally the president's) programs. Thus, witnesses before a Senate Appropriations Committee subcommittee may "happen" to be from the states of the senators on the subcommittee.[105]

Richard Fenno argues that on most issues members of Congress are free from strong constituency influences and can vote as they want as long as they can explain their votes to the satisfaction of interested constituents.[106] Thus, presidents sometimes try to make it easier for members to vote for their policies and remain popular in the members' constituencies by providing an "umbrella," which is usually a senior and highly respected member of Congress whose support for a bill can be cited by other members as evidence that their support for the bill is not a deviation from established principles.

Representative Phil Landrum of Georgia was the leading Southern Democrat on the House Education and Labor Committee. Thus, his support of the 1963 Vocational Education Bill helped pick up votes among southern members of the House.[107] President Kennedy successfully courted another prominent southerner, Carl Vinson, whose support for New Frontier policies helped swing additional southern votes the president's way.[108]

President Johnson, as we would expect, was also sensitive to this tactic. He personally selected the sponsors of his programs in both the House and the Senate, breaking congressional custom. Thus, he had both the Senate majority leader, Mike Mansfield, and the minority leader, Everett Dirksen, introduce the 1965 Voting Rights Act. He also arranged for Phil Landrum to sponsor the War on Poverty legislation in 1964, and the Georgian's sponsorship is widely attributed to have made the legislation more palatable to the South. Appealing to rural interests, he had Senator Edmund Muskie of Maine sponsor the Model Cities program.[109]

A president himself may serve as an umbrella. Richard Nixon's long history of taking a hard line on national security matters and on dealing with communist nations probably made it easier for conservative members of Congress to support such policies of Nixon's administration as giving Okinawa to Japan, the arms accord and joint space efforts with the Soviet Union, and reducing the U.S. germ warfare capability. Nixon's advocacy of these policies made it more difficult for conservative groups to oppose them.[110] Similarly, President Johnson, a southerner and a Protestant, successfully proposed strong civil rights laws and aid to Catholic schools; President Kennedy, the founder of the Green Berets and a hard-liner on Cuba, successfully led a nuclear test ban treaty to ratification.[111]

Presidents can employ additional tactics to help congressional supporters with their constituents. They may tell members of Congress, "Vote with us here and you're off the hook next time," or they may request support on an amendment or a recommital motion while allowing a no vote on the more visible, but often less crucial vote on final passage.[112] Other tactics are more involved. When Congress was considering the rent supplements program, Johnson made sure that members had information to use in newsletters and constituency speeches to account for their votes. For example, data were provided on the relatively low cost of the program in relation to other subsidy programs.[113] To "ease the path" for legislators willing to support the 1968 tax surcharge, the White House had national business leaders call local business persons, who in turn phoned their representatives and asked them to support the tax. Efforts were also made to soften the opposition of labor.[114] When two members who supported civil rights told White House staffers that their constituents wanted to hear the president say that he wanted to help all people (and not just blacks), Johnson included a paragraph to this effect in his State of the Union speech two weeks later.[115]

Johnson (and undoubtedly other presidents) felt that the best way to the hearts of members was to create the impression that a proposed bill would serve the best interests of both the nation and the members' constituencies.[116] At the same time, neither the president nor his aides are likely to press a member of Congress to commit political suicide. To avoid this problem, Lawrence O'Brien tried to get to know each member to learn how far each could go in supporting the president without politically hurting himself or herself. To this end he kept a card file on every member, complete with political and personal information and constituency data. The next step was to convince members that supporting the president was in the interests of their constituents and their political careers,[117] which was done in different ways. When the Area Redevelopment Act was being debated in 1961, a map circulated on the floor showing how the guidelines would substantially benefit rural southern areas. During consideration of the 1963 public works appropriations bill, key representatives were provided with lists of projects approved by the president and needing funding, which showed that projects had been allocated to nearly 250 congressional districts.[118]

Lacking information on the impact of a vote on a constituency can not only cost votes but also lead to poor relations with members of Congress in the future, even when the president gets support in the short run. When Richard Nixon nominated G. Harrold Carswell to the Supreme Court, the White House asked and received the support of Senate Republican leader Hugh Scott. They failed to inform him, however, of the certain opposition of labor and civil rights groups to the nomination, although Scott was up for reelection that year and needed the votes of these groups to win.[119]

Public Opinion and Interest Group Support

President Johnson labored to build public support for his bills when they were introduced to discourage opposition and encourage support. He worked especially hard in obtaining support from likely opponents, such as conservatives and business interests.[120] He worked incessantly to make poverty an issue of public concern, meeting with all kinds of groups, making numerous speeches, and visiting poverty areas before he went to Congress with legislation. As a result, he claimed, he got thousands of editorials, visits, letters, and petitions in support of his poverty program. He spoke out frequently on other issues, ranging from rat control to civil rights, creating a broad support for social action. On the 1964 tax cut he made headlines with announcements of defense savings in order to generate headlines and favorable editorials that would reassure the public on government spending and add pressure on the Senate Finance Committee to cut taxes.[121]

Presidents also seek the support of organized interests. On his War on Poverty legislation, Johnson sought the support of conservationists, pointing out that 40 percent of the funds would go for conservation. On the Elementary and Secondary Education Act of 1965, he forged a coalition of Protestants, Catholics, Jews, and education groups, refusing to go to Congress with a bill until he had agreement between the National Education Association and National Catholic Welfare Conference.[122]

On the 1964 tax cut Johnson needed business support to move the bill out of the Senate Finance Committee. He held a meeting with business leaders and established rapport with them by promising increased profits because of the economic stimulus that would result from the tax cut and less class conflict because of increased prosperity. He also eschewed any desire to run their businesses. He also kept the budget down because of the importance that the business community places on fiscal responsibility. By placing himself in the role of a business person and then giving the business community what it wanted, Johnson enhanced the prospects for the ground-breaking tax cut.[123]

President Kennedy made the Trade Expansion Act his top priority in 1962. To prevent textile industry opposition, he pressured Japan and Hong Kong manufacturers to restrict their textile exports to the United States, increased tariffs on Belgian carpets, negotiated an international cotton quota agreement (gaining the support of the American Cotton Manufacturers Institute), proposed bills to bar cotton textile imports from any country not party to the international agreement, and promised similar consideration for manufacturers of woolen textiles.[124] In the summer of 1963, Kennedy met with more than 1700 opinion leaders to seek support for his civil rights bill.[125]

In general, the Kennedy and Johnson administrations worked closely with lobbyists from the AFL-CIO and with other interest groups as was necessary. Interest group lobbyists were especially useful in wooing Republicans, who were difficult for the president's men to approach. Special groups were set up in the White House to coordinate action with other lobbying groups on behalf of bills. These groups engaged in activities ranging from encouraging groups to issue statements on behalf of rat control to working with nonpartisan groups to distribute information on the 1964 tax cut.[126] The groups also organized local support, conducted research, gave information to congressional sponsors of legislation, publicized issues in the media, pressured key members of Congress, and stimulated constituency mail.[127]

Sometimes presidents encourage private groups to show members of Congress where their interests lay. Both Kennedy and Johnson energized groups (religious, racial, business, labor, etc.) to act on behalf of civil rights legislation. On the 1964 Civil Rights Act, for example, Johnson told black leaders Roy Wilkens and Whitney Young to go to Senate Republican leader Everett Dirksen and convince him that supporting civil rights was in the best interests of Republicans. Johnson later termed group pressure the critical factor in the act's passage.[128]

On a mass transit bill that same year, White House aide Henry Wall Wilson called a Westinghouse official to the White House (Westinghouse would receive contracts if the bill passed) and suggested that the official establish an informal group of lobbyists representing similar companies. These lobbyists would in turn try to bring pressure on Southern Democrats, whose votes were crucial, through plants, banks, and other business interests in their constituencies that stood to gain by the bill.[129] Similarly, the Kennedy White House mobilized local lobbies among those who would gain from the Area Redevelopment Act and the Accelerated Public Works Act.[130]

Republican presidents have also worked with interest groups, although their relationships with such groups do not appear to have been as close as those of Kennedy and Johnson. Nevertheless, Eisenhower's aides worked with conservative lobbies, Nixon activated business interests against the Clean Water Bill of 1971, and Ford was not at all reluctant to be involved with interest groups.[131]

Johnson preferred not to go over the heads of Congress and appeal directly to the people, favoring private negotiation and compromise instead. One reason was that it may be necessary to be quite critical of Congress to pique the interests of the media, through which presidents communicate with the public. By criticizing Congress, a president, according to Johnson, "may serve to galvanize support in the Congress and the country, but it may also shorten tempers and polarize thought and emotion."[132]

Nevertheless, sometimes Johnson found it necessary to appeal to the public in order to move Congress. When his tax surcharge bill remained locked in the House Ways and Means Committee, he took the issue to the people, expressing his concern in a variety of forums, including his 1968 State of the Union address. When the bill was later stalled in conference committee, he used a televised press conference to appeal to the people again. Although some members of Congress were angered, he felt his actions helped to break the logjam.[133]

Despite his mastery of public relations, Kennedy also did not favor appealing to the people over the heads of Congress, fearing both failure and antagonizing Congress.[134] Aide Theodore Sorensen argues that the president did not like rhetorical appeals to the public on issues for which support was uncertain, and he was not good at dramatizing specific issues on the stump. His talents lay in projecting an image, developing diffuse support, and fashioning an electoral coalition.[135] In 1962 he took Medicare to the people, making a nationally televised address at a pro-Medicare rally sponsored by the National Council of Senior Citizens. The next day he was dramatically rebuked by an American

Medical Association speaker lecturing to an empty Madison Square Garden. He made numerous other, although less dramatic, attempts to influence public opinion in his speeches and press conferences in the hopes of stimulating congressional support, but there is no conclusive evidence of his success.[136]

Eisenhower did not ignore public opinion either. In 1953 in an attempt to appeal to the conservative Republican leadership in Congress, he asked the recently retired chairperson of Inland Steel to study and then recommend a free trade policy before Eisenhower sent his bill to Congress. Later he made more efforts to gain public support for trade policies, especially within the business community, assigning Secretary of Commerce Sinclair Weeks and other officials to this task. In 1957 the president established a cabinet-level Trade Policy Committee to bring the views of business people closer to the decision making on the trade agreement. The next year his subordinates helped to stage with impressive fanfare a Conference on Trade Policy in Washington, which ended with a dinner at which he again strongly stated the case for free trade. Despite these efforts, he was only slightly successful in the free-trade area.[137]

Most of Eisenhower's public appeals were on foreign policy, especially foreign aid. In 1957 he held a public demonstration on behalf of foreign aid that was attended by notables from all walks of life. He also tried to mobilize notables on behalf of his efforts to reorganize the defense department and to control spending. (Nevertheless, Speaker Martin later criticized Eisenhower for failing to mobilize his influential friends in the country.) Broad public appeals were made on issues ranging from labor legislation and extending the excess profits tax to support for his vetoes and attacking spending.[138] Despite these actions, Eisenhower never appealed to the public directly in a coherent or sustained campaign, despite his enormous popularity, and he minimized his use of the media as much as his advisers would allow.[139]

Eisenhower made no attempt to mobilize blacks or public opinion in general behind his civil rights legislation. He even refused to meet with black leaders in the White House until June 1958. He would not meet with them in 1957 because he feared that such an act would be interpreted by senators as pressure to make them vote for his proposed civil rights bill![140]

Presidents Nixon and Ford appealed to the public on many occasions, sometimes seeking general support for foreign policy decisions and other times requesting support for specific legislative stands, including vetoes. As was the case with other presidents, these efforts were not especially successful.

At times President Johnson carefully orchestrated bill-signing ceremonies to call public attention to what had been accomplished and, according to his biographer, to notify the public of the next legislative endeavor. In 1965 he signed the Elementary and Secondary Education Act in a one-room schoolhouse near his birthplace in Texas in the presence of his first teacher; he signed the Voting Rights Act in the President's Room next to the senate chamber, where Lincoln signed the Emancipation Proclamation; he signed the Immigration Act in the shadow of the

Statue of Liberty; and he signed the Medicare Bill in Independence, Missouri, so that Harry Truman, who first introduced the legislation, could attend.[141]

Johnson, like other presidents, sometimes supported legislation that he knew would not pass. Thus, after becoming president in 1963, he put the tax cut and civil rights bills at the head of his list of priorities to lay the groundwork for eventual passage in 1964.[142] President Kennedy submitted to Congress controversial legislation that he did not expect would pass, hoping his accompanying message and the ensuing debate would help to educate the public and pave the way for future passage.[143]

Presidents not only try to lead public opinion but also may attempt to exploit opportunities presented by events beyond their control. Within hours of the assassination of Martin Luther King, Jr., in 1968, President Johnson was on the phone to House leaders of both parties and several other representatives, urging them to bring the Fair Housing Act to the floor for a vote. (It had been bottled up in the House Judiciary Committee for more than two years.) In addition, the White House staff called the remaining members of the House, pressing for majority support. Six days after King's death the House passed the bill, and the president signed it into law a day later.[144] On a broader scale, he immediately moved to direct the powerful public reaction to President Kennedy's assassination toward support for Kennedy's legislative program.[145]

Johnson did not originally feel that 1965 was a propitious time for the passage of a voting rights act, but he was forced into supporting such a law after the violent reception given blacks in their voter registration drive in Selma, Alabama. Nevertheless, he did not intervene until it was clear that the country (at least outside the South) was convinced that a problem existed. Under these conditions he could send in federal troops to prevent further violence and not be accused of federal imposition on the South. This violence also set the stage for his televised, prime-time address before a joint session of Congress and helped him to obtain support for his legislation.[146] Similarly, in 1963, President Kennedy introduced the most far-reaching civil rights bill in history after the issue was dramatized by marches and sit-ins and the use of police dogs, fire hoses, and billy clubs against civil rights leaders and their followers.

Jimmy Carter's Legislative Skills

President Jimmy Carter's legislative skills in the Ninety-fifth Congress received decidedly mixed reviews. *Congressional Quarterly* reported in the fall of 1978 that there was "near unanimity in Congress that Carter and his staff had blundered repeatedly in pushing their proposals."[147] That summer Secretary of the Treasury Michael Blumenthal stated that he was "sick and tired of seeing the President and the administration two and three and four months behind the curve on everything." He felt that this was "ruining his Presidency, looking so foolish, being dragged hind tail by events."[148]

Perhaps the most frequent and most damaging complaint heard about President Carter is his lack of advance consultation with or even advance notice to Congress on legislation, patronage, and project matters.[149] This applies even to the congressional leadership. Speaker Tip O'Neill was upset that the president appointed Republicans from O'Neill's home state of Massachusetts to the positions of White House chief of protocol and ambassador-at-large without checking with him. He was also upset at the perfunctory manner in which his friend Robert Griffin was fired from the General Services Administration.[150] Senate Majority Leader Robert Byrd sent the president a letter expressing the Senate's "anger and frustration" at not being consulted on the cutting of water projects from the budget, and he was not the only congressional leader to be upset.[151] The president also failed to warn Jewish leaders and Congress of an impending controversial joint statement with the Soviet Union regarding the Middle East. Likewise, he failed to warn liberal Democratic senators Howard Metzenbaum and James Abourezk that their filibuster to block the deregulation of natural gas, which they thought was supporting administration policy, would be broken. The president's reversal on his $50 tax rebate proposal likewise left Ways and Means Committee chairperson Al Ullman and others fighting for it high and dry.[152]

Some of the consultation that *has* taken place has not been viewed by members of Congress as being very useful. Stuart Eizenstat, Carter's chief domestic policy adviser, consulted Congress extensively during the development of the president's urban policy initiatives. He went to Capitol Hill, twenty or thirty times in the final two months before they were made public, to answer questions or to brief members, but members were not shown the final set of options that were laid before the president. Thus, they were not committed to specifics and some complained that the consultation was one-way, from the White House to the Congress.[153]

Similarly, Carter did not make calls to members of Congress alerting them about cuts in water projects until many members had left for the weekend. Thus, many of them read of the cuts in their hometown newspapers.[154] Al Ullman was invited to the White House the day before Carter presented his welfare plan to Congress, but when he objected to some parts of it, the president said it was too late to make changes. Others felt that the White House's consultation with Congress was often perfunctory or, worse, that some administration officials were disdainful of cabinet advice.[155]

On the matter of consultation with Congress, the president replied in a July 1977 news conference that he had learned of its members' sensitivities on consultation and would try to check with them before announcing his own positions. Earlier he had sent a letter of apology to Congress for his handling of the water projects. At his very first press conference, Carter emphasized improving relations with Congress and said that he was initiating almost daily meetings with members of Congress and biweekly breakfasts with Democratic leaders. Over a year later, however, he was still attempting to quell criticism of his isolation from the Hill, this time with a series of receptions for members of Congress at the Blair House that top White House aides also attended.[156]

Carter is also charged with sending too much too fast to Congress. The House Ways and Means Committee had, at the same time, the president's income tax, welfare, hospital cost control, and energy tax proposals. This legislative glut, it is said, has baffled Congress about his priorities and stretched his prestige too thin.[157]

Particularly on the energy program, the White House has been charged with sloppy drafting of legislation and providing poorly presented and weak supporting evidence. Moreover, the administration's lobbyists have been accused of not understanding the legislation that they are supporting.[158]

Amenities are not part of Carter's personal style. Thus, he raised congressional hackles by sending senators unsigned photos for their offices and identical "personal" letters, by failing to make "bread-and-butter" calls, by not administering niceties (he sold the presidential yacht, a frequent scene of wooing and flattery), and by neglecting small talk.[159]

There have also been some instances of personal effrontery. The president criticized a bill in front of its sponsors at a White House bill-signing ceremony; he forgot to invite Senator Birch Bayh (from the steel-producing state of Indiana) to a White House conference on steel; he invited eighteen senators from "water states" to the White House and scolded them for their parochial stands on water projects, admonishing them to see things in his own "mature and businesslike" way. When Representative Toby Moffett, a strong Carter supporter, requested a bill-signing ceremony for a bill on which he had worked hard, the White House replied no.[160] These problems have also arisen among Carter's staff. Tip O'Neill complained that top White House aides Jody Powell, Hamilton Jordan, and Gerald Rafshoon had never been friendly to him. Other members of Congress objected to the lack of personal relations with White House and liaison officials.[161]

Carter's unwillingness to bargain and make trades has been cited numerous times, and he tends to adopt a pious, moral approach to seeking votes rather than a "Can you help me with this?" approach, with which most members of Congress are used to being treated.[162]

The president freely admits his reluctance to trade. In an August 1978 interview, he said that

> horse-trading and compromising and so forth have always been very difficult for me to do. I just don't feel at ease with it, and it is a very rare occasion when any member of Congress or anyone else even brings up a subject that could be interpreted by the most severe cynic as a horse-trade. We were interested and amused, somewhat, during the Panama Canal treaty votes that every time a senator came in here, there were a rash of stories saying that certain things must have been promised to that senator to vote for the bill. This is not the case.[163]

When Carter appeared to have made a deal a few days after making the above statement, it was ineptly handled and only caused him problems. The deal, which the administration denied, seems to have involved administration support for an energy research project in Idaho and a breeder reactor in return for Senator James McClure's support for the natural gas bill and the termination of the Clinch River breeder reactor. When word of the deal leaked to the press, both sides seemed confused about just what agreements had been made.[164]

Carter has also had problems with his professional reputation. On the energy bill there were complaints of mixed signals from the White House, of Carter's failure to support the initiatives of senators supporting the administration, of his ready abandonment of major aspects of the bill, and of Secretary of Energy James Schlesinger's public outline of the White House's bottom line on an acceptable energy bill before the negotiations in the conference committee were completed. These criticisms were echoed on other bills.[165] To combat these criticisms, in the summer of 1978 the White House threatened to get tough with Democrats who failed to support the president, announcing that offending members of Congress would lose benefits such as presidential fund-raising appearances and patronage.[166]

Other criticisms of Carter include his slowness in using patronage to replace Republican officials in the executive branch with Democrats suggested by party leaders, his devoting too little attention to his energy program, his lack of briefings for members of Congress, his failing to check on the needs and doubts of representatives, the poor service by executive departments in meeting congressional requests, and the inexperience, incompetence, and lack of "clout" with the president of the White House and the department legislative liaison staffs.[167]

On the other hand, there is substantial evidence that Carter has the capacity to learn and to improve his legislative operation. At the end of the 1978 session, Speaker Tip O'Neill proclaimed that "their operation is really good now" and that the White House had "learned the things I've been advocating."[168]

The White House was perhaps at its best in dealing with Congress on the Panama Canal treaties. A massive public relations campaign was conducted from the White House as the president sensed that public opinion was the primary stumbling block to ratification. Hundreds of opinion leaders were invited to the White House and briefed by the president and other high administration officials in the hopes of molding public opinion. The president also had pictures taken with those people who wanted them. High officials, including Secretary of State Cyrus Vance and Secretary of Defense Harold Brown, made hundreds of appearances around the country, especially in states whose senators were undecided. The president answered questions at several town meetings and invited influential constituents of senators to the White House. The Democratic National Committee arranged for nearly 5,000 prominent Democrats in twelve key states to call wavering senators. Most dramatically, Carter addressed the nation on the treaty in a fireside chat.[169]

The president did not rely solely upon public relations, however. Interested senators were flown to Panama to see the canal and talk to Panamanian leader General Omar Torrijos. Each senator was contacted by the administration, some several times. Administration heavyweights like Vance, Brown, Vice President Mondale, the Joint Chiefs of Staff, Ambassador Ellsworth Bunker, Deputy Secretary of State Warren Christopher, White House aides Zgibniew Brzezinski and Hamilton Jordan, pollster Patrick Caddell, and "outsiders" Clark Clifford and Bert Lance were mobilized in the effort to persuade senators to support the treaties. Senate Majority Leader Robert Byrd and Senator Frank Church, a senior member of the Foreign Relations Committee, were also active in rounding up votes for the president. According to one count, Carter himself made eighty-seven phone calls to senators in the two weeks before the first vote, and he met or spoke to each senator at least once. At one point he spent three hours calling sixteen staunchly opposed senators and moved one of them to support him. Although most of the arguments were on the merits of the treaty and did not involve trading, the president did show flexibility in accepting amendments that garnered critical support for the treaties. He also got Senator Jennings Randolph's promise to vote yes if his vote was absolutely needed (it wasn't).[170]

(As is the case for other presidents, these efforts did not always succeed. Edward Zorinsky, a freshman senator from Nebraska, was undecided on the Panama Canal treaties. Carter saw to it that he was visited by Secretary of State Cyrus Vance, Secretary of Defense Harold Brown, White House national security advisor Zbigniew Brzezinski, and Pentagon generals. Secretary of the Treasury Michael Blumenthal called and treaty negotiator Sol Linowitz met him for tennis. Carter called him, later invited him and 190 visiting Nebraskans to the White House, and then invited the senator back to the White House for a more private meeting. Rosalyn Carter even called Mrs. Zorinsky to offer her a briefing on the treaties. Nevertheless, Zorinsky voted against the president.)[171]

Probably the most difficult legislative task faced by Carter was passage of his energy program, especially the natural gas bill. We have seen that his early efforts, at least in the Senate, were unproductive and sometimes even detrimental to his goal of passage. But by the end of the summer of 1978 things had changed. The president concluded that the greatest hindrance to passage of the bill was public opinion, and he set about to change it.

A dozen meetings with key industrial consumers of natural gas, including the glass, paper, textile, steel, automobile, aerospace, insurance, and construction industries, were held at the White House in the weeks before the natural gas bill came to the Senate floor from the conference committee. There these company representatives were briefed by officials such as Energy Secretary James Schlesinger, top Carter aide Robert Strauss, and Federal Reserve chairperson William Miller. A group of bankers lunched with Carter in the family dining room, and 130 of the most ardent industrial opponents were called to the East Room of the White House for an energy briefing.[172]

Thus, the intention of the White House efforts was to seek the support of interest groups, who in turn would attempt to influence senators. Presidential assistant Anne Wexler found out from senators which groups were leaning most heavily on them to oppose the bill and then invited representatives from these groups to the White House. Part of the strategy was to split an industry that was previously united in opposition. For example, Senator Robert Griffin of Michigan could not support the bill as long as all the major automobile companies opposed it. When Chrysler came out for the bill, however, Griffin felt free to do so also. The Department of Energy also supplied all senators with a list of fifty-five major industrial and financial corporations and twenty trade associations that were backing the bill.[173]

These efforts were supplemented with more direct contact from the administration. Schlesinger, Strauss, and Vice President Mondale were active lobbyists, and the president made many calls. This lobbying was directed by a daily meeting of top White House aides and Energy Department officials at congressional liaison chief Frank Moore's office. In addition, the Democratic National Committee mailed public relations packets on the energy program around the country and made more than 1,500 phone calls to organize grass roots lobbying.[174]

As noted earlier, one of President Carter's first conflicts with Congress in 1977 was over his opposition to eighteen water projects. In the end he compromised and deleted about half of the projects. In an August 1978 press conference he said, "I think that last year I should have vetoed the appropriations bill that authorized unnecessary water projects. If I had to do it over again, I would have vetoed it." He soon followed his own advice and vetoed the 1978 public works bill, despite strong support for it by his own party's leadership in both houses.[175]

Again, the White House applied both personal and constituency pressure on Congress. The president called several dozen members of the House, and members of the cabinet and top White House aides called also. One Southern Democrat said that the president said he would remember a vote to sustain his veto and return the favor. The White House staff traded a variety of presidential largess, including photographs, campaign appearances, and appointments to obscure commissions. Interior Secretary Cecil Andrus, budget director James McIntyre, Council of Economic Advisers chairperson Charles Schultze, and Army Secretary Clifford Alexander were dispatched to defend the veto on the Hill. About thirty Republican representatives were invited to a White House breakfast to talk about the veto.[176]

The outside strategy was equally elaborate. The White House sent out press kits explaining and defending the veto, briefed business leaders, obtained the support of antispending advocate Howard Jarvis in a full-page ad in the *Washington Post,* and had bankers, corporate executives, defense contractors, environmental group members, governmental contractors, and western governors call their local representatives in favor of the veto.[177]

In the end Carter won a stunning victory, having his veto sustained by a 53-vote margin, receiving the support of 62 of 135 Republicans voting (as opposed to 128 out of 278 Democrats).[178] The victory was all the more impressive because it was over the active opposition of the Democratic congressional leadership and because it concerned pork barrel legislation with a congressional election only a few weeks off.

The support that Carter received from Republicans on his public works veto was not unprecedented. On the vote to end the Turkish arms embargo, a majority of Democrats in each house opposed the president, but he received a large enough majority from Republicans to win on the issue. A majority of Senate Democrats also opposed the president on the sale of F-15 fighters to Saudi Arabia, but Republicans again gave him enough of a majority of their votes to carry the issue. Carter also received sixteen of thirty-eight Republican senators' votes on each of the Panama Canal treaties, which were essential for him to achieve the necessary two-thirds majority required.[179]

Carter's use of his legislative liaison office also shows signs of promise. Since mid-1977, the White House legislative liaison operation has had computerized files containing information on all members of Congress, including their party, committee assignments, seniority, margin of victory in their last election, interest group ratings, and votes in the current and past Congresses categorized by issue areas. This information allows the administration to cross-reference past voting with political indexes and possibly spot swing votes on crucial issues in a much shorter time than in the past. For example, the White House found the members of Congress who were undecided on a consumer protection agency but who had voted proconsumer in the past. Viewing these members as susceptible to persuasion, it focused its efforts on them. As of 1978 the computer had not been used on the Senate, contains no sensitive information, and cannot tell the White House *how* to lobby a representative. While use of the computer is certainly no guarantee of success (the consumer protection agency failed), it can make the liaison operation more efficient and perhaps isolate potential votes that may have otherwise been overlooked.[180]

The computer is also useful for tracking legislation and providing a full legislative background of each bill (from Congress's computer) and for providing issue briefs on specific topics (from the Library of Congress). In addition, the White House is using the computer to handle mail from Congress. Each piece is logged in and the date and subject are noted, permitting the administration to ensure that letters are answered promptly by the right person in the executive branch. Since the president believes in cabinet government, much of the mail goes to the departments. The computer prepares a daily summary of congressional letters received and of the correspondence that still needs cabinet or White House follow-up. The computer is also used to sample the mail to get congressional reaction to an issue.[181]

The congressional liaison staff itself has been increased and organized on a geographical basis for the House, allowing greater rapport between White House lobbyists and members of Congress to develop. Tighter controls have been imposed on Departmental lobbyists, and their tasks have been coordinated more. The task force operation that was used on the energy program and the Panama Canal treaties has been extended to other important legislation. Sometimes the White House lobbies at early stages of legislation, and the number of bills that it considers priority has been reduced. Patronage and service for members of

Congress are better organized, and they are used more flexibly than at the beginning of Carter's term. Similarly, the White House now works more closely with Democratic congressional leaders, and the president meets with them every Tuesday when Congress is in session. Thus, in many ways the Carter White House has been attempting to improve what we have broadly termed presidential legislative skills.[182]

Notes

1. Joseph A. Pika, "White House Office of Congressional Relations: A Longitudinal Analysis," paper presented at the annual meeting of the Midwest Political Science Association, Chicago, April 1978, p. 12.

2. Pika, "White House Office of Congressional Relations," p. 16; "Turning Screws: Winning Votes in Congress," *Congressional Quarterly Weekly Report,* April 24, 1976, p. 952.

3. See, for example, Jack Bell, *The Johnson Treatment* (New York: Harper & Row, 1965), p. 181. See John W. Kingdon, *Congressmen's Voting Decisions* (New York: Harper & Row, 1973), p. 187, for a questioning of the importance of favors.

4. Neil MacNeil, *Forge of Democracy: The House of Representatives* (New York: McKay, 1963), p. 260; Theodore C. Sorensen, *Kennedy* (New York: Bantam, 1966), p. 392.

5. "Carter Seeks More Effective Use of Departmental Lobbyists' Skills," *Congressional Quarterly Weekly Report,* March 4, 1978, p. 586; Ralph K. Huitt, "White House Channels to the Hill," in *Congress against the President,* ed. Harvey C. Mansfield, Sr. (New York: Praeger, 1975), p. 74.

6. MacNeil, *Forge of Democracy,* p. 260; Stephen J. Wayne, *The Legislative Presidency* (New York: Harper & Row, 1978), pp. 155–156; Rowland Evans, Jr., and Robert D. Novak, *Nixon in the White House: The Frustration of Power* (New York: Vintage, 1972), p. 105.

7. Abraham Holtzman, *Legislative Liaison: Executive Leadership in Congress* (Chicago: Rand McNally, 1970), pp. 251–252; MacNeil, *Forge of Democracy,* p. 261; Russell D. Renka, "Legislative Leadership and Marginal Vote-Gaining Strategies in the Kennedy and Johnson Presidencies," paper presented at the annual meeting of the Southwest Political Science Association, Houston, April 1978, p. 9.

8. Wayne, *Legislative Presidency,* p. 162.

9. "Turning Screws," pp. 949, 951.

10. Ibid., pp. 951–952.

11. Wayne, *Legislative Presidency,* pp. 144, 153; Holtzman, *Legislative Liaison,* p. 251; Lawrence F. O'Brien, *No Final Victories: A Life in Politics from John F. Kennedy to Watergate* (New York: Ballantine, 1975), pp. 139, 185–186. For a discussion of some problems with this system, see Renka, "Legislative Leadership," p. 10.

12. O'Brien, *No Final Victories,* pp. 185–186.

13. Wayne, *Legislative Presidency,* p. 162.

14. Pika, "White House Office of Congressional Relations," p. 15.

15. See Arthur Larson, *Eisenhower: The President Nobody Knew* (New York: Scribner's, 1968), p. 29.

16. Pika, "White House Office of Congressional Relations," pp. 14–15, fig. 5; Wayne, *Legislative Presidency,* pp. 153, 161; John F. Manley, "White House Lobbying

and the Problem of Presidential Power," paper presented at the annual meeting of the American Political Science Association, Washington, D.C., September 1977, pp. 14–15, 17; "Carter Seeks More Effective Use," p. 586; Dom Bonafede, "Ford's Lobbyists Expect Democrats to Revise Tactics," *National Journal,* June 21, 1975, p. 927; William Chapman, "LBJ's Way: Tears, Not Arm-Twists," *Washington Post,* October 17, 1965, p. E-1.

17. MacNeil, *Forge of Democracy,* p. 264.

18. Huitt, "White House Channels," p. 83.

19. MacNeil, *Forge of Democracy,* p. 262; Sorensen, *Kennedy,* p. 399; Bonafede, "Ford's Lobbyists," p. 926; Dwight D. Eisenhower, *Mandate for Change, 1953–1956* (New York: New American Library, 1965), p. 245; Jeb S. Magruder, *An American Life: One Man's Road to Watergate* (New York: Pocket Books, 1975), p. 102.

20. O'Brien, *No Final Victories,* p. 185 (Greigg lost the election anyway).

21. For example, see Sorensen, *Kennedy,* pp. 392, 395; Eisenhower, *Mandate for Change,* p. 519; Jack Valenti, *A Very Human President* (New York: Norton, 1975), p. 189.

22. Eisenhower, *Mandate for Change,* pp. 515–517; Sherman Adams, *Firsthand Report* (New York: Popular Library, 1962), pp. 167–168. See also Joe Martin, *My First Fifty Years in Politics* (New York: McGraw-Hill, 1960), p. 226.

23. Martin, *My First Fifty Years,* pp. 222–223; Dwight D. Eisenhower, *Waging Peace, 1956–1961* (Garden City, N.Y.: Doubleday, 1965), p. 642; Emmet J. Hughes, *The Ordeal of Power: A Political Memoir of the Eisenhower Years* (New York: Atheneum, 1975), pp. 130–131; Gary W. Reichard, *The Reaffirmation of Republicanism: Eisenhower and the Eighty-third Congress* (Knoxville: University of Tennessee Press, 1975), p. 224; Robert J. Donovan, *Eisenhower: The Inside Story* (New York: Harper & Row, 1956), p. 99; Stanley Kelly, Jr., "Patronage and Presidential Legislative Leadership," in *The Presidency,* ed. Aaron Wildavsky (Boston: Little, Brown, 1969), p. 275. For seeming exceptions to Eisenhower's nonuse of patronage, see Reichard, *Reaffirmation of Republicanism,* pp. 105, 112, 226.

24. Donovan, *Eisenhower,* pp. 99, 229; Martin, *My First Fifty Years,* pp. 225–226.

25. Martin, *My First Fifty Years,* p. 224; William S. White, *The Taft Story* (New York: Harper & Row, 1954), pp. 207–208 (for an exception to this lack of consultation, see p. 250).

26. Neil MacNeil, *Dirksen: Portrait of a Public Man* (New York: World, 1970), pp. 352–353; Evans and Novak, *Nixon in the White House,* pp. 66–70. See also Frederic V. Malek, *Washington's Hidden Tragedy: The Failure to Make Government Work* (New York: Free Press, 1978), p. 84.

27. O'Brien, *No Final Victories,* p. 121.

28. MacNeil, *Dirksen,* pp. 282–283, 352.

29. Ibid., p. 343.

30. MacNeil, *Forge of Democracy,* p. 252; Sorensen, *Kennedy,* p. 391.

31. O'Brien, *No Final Victories,* p. 121. However, Holtzman (*Legislative Liaison,* p. 250) quotes O'Brien that "we could never have survived unless we had used patronage."

32. O'Brien, *No Final Victories,* p. 121; MacNeil, *Dirksen,* p. 283; "Turning Screws," p. 952; Merlo J. Pusey, *Eisenhower the President* (New York: Macmillan, 1956), p. 213. Renka ("Legislative Leadership," p. 35) reports that Kennedy gave patronage to nearly all Democrats.

33. Eisenhower, *Waging Peace,* pp. 138, 144; Larson, *Eisenhower,* p. 29.

34. MacNeil, *Dirksen,* pp. 348–350, 353–361.

35. Evans and Novak, *Nixon in the White House,* pp. 68–69.

36. MacNeil, *Forge of Democracy,* pp. 255, 263; O'Brien, *No Final Victories,* pp. 110–111; Richard L. Schott and Dagmar Hamilton, "The Politics of Presidential Appointments in the Johnson Administration," paper presented at the annual meeting of the Southern Political Science Association, New Orleans, November 1977, p. 6; Pika, "White House Office of Congressional Relations," p. 13; Wayne, *Legislative Presidency,* p. 153.

37. MacNeil, *Forge of Democracy,* pp. 249–251.

38. Quoted in John A. Ferejohn, *Pork Barrel Politics: Rivers and Harbors Legislation, 1947–1968* (Stanford, Calif.: Stanford University Press, 1974), p. 106.

39. Pika, "White House Office of Congressional Relations," p. 15.

40. Eisenhower, *Waging Peace,* p. 13.

41. MacNeil, *Forge of Democracy,* p. 256.

42. Alan L. Otten, "By Courting Congress Assiduously, Johnson Furthers His Program," *Wall Street Journal,* April 9, 1965, p. 1.

43. O'Brien, *No Final Victories,* p. 113.

44. Bell, *Johnson Treatment,* pp. 47, 97; Eric F. Goldman, *The Tragedy of Lyndon Johnson* (New York: Dell, 1974), p. 33.

45. O'Brien, *No Final Victories,* p. 113; MacNeil, *Dirksen,* pp. 146, 190; "The Congress: The Gut Fighters," *Time,* June 8, 1959, p. 18.

46. Valenti, *Very Human President,* pp. 193–194, 304. See also Otten, "By Courting Congress," p. 1; Doris Kearns, *Lyndon Johnson and the American Dream* (New York: Harper & Row, 1976), p. 237.

47. Chapman, "LBJ's Way," p. 1.

48. Donovan, *Eisenhower,* p. 85; Wayne, *Legislative Presidency,* p. 145; Pusey, *Eisenhower the President,* pp. 210–211; Eisenhower, *Mandate for Change,* p. 245.

49. O'Brien, *No Final Victories,* p. 113; MacNeil, *Forge of Democracy,* p. 260; Wayne, *Legislative Presidency,* pp. 147, 152; Holtzman, *Legislative Liaison,* p. 246.

50. Sorensen, *Kennedy,* p. 391; Harry McPherson, *A Political Education* (Boston: Little, Brown, 1972), p. 190.

51. O'Brien, *No Final Victories,* pp. 114–115, 150–151; MacNeil, *Forge of Democracy,* p. 260.

52. Valenti, *Very Human President,* pp. 192–193, 304. See also Johnson, *Vantage Point: Perspectives on the Presidency, 1963–1969* (New York: Popular Library, 1971), p. 40; Goldman, *Tragedy of Lyndon Johnson,* pp. 36–37; Bell, *Johnson Treatment,* pp. 59–64; Rowland Evans and Robert Novak, *Lyndon B. Johnson: The Exercise of Power* (New York: Signet, 1966), p. 382.

53. Goldman, *Tragedy of Lyndon Johnson,* p. 72; Bell, *Johnson Treatment,* pp. 37–38; Wayne, *Legislative Presidency,* p. 152.

54. Wayne, *Legislative Presidency,* pp. 161–163.

55. Johnson, *Vantage Point,* pp. 157, 159, 166.

56. Goldman, *Tragedy of Lyndon Johnson,* p. 79. See also pp. 363–364 for Johnson's distribution of praise after the passage of the Elementary and Secondary Education Act of 1965.

57. Louis W. Koenig, *The Chief Executive,* 3rd ed. (New York: Harcourt Brace Jovanovich, 1975), p. 175.

58. Kearns, *Lyndon Johnson,* p. 300.

59. Goldman, *Tragedy of Lyndon Johnson,* pp. 33, 73; MacNeil, *Dirksen,* pp. 280–281; Otten, "By Courting Congress," p. 1.

60. Goldman, *Tragedy of Lyndon Johnson,* p. 70; Huitt, "White House Channels," p. 73.

61. Valenti, *Very Human President,* pp. 178–179.

62. Goldman, *Tragedy of Lyndon Johnson,* p. 334.

63. "Ford's Lobbyists," p. 924.

64. Richard Harris, *Decision* (New York: Dutton, 1971), pp. 155–156, 158, 209; Evans and Novak, *Nixon in the White House,* pp. 106–108, 166, 170–172.

65. Dan Rather and Gary P. Gates, *The Palace Guard* (New York: Warner, 1975), p. 271.

66. Donovan, *Eisenhower,* pp. 177–178; Eisenhower, *Waging Peace,* p. 587; Wayne, *Legislative Presidency,* p. 145.

67. Hughes, *Ordeal of Power,* pp. 76–77; Larson, *Eisenhower,* p. 22; Eisenhower, *Waging Peace,* p. 137.

68. Randall B. Ripley, *Kennedy and Congress* (Morristown, N.J.: General Learning Press, 1972), p. 16.

69. Kearns, *Lyndon Johnson,* pp. 224–225, 448.

70. Reichard, *Reaffirmation of Republicanism,* p. 221.

71. Randall B. Ripley, *Majority Party Leadership in Congress* (Boston: Little, Brown, 1969), p. 18. But see Kenneth P. O'Donnell and David F. Powers, *Johnny, We Hardly Knew Ye* (New York: Pocket Books, 1973), pp. 372, 378–380.

72. William Safire, *Before the Fall: An Inside View of the Pre-Watergate White House* (New York: Ballantine, 1977), pp. 190–191, 193, 518.

73. Johnson, *Vantage Point,* p. 459.

74. Eisenhower, *Waging Peace,* p. 642.

75. "House GOP: Its Survival May Be at Stake," *Congressional Quarterly Weekly Report,* June 26, 1976, p. 1634.

76. McPherson, *Political Education,* p. 198.

77. Kearns, *Lyndon Johnson,* pp. 236–237; Sorensen, *Kennedy,* p. 390; Goldman, *Tragedy of Lyndon Johnson,* pp. 71–72; Otten, "By Courting Congress," p. 1.

78. MacNeil, *Dirksen,* pp. 134–139, 144–145, 177, 190, 193, 214, 284, 346, 358.

79. Ibid., pp. 137, 149–151, 156–157, 189–192, 194–196, 207; Hughes, *Ordeal of Power,* p. 126.

80. White, *Taft Story,* pp. 213, 215, 228.

81. Reichard, *Reaffirmation of Republicanism,* pp. 107–108.

82. Valenti, *Very Human President,* p. 193. See also Otten, "By Courting Congress," p. 1.

83. Evans and Novak, *Lyndon B. Johnson,* p. 386.

84. Sorensen, *Kennedy,* p. 386. For possible exceptions to the norm of amenities not bringing the president support, see O'Brien, *No Final Victories,* p. 155; Sorensen, *Kennedy,* p. 432.

85. Donovan, *Eisenhower,* p. 85.

86. See, for example, Reichard, *Reaffirmation of Republicanism,* p. 172; Donovan, *Eisenhower,* p. 279.

87. Kearns, *Lyndon Johnson,* pp. 164–165; Arthur M. Schlesinger, Jr., *A Thousand Days: John F. Kennedy in the White House* (New York: Houghton Mifflin, 1965), pp. 706–707; McPherson, *Political Education,* pp. 190–191; Evans and Novak, *Lyndon B. Johnson,* pp. 324–326; Hubert H. Humphrey, *The Education of a Public Man: My Life and Politics* (Garden City, N.Y.: Doubleday, 1976), p. 243.

88. Schlesinger, *Thousand Days,* p. 707; McPherson, *Political Education,* p. 190.

89. Holtzman, *Legislative Liaison,* p. 258; Otten, "By Courting Congress," p. 1; Stephen Horn, *Unused Power: The Work of the Senate Committee on Appropriations* (Washington, D.C.: Brookings Institution, 1970), p. 200; Humphrey, *Education of a Public Man,* pp. 409–414.

90. MacNeil, *Dirksen,* pp. 376–378; Congressional Quarterly, *The Washington Lobby,* 2nd ed. (Washington, D.C.: Congressional Quarterly, 1974), pp. 107–108.

91. Congressional Quarterly, *Washington Lobby,* pp. 107–108.

92. Goldman, *Tragedy of Lyndon Johnson,* p. 74.

93. Ibid., p. 340; Johnson, *Vantage Point,* pp. 83, 215–216; 449; Bell, *Johnson Treatment,* p. 169; James L. Sundquist, *Politics and Policy: The Eisenhower, Kennedy, and Johnson Years* (Washington, D.C.: Brookings Institution, 1968), p. 110.

94. Kearns, *Lyndon Johnson,* pp. 186, 189, 234–235.

95. Eisenhower, *Mandate for Change,* p. 270; Donovan, *Eisenhower,* pp. 133, 135, 240; Adams, *Firsthand Report,* p. 381; Reichard, *Reaffirmation of Republicanism,* pp. 71, 80, 98, 226; Malcolm Jewell, *Senatorial Politics and Foreign Policy* (Lexington: University of Kentucky Press, 1962), p. 151; Sundquist, *Politics and Policy,* p. 265; MacNeil, *Dirksen,* pp. 222, 225; Ripley, *Majority Party Leadership,* pp. 18–19; Sorensen, *Kennedy,* pp. 394–395; Congressional Quarterly, *Congressional Quarterly Almanac, 1962* (Washington, D.C.: Congressional Quarterly, 1963), p. 250; "Ford's Lobbyists," p. 926; Rather and Gates, *Palace Guard,* p. 240; Evans and Novak, *Nixon in the White House,* chap. 5 passim. But see Adams, *Firsthand Report,* p. 373; Reichard, *Reaffirmation of Republicanism,* pp. 62–63, 111, 113.

96. O'Brien, *No Final Victories,* pp. 172–173; Joseph A. Califano, Jr., *A Presidential Nation* (New York: Norton, 1975), p. 213.

97. Bell, *Johnson Treatment,* p. 38; Valenti, *Very Human President,* p. 184; MacNeil, *Dirksen,* pp. 274, 281. Dirksen once told Lawrence O'Brien that he criticized Johnson to please Republicans; MacNeil, *Dirksen,* p. 282. See also p. 303 and chap. 12.

98. Valenti, *Very Human President,* pp. 184–185; George Christian, *The President Steps Down: A Personal Memoir of the Transfer of Power* (New York: Macmillan, 1970), p. 31. An exception to this seems to have been Fulbright; Califano, *Presidential Nation,* p. 213.

99. Sorensen, *Kennedy,* p. 393; Schlesinger, *Thousand Days,* p. 712.

100. Reichard, *Reaffirmation of Republicanism,* p. 131; Donovan, *Eisenhower,* p. 111.

101. Evans and Novak, *Nixon in the White House,* p. 109.

102. Califano, *Presidential Nation,* p. 215; Sorensen, *Kennedy,* p. 400; Chapman, "LBJ's Way," p. 1; Wayne, *Legislative Presidency,* pp. 159–160; Tom Wicker, *JFK and LBJ: The Influence of Personality upon Politics* (Baltimore: Penguin, 1969), pp. 34–35; Holtzman, *Legislative Liaison,* pp. 252, 254. For failures at influencing members of Congress by mobilizing their constituents, see O'Brien, *No Final Victories,* p. 137; Sorensen, *Kennedy,* p. 385.

103. Holtzman, *Legislative Liaison,* pp. 253–254.

104. Wilfred E. Binkley, *President and Congress* (New York: Vintage, 1962), p. 362.

105. Horn, *Unused Power,* p. 197.

106. Richard F. Fenno, "U.S. House Members in Their Constituencies: An Exploration," *American Political Science Review* 71 (September 1977): 911.

107. Sundquist, *Politics and Policy*, pp. 209–210.

108. MacNeil, *Forge of Democracy*, p. 295; O'Brien, *No Final Victories*, p. 119.

109. Kearns, *Lyndon Johnson*, pp. 226–227; MacNeil, *Dirksen*, p. 254; Johnson, *Vantage Point*, pp. 77–78; Bell, *Johnson Treatment*, p. 97; Sundquist, *Politics and Policy*, pp. 146–147. It appears that in return for Landrum's support, the White House influenced the AFL-CIO to stop local union efforts to build a campaign chest against him; Renka, "Legislative Leadership," pp. 31–32.

110. Safire, *Before the Fall*, pp. 162–163, 366–367, 458.

111. McPherson, *Political Education*, p. 196. See also Johnson, *Vantage Point*, p. 178. McPherson argues that where there is no natural camouflage for change, it is good to construct one.

112. Holtzman, *Legislative Liaison*, p. 254; Sorensen, *Kennedy*, p. 392.

113. Valenti, *Very Human President*, pp. 189–191.

114. Johnson, *Vantage Point*, p. 458.

115. Huitt, "White House Channels," pp. 75–76.

116. Valenti, *Very Human President*, p. 189.

117. O'Brien, *No Final Victories*, pp. 120–121; Wayne, *Legislative Presidency*, p. 147; Sorensen, *Kennedy*, p. 400; Holtzman, *Legislative Liaison*, p. 252. More generally, see Pika, "White House Office of Congressional Relations," p. 14.

118. Ripley, *Majority Party Leadership*, p. 18.

119. Harris, *Decision*, p. 31.

120. Goldman, *Tragedy of Lyndon Johnson*, pp. 308–309.

121. Johnson, *Vantage Point*, pp. 37, 79, 82–83, 85, 157; Kearns, *Lyndon Johnson*, p. 188.

122. Johnson, *Vantage Point*, pp. 79–81, 209; Goldman, *Tragedy of Lyndon Johnson*, pp. 356–357; Sundquist, *Politics and Policy*, p. 212; Kearns, *Lyndon Johnson*, p. 227. For further comments on her view of the importance of obtaining a consensus among interest groups, see Kearns, *Lyndon Johnson*, p. 391.

123. Kearns, *Lyndon Johnson*, p. 187. He also brought the business community to the White House to gain support for his Great Society programs. Valenti, *Very Human President*, p. 199. See also Renka, "Legislative Leadership," p. 34.

124. Raymond A. Bauer, Ithiel de Sola Pool, and Lewis A. Dexter, *American Business and Public Policy* (New York: Atherton, 1963), pp. 78–79; Renka, "Legislative Leadership," pp. 34–35. See also O'Brien, *No Final Victories*, p. 133.

125. Donald C. Lord, "JFK and Civil Rights," *Presidential Studies Quarterly* 8 (Spring 1978): 157.

126. Goldman, *Tragedy of Lyndon Johnson*, pp. 82, 341; Sorensen, *Kennedy*, p. 400; MacNeil, *Forge of Democracy*, pp. 262–263; Holtzman, *Legislative Liaison*, p. 252; "Larry O'Brien Discusses White House Contacts with Capitol Hill," in *The Presidency*, ed. Aaron Wildavsky (Boston: Little, Brown, 1969), pp. 483–484; Johnson, *Vantage Point*, pp. 37, 85; *Congressional Quarterly Almanac, 1962*, p. 250.

127. Sundquist, *Politics and Policy*, p. 509.

128. Johnson, *Vantage Point*, p. 159; Kearns, *Lyndon Johnson*, p. 192. See also Sundquist, *Politics and Policy*, p. 509.

129. Manley, "White House Lobbying," pp. 31–32.

130. Renka, "Legislative Leadership," pp. 34–35.

131. MacNeil, *Forge of Democracy*, p. 235; Mark J. Green, James M. Fallows, and David R. Zwick, *Who Runs Congress?* (New York: Bantam, 1972), pp. 106–107; "Ford's

Lobbyists," p. 927.

132. Johnson, *Vantage Point,* pp. 450–451. See also Goldman, *Tragedy of Lyndon Johnson,* p. 68.

133. Johnson, *Vantage Point,* pp. 450–451, 453–454.

134. MacNeil, *Forge of Democracy,* pp. 266–267.

135. Sorensen, *Kennedy,* p. 392. See also O'Brien, *No Final Victories,* p. 136.

136. "Larry O'Brien Discusses," p. 484; Sorensen, *Kennedy,* p. 392; Schlesinger, *Thousand Days,* p. 715.

137. Adams, *Firsthand Report,* pp. 377, 380, 386–387.

138. Eisenhower, *Waging Peace,* pp. 133, 135–136, 387–388; Adams, *Firsthand Report,* pp. 368, 372–373; Ripley, *Majority Party Leadership,* pp. 126, 130, 159–160; Jewell, *Senatorial Politics,* pp. 164–165; Larson, *Eisenhower,* pp. 30–32; Martin, *My First Fifty Years,* pp. 234–235; Reichard, *Reaffirmation of Republicanism,* p. 103; Marquis Childs, *Eisenhower: Captive Hero* (New York: Harcourt, Brace, 1958), p. 283. Jewell (*Senatorial Politics,* p. 165) points out, however, that Eisenhower said little publicly about the Bricker amendment.

139. See Hughes, *Ordeal of Power,* pp. 131–132.

140. E. Frederic Morrow, *Black Man in the White House* (New York: Coward-McCann, 1963), pp. 163, 233.

141. Kearns, *Lyndon Johnson,* pp. 249–250.

142. Johnson, *Vantage Point,* p. 35.

143. Sorensen, *Kennedy,* p. 392; Schlesinger, *Thousand Days,* pp. 709–710.

144. Califano, *Presidential Nation,* p. 205.

145. Kearns, *Lyndon Johnson,* p. 179.

146. Ibid., pp. 228–229.

147. "Changes on the Hill Worsen End-of-Year Logjam," *Congressional Quarterly Weekly Report,* September 2, 1978, p. 2303.

148. "Slings and Arrows," *Newsweek,* July 31, 1978, p. 20.

149. "Friend and Foe Alike Fault Administration . . . for Poor Lobbying Job on Energy Package," *Congressional Quarterly Weekly Report,* October 1, 1977, pp. 2062–2063; Congressional Quarterly, *Guide to Current American Government, Fall 1978* (Washington, D.C.: Congressional Quarterly, 1978), p. 123; "Changes on the Hill," p. 2305; "Senate Rejection of Carter Energy Proposals Attributed to Belief They Were Unwise," *Congressional Quarterly Weekly Report,* October 22, 1977, p. 2236; "The Carter-Congress Rift—Who's Really to Blame?" *National Journal,* April 22, 1978, p. 632.

150. "Carter and Congress: Fragile Friendship," *Congressional Quarterly Weekly Report,* February 26, 1977, p. 361; "Carter's Relationship with Congress—Making a Mountain out of a 'Moorehill,'" *National Journal,* March 26, 1977, p. 460; "Tiffling with Tip," *Newsweek,* August 14, 1978, p. 19.

151. "What Price Candor?" *Newsweek,* March 21, 1977, p. 28; "Turning Off the Water," *Newsweek,* April 4, 1977, p. 29; "Meanwhile, Back on the Hill," *Newsweek,* March 28, 1977, p. 17; "Congress Protests Water Project Cuts," *Congressional Quarterly Weekly Report,* February 26, 1977, p. 379; Martin Schram, "A New Role for the Vice President of the United States," *Houston Chronicle,* December 3, 1978, sec. 1, p. 18; "Carter and Congress," p. 361.

152. Charles Mohr, "Carter's First Nine Months: Charges of Ineptitude Rise," *New York Times,* October 23, 1977, pp. 1, 36.

153. "Carter Aides Proud of Urban Policy Process," *Congressional Quarterly Weekly Report,* April 1, 1978, pp. 783–784.

154. "Carter and Congress," *Newsweek,* March 7, 1977, p. 18.

155. "Carter-Congress Rift," pp. 630–631.

156. "Congress Impresses Carter," *Congressional Quarterly Weekly Report,* July 30, 1977 p. 1592; "Carter's Relationship with Congress," p. 461; "Meanwhile, Back on the Hill," pp. 16–17; "Senate Committee Debates Carter Reorganization Plan: House Roadblocks Possible," *Congressional Quarterly Weekly Report,* February 12, 1977, p. 270; "Receptions Planned as Balms to House Members' Feelings," *Congressional Quarterly Weekly Report,* February 25, 1978, pp. 520–521.

157. "Carter-Congress Rift," pp. 631–632; "Changes on the Hill," p. 2308; "Can Carter . . . Cope," *Newsweek,* October 24, 1977, p. 37.

158. "Friend and Foe Alike," pp. 2062–2063; "Changes on the Hill," p. 2305; Gil Thelen, "How Carter Bungled Energy Plan," *New Orleans Times-Picayune,* October 11, 1977, p. 14; "Senate Rejection of Carter Energy Proposals," p. 2236.

159. "Proving Ground," *Newsweek,* May 2, 1977, p. 45; "The Hard View from the Hill," *Newsweek,* October 10, 1977, p. 30; "Carter and Congress," pp. 18, 21; "Can Carter . . . Cope?," p. 38; Eric Davis, "Legislative Liaison in the Carter Administration," paper presented at the annual meeting of the Midwest Political Science Association, Chicago, April 1978, pp. 18–19.

160. Mohr, "Carter's First Nine Months," pp. 1, 36; "Proving Ground," p. 45; Nicholas Lemann, "Why Carter Fails: Taking the Politics out of Government," *Washington Monthly,* September 1978, p. 22.

161. "O'Neill Shows Antipathy to White House Staff," *Houston Chronicle,* August 11, 1978, sec. 1, p. 10; "Senate Rejection of Carter Energy Proposals," p. 2236; "Carter-Congress Rift," p. 631.

162. "Carter-Congress Rift," p. 630; "The Cabinet's Ambassadors to Capitol Hill," *National Journal,* July 29, 1978, p. 1200; "Changes on the Hill," pp. 2304–2305; Davis, "Legislative Liaison," p. 20; "House Committee Scraps President's Hospital Cost Control Proposal," *Congressional Quarterly Weekly Report,* July 22, 1978, p. 1886.

163. "His Mood at Mid-Term," *Newsweek,* August 28, 1978, p. 21. See also, "Rebates Dropped as Honeymoon Spirit Ebbs," *Congressional Quarterly Weekly Report,* April 16, 1977, p. 691; televised press conference by President Carter, December 28, 1977.

164. "McClure Wins Concessions; Agrees to Support Carter on Gas Bill, Clinch River," *Congressional Quarterly Weekly Report,* September 2, 1978, p. 2396. See "Carter's Kiddie Corps," *Newsweek,* April 10, 1978, p. 33, for a similar view of his staff's efforts at logrolling.

165. Jim Luther, "Carter Accused of Energy 'Doublespeak,'" *New Orleans Times-Picayune,* November 30, 1977, sec. 1, p. 2; "Friend and Foe Alike," pp. 2062–2063; "Energy Fallback," *Newsweek,* December 5, 1977, p. 37; "Rebates Dropped," p. 691; "Carter-Congress Rift," p. 630; "Confronting Congress," *Newsweek,* July 3, 1978, p. 22; Terrence Smith, "Carter's Courtship of Congress," *Houston Chronicle,* August 13, 1978, sec. 1, p. 12.

166. "A Friendly Enemies List," *Newsweek,* July 8, 1978, p. 27; "Carter Reported Planning Get Tough Strategy against Dem Critics," *Houston Chronicle,* August 16, 1978, sec. 1, p. 2.

167. "A Party of One," *Newsweek,* July 4, 1977, pp. 13–14; Congressional Quar-

terly, *Guide to Current American Government*, p. 120; "Carter-Congress Rift," p. 631; "Cabinet's Ambassadors," p. 1198; Renka, "Legislative Leadership," pp. 46–47; "Friend and Foe Alike," pp. 2062–2063.

168. "A Last-Minute Rush," *Newsweek*, October 23, 1978, p. 44.

169. "Carter Sent the Heavy Artillery to Lobby for Treaty," *Congressional Quarterly Weekly Report*, March 18, 1978, p. 678; "Heading for a Win?" *Newsweek*, February 13, 1978, pp. 18–19; "Victory and the Canal," *Newsweek*, May 1, 1978, p. 25; "Panama: A Big Win," *Newsweek*, March 27, 1978, pp. 42, 45–47.

170. "Panama: A Big Win," pp. 42, 45–47.

171. "Courting Zorinsky," *Newsweek*, March 27, 1978, p. 45.

172. "White House Lobbyists Employ the Hard Sell . . . to Win Senate Support for Natural Gas Bill," *Congressional Quarterly Weekly Report*, September 16, 1978, p. 2452.

173. Ibid., pp. 2452–2453.

174. Ibid., p. 2452; "The Battle Begins," *Newsweek*, May 9, 1977, pp. 22–23.

175. "House Sustains Carter Public Works Veto," *Congressional Quarterly Weekly Report*, October 7, 1978, p. 2722.

176. Ibid., p. 2721; "Hail to the Chief," *Newsweek*, October 16, 1978, pp. 32–33.

177. "Hail to the Chief," pp. 32–33.

178. "House Sustains Carter," pp. 2721–2722.

179. "Helping Hand: Republican Votes in Congress Are Giving Carter Key Foreign Policy Wins," *Congressional Quarterly Weekly Report*, August 5, 1978, p. 2042.

180. Congressional Quarterly, *Guide to Current American Government*, pp. 124–125.

181. Ibid.

182. "White House Lobby Gets Its Act Together," *Congressional Quarterly Weekly Report*, February 3, 1979. For other examples of President Carter's legislative skills, see "Carter's Courtship," p. 12; "Cabinet's Ambassadors," pp. 1196–1197, 1199; "A Show of Force," *Newsweek*, August 28, 1978, p. 19; Davis, "Legislative Liaison," p. 28; James Wooten, "Carter Tries Some One-to-One Lobbying on Energy," *New York Times*, October 21, 1977, p. A-12; "Meanwhile, Back on the Hill," p. 17; "Senate Committee Debates Carter Reorganization Plan," p. 267; "House Passes Wiretap Control Bill," *Congressional Quarterly Weekly Report*, September 9, 1978, p. 2419; "White House Lobbying Helps Kill B-1," *Congressional Quarterly Weekly Report*, February 25, 1978, p. 519; "Setting the Style," *Newsweek*, February 21, 1977, p. 15; "House Easily Sustains Carter Weapons Veto," *Congressional Quarterly Weekly Report*, September 9, 1978, p. 2415; "Carter Plan Would Reshuffle LEAA Program," *Congressional Quarterly Weekly Report*, July 15, 1978, p. 1821; "Middle East Plane Sales Backed by Senate Vote in Major Carter Victory," *Congressional Quarterly Weekly Report*, May 20, 1978, p. 1263; "Carter Administration Pits Its Lobbying Efforts . . . against Hospital Industry's on Cost Control Issue," *Congressional Quarterly Weekly Report*, March 17, 1979; Congressional Quarterly, *Guide to Current American Government*, p. 117; "Carter Can't Get Up the Hill," *Newsweek*, October 1, 1979, p. 18; Dom Bonafede, "The Tough Job of Normalizing Relations with Capitol Hill," *National Journal*, January 13, 1979; William J. Lanouette, "Who's Setting Foreign Policy—Carter or Congress?," *National Journal*, July 15, 1978.

Presidential Legislative Skills as a Source of Influence

7

In the previous chapters we have considered presidential legislative skills. We have also seen that there is disagreement concerning their effectiveness in influencing Congress. While presidents and observers have often perceived presidential legislative skills as an effective source of infuence, our rigorous, detailed analysis has raised some serious questions about this view. In this chapter we shall systematically evaluate presidential legislative skills to determine how important they are as a source of influence in Congress.

Usually when we evaluate presidential performance in Congress, we focus on Congress's output under the president being studied or on the president's behavior toward Congress, as we did in Chapters 5 and 6. Yet discussions of bills passed or of presidential behavior avoid a more significant question: What are the consequences of the president's and his administration's behavior toward Congress on support for his policies? We must examine the independent (presidential legislative skills) and the dependent (congressional support) variables together rather than separately.

Evaluating Presidential Legislative Skills

How can we evaluate and compare the performances of presidents? We cannot use the boxscores or victories-on-votes figures presented in Chapter 1, because winning votes and passing legislation heavily depend on the party composition of Congress and on whether Democrats are from the North or the South. Also, the boxscore is directly influenced by the strategic positions held by opponents. If they are situated so as to increase the likelihood of blocking consideration of legislation, then the legislation will be less likely to come to a vote.

The most productive analysis seems to be a comparison of presidential support among different groups of members of Congress. We can control for the factors of party and region by comparing the support that similar groups gave different presidents. Naturally, the party of the president also plays an important role in determining the level of support given by various groups in Congress. Thus, our formal comparisons must be restricted to presidents of the same party.

Our interest, of course, is not in just comparing the records of various presidents; we want to evaluate the importance of presidents' legislative skills. To do so, we would ideally measure the extent to which presidents exercised these skills on each member of a Congress or on the same members over several Congresses. After controlling for other sources of influence, we would determine whether members of Congress on whom presidential legislative skills were employed provided more support than other members or whether members' support over time fluctuated with the degree to which the president exercised his skills on them.

Unfortunately, we do not have sufficient data on individuals, but we do have the information to compare groups within different Congresses. If these groups provided more skilled presidents with greater support, we may conclude that legislative skills are an important source of presidential influence.

At this point we should recall a point made in Chapter 2. It is reasonable to examine presidential support here in the aggregate rather than on just a few votes in which the president was especially interested. In the previous two chapters we have seen that presidential legislative skills are generally aimed at generating goodwill and not at gaining a particular person's vote on a particular issue. Moreover, presidential efforts for specific votes are not necessarily the best tests of the effectiveness of presidential legislative skills, because members of Congress receiving the president's attentions may not be resistant on these issues. Finally, as mentioned above, we lack data on the individual level, such as whom the president called and how those whom he called were affected by the calls.

Tables 3.1 and 3.2 presented the average presidential support by party for the House and the Senate, respectively. Tables 7.1 and 7.2 present the average presidential support for Northern and Southern Democrats in the House and Senate, respectively. The data in these tables will serve as the basis for the analysis that follows.

Democratic Presidents

To simplify matters, we will examine Democratic presidents first and then Republicans, limiting our discussion to overall presidential support scores (these are all we have for Presidents Ford and Carter). On the basis of our earlier description of presidential legislative skills, we would certainly expect President Johnson's record of presidential support to be better than those of Presidents Kennedy and Carter. Johnson was the master legislative technician, giving Congress top priority (at least until 1967) and leaving no stone unturned in his efforts to exercise his influence. If we cannot find clear evidence of the significance of legislative skills for Johnson, we will be unlikely to find it for anyone.

Table 7.1

Democratic House Members' Average Presidential Support by Region (Percent)

	NORTHERN DEMOCRATS			SOUTHERN DEMOCRATS		
YEAR	OVERALL POLICY	DOMESTIC POLICY	FOREIGN POLICY	OVERALL POLICY	DOMESTIC POLICY	FOREIGN POLICY
1953	50	——	——	47	——	——
1954	50	——	——	41	——	——
1955	55	48	72	50	45	64
1956	56	53	89	47	47	58
1957	59	60	57	37	38	33
1958	65	63	73	42	40	50
1959	42	35	79	37	35	46
1960	49	43	64	35	35	35
1961	83	82	84	57	57	55
1962	81	81	81	57	58	53
1963	81	81	80	58	60	49
1964	82	82	85	59	58	62
1965	82	82	85	54	53	58
1966	71	71	69	46	47	40
1967	77	77	75	54	55	50
1968	70	70	76	51	52	46
1969	49	46	73	47	47	45
1970	53	53	63	52	54	41
1971	41	——	——	60	——	——
1972	47	——	——	48	——	——
1973	32	——	——	45	——	——
1974	41	——	——	50	——	——
1975	35	——	——	45	——	——
1976	27	——	——	46	——	——
1977	67	——	——	53	——	——
1978	65	——	——	48	——	——

Tables 7.3 and 7.4 summarize the records of support for Presidents Kennedy, Johnson, and Carter in the House and Senate, respectively. The data on presidential support in these tables do not support the hypothesis that Johnson's legislative skills were important in influencing members of Congress. Kennedy received more support in the House from both Northern and Southern Democrats than did Johnson, while Johnson received more support from Republicans. (Johnson's support among all Democrats exceeds Kennedy's, despite Johnson's lower scores for both Northern and Southern Democrats, because a greater percentage of House Democrats were from the more liberal North during Johnson's tenure in office.) Carter's scores are only slightly less than Johnson's among Republicans

Table 7.2

Democratic Senators' Average Presidential Support by Region (Percent)

	NORTHERN DEMOCRATS			SOUTHERN DEMOCRATS		
YEAR	OVERALL POLICY	DOMESTIC POLICY	FOREIGN POLICY	OVERALL POLICY	DOMESTIC POLICY	FOREIGN POLICY
1953	45	——	——	50	——	——
1954	41	——	——	38	——	——
1955	56	35	71	57	38	71
1956	42	30	65	37	30	50
1957	55	46	66	49	41	59
1958	46	43	58	43	42	48
1959	35	28	57	44	40	49
1960	42	35	60	43	44	42
1961	74	73	78	49	50	46
1962	69	65	77	50	48	54
1963	71	71	71	45	49	39
1964	66	69	61	52	53	51
1965	70	73	63	49	48	53
1966	62	60	66	44	41	55
1967	64	62	68	55	55	55
1968	53	53	54	38	37	44
1969	47	37	74	47	47	47
1970	42	41	48	51	48	78
1971	35	——	——	54	——	——
1972	35	——	——	64	——	——
1973	34	——	——	48	——	——
1974	35	——	——	50	——	——
1975	43	——	——	58	——	——
1976	33	——	——	55	——	——
1977	72	——	——	65	——	——
1978	70	——	——	54	——	——

Table 7.3

House Members' Average Support for Democratic Presidents (Percent)

	KENNEDY (1961–1963)	JOHNSON (1964–1968)	CARTER (1977–1978)
Democrats	63	69	62
Northern Democrats	82	76	66
Southern Democrats	57	53	51
Republicans	37	43	39

Table 7.4

Senators' Average Support for Democratic Presidents (Percent)

	KENNEDY (1961–1963)	JOHNSON (1964–1968)	CARTER (1977–1978)
Democrats	64	59	68
Northern Democrats	71	63	71
Southern Democrats	48	48	60
Republicans	40	47	47

and Southern Democrats and less among Northern Democrats (consequently, the support percentage of all Democrats was also lower for Carter than Johnson). In the Senate, Kennedy did better than Johnson among Northern Democrats, the same as Johnson among Southern Democrats, and more poorly only among Republicans. Carter did better than his Democratic predecessor among all Democrats and the same as Johnson among Republicans.

The Johnson-Carter comparison is especially interesting, since it involves the ultimate professional and "insider" Lyndon Johnson, with the amateur with no Washington experience at all, Jimmy Carter. In a news conference in April 1978, Carter declared that dealing with Congress was a "new experience for me altogether." He added that he "never dreamed a year ago" that his energy bill would not have been passed by then and that "I have found it is much easier for me in my own administration to evolve a very complex proposal for resolving a difficult issue than it is for Congress to pass legislation and to make the same decision."[1]

Table 7.5 shows Johnson's support in Congress in 1965, the first year of his full term in office, when he was at the height of his legislative powers, and Carter's support in 1977, his first year in office. This table has findings that are similar to those of our previous comparison. Only among Northern Democrats in the House did Johnson receive more support than Carter (ignoring the 1 percent difference for House Southern Democrats). This is particularly striking when one considers that Carter's task in influencing members of Congress has been more demanding than was Johnson's.

Carter's Burden

Why might President Carter be having a more difficult time in gaining support from Congress than his Democratic predecessors in the 1960s? One reason is the increased dispersion of power in Congress, especially the House. The face of Congress has changed over the past two decades. Seniority is no longer an automatic path to committee or subcommittee chairs, and chairpersons must be more responsive to the desires of committee members. In the words of Represen-

Table 7.5

Average Support from Congress for President Johnson in 1965 and President Carter in 1977 (Percent)

	HOUSE		SENATE	
	JOHNSON	CARTER	JOHNSON	CARTER
Democrats	74	63	65	68
Northern Democrats	82	67	70	72
Southern Democrats	54	53	49	65
Republicans	42	42	48	52

tative Thomas Foley, "If I as Agriculture Committee chairman say to a member, 'I don't like your bill and I'm not going to schedule it,' I'll walk into the committee room and find a meeting going on without me."[2]

There are also more subcommittees and more subcommittee chairpersons now, and these subcommittees have a more important role in handling legislation.[3] While the power of subcommittees has increased, that of the Southern oligarchies has declined. Members of both parties have larger personal, committee, and subcommittee staffs at their disposal as well as new service adjuncts such as the Congressional Budget Office. This new freedom and these additional resources, combined with more opportunities to amend legislation, make it easier for members of Congress to challenge the White House (and the congressional leadership) and to provide alternatives to the president's policies.[4]

Yet other reforms have increased Carter's burden. In 1970 the House ended unrecorded teller votes (in which only the number of votes on each side is reported), and in 1973 it began electronic voting. Both changes led to an increase in the number of roll call votes and thus an increase in the visibility of representatives' voting behavior. This has generated more pressure on House members to abandon party loyalty, making it more difficult for the president to gain passage of legislation. These changes are obviously beyond President Carter's control.

The faces of Congress have also changed since the 1960s. Most of the members of the Ninety-fifth Congress (60 senators and 280 representatives) were elected in the 1968 elections (the year the Republicans regained the presidency) or later.[5] These newer members have tended to adopt the rules of apprenticeship and specialization to a much lesser degree than their first-term predecessors. Instead, they have eagerly taken an active role in all legislation.[6]

Thus, the president now has more decision makers to influence. He can no longer rely on dealing with the congressional aristocracy and expect the rest of the members to follow. "Ten years ago," said Terry Bracy, the chief lobbyist for the Department of Transportation, "if you wanted a highway bill, you went to see [former House Public Works Committee chairperson John] Blatnik, the Speaker, and the chairman of the Rules Committee. There would be a small collegial discussion—and all the political decisions would be made. Now there's no one person to see. . . . You have to deal with everybody." Andrew Manatos, the Commerce Department's chief lobbyist, and his father Mike, a Johnson White House congressional liaison aide, recently wrote a report in which they concluded that the Ninety-fifth (1977–1978) Congress was different from the Democratic Congresses Johnson faced. "In the early 1960s," they wrote, "the 'Club' still controlled the congressional levers of power," but now the president must persuade more people.[7]

We also must consider the historical context of administrations. Perhaps the most obvious difference between the Democratic administrations of the 1960s and Jimmy Carter's in the late 1970s is that Carter is serving during the post-Vietnam and post-Watergate period of congressional assertiveness. The nation was severely shocked by the war in Southeast Asia and the scandals in the White House, both of which, many believe, were due to abuses of presidential power. These traumas have had many consequences, but for our purposes the most important is the increase in congressional assertiveness. The diminished deference to the president by individual members of Congress and by the institution as a whole naturally makes presidential influence more problematical. As one Democratic senator said in 1977, "We got such fun out of popping Nixon and Ford. We don't want to give it up and be good boys any more."[8]

Carter has also had the misfortune to preside during a period of substantial inflation and unemployment, whereas the Kennedy-Johnson years were characterized by stable prices, sustained economic growth, and general prosperity. The prosperity of the 1960s provided the federal government with the funds for new policies, with little political risk. Taxes did not have to be raised and sacrifices did not have to be made in order to help the underprivileged. In the late 1970s resources are more limited, helping to make the passage of new welfare or health programs, for example, more problematical.

Vietnam, Watergate, and the sagging economy have also combined to make the public more skeptical of government policies. Public opinion polls indicate that trust and confidence in government are very low.[9] The optimism that resulted from the race to the moon and the idealism that fueled the war on poverty in the 1960s has been replaced by anxiety over future energy resources and the skepticism of the tax revolt. For a president who desires to establish new programs, the outlook is not promising.

President Johnson also had some unique advantages in dealing with Congress that were unrelated to his legislative skills. As mentioned, the years of his presidency were more prosperous than those of any other modern president. Furthermore, he took office following Kennedy's assassination, a tragedy that provided, at least in the short run, a sense of national unity, overwhelming support for the new president, and new support for the slain president's policies (which Johnson adopted as his own). In 1964 Johnson was elected in a landslide, which provided him increased congressional support, as we saw in Chapter 4, and many first-term Democrats undoubtedly perceived that they owed their seats to his coattails.

On the other hand, Johnson did labor under some special burdens. One was the absence of a sense of national crisis, such as existed during the Depression of the 1930s, which generates support for reform or progressive policies. The second burden was the war in Vietnam, especially during the latter part of his tenure. The growing opposition to the war shattered national unity, produced schisms within his own party, and caused his popularity to take a dramatic and sustained plunge. Nevertheless, Carter's burdens seem far greater, and we should remember that Carter's record compares favorably with Johnson's even in 1965, before Vietnam began taking its toll.

Program Innovativeness

The innovativeness of presidents' legislative programs may also vary. It may be more difficult to obtain support for innovative legislation because of its greater controversy. Thus, greater efforts may be required to build support after innovative legislation has been introduced. Moreover, disputes over new issues may jeopardize an entire legislative program, causing division even on routine and noncontroversial issues. We have probably controlled for this influence to a large extent by comparing only presidents of the same party, since recent Democratic presidents seem to have pressed for greater changes than Republican presidents. Thus, we are comparing innovative presidents with other innovative presidents and less innovative presidents with other less innovative presidents.

However, we might question whether what we commonly consider innovative legislation is really new, at least in regards to building a consensus. At first thought, we might regard the New Frontier legislation as innovative, but perhaps this belief is more the result of rhetoric than of substance. Much of Kennedy's top-priority legislation on public housing, federal aid to education, Medicare, manpower training, federal aid to depressed areas, the Peace Corps, increasing the minimum wage and extending its application, and space exploration had all been before Congress in some form during the Eisenhower years and, in the words of one observer, were "as familiar in Congress as Sam Rayburn's bald head."[10]

Commentary by close Kennedy aides supports this view. Theodore Sorensen writes of Kennedy's quoting Jefferson that "great innovations should not be forced on slender majorities" and argues that there was no virtue in fighting and losing.[11] Similarly, Arthur Schlesinger, Jr., reports that the narrow victory in the early 1961 fight to expand the House Rules Committee after an all-out effort laid a restraining hand on Kennedy's legislative program. He had to husband his bargaining power (for example, he selected the trade expansion bill in 1962 as his "controversial" legislation) and await better times in Congress to propose legislation requiring extensive consensus building. Knowing that he did not have the votes to pass much controversial legislation, he saw no point in alienating members of Congress and possibly losing on noncontroversial bills.[12]

Johnson adopted most of Kennedy's legislative programs. If these programs were not new in Kennedy's term, then they were even less so in Johnson's. Nevertheless, Johnson did propose innovative legislation, such as the 1965 Voting Rights Act, rent supplements, the 1968 Fair Housing Act, and the war on poverty. He also successfully pushed controversial Kennedy bills such as the 1964 tax cut and the 1964 Civil Rights Act.

Both Kennedy and Johnson did propose some innovative legislation, especially Johnson. However, we should not assume that programs passed for the first time are necessarily new or that they all require the same amount of consensus building. Thus, although we have not developed a measure of innovativeness, we have shown that consensus building may have been less difficult than is usually assumed.

What about the innovativeness of President Carter's legislative programs? William H. Cable, Carter's chief lobbyist in the House, argues "that Jimmy Carter has taken a number of issues for which there is no easy answer and no consensus." He adds that issues "like energy and taxes and civil service reform—those are tough nuts to crack."[13] Indeed they are. So are the elimination of pork barrel water projects, the Panama Canal treaties, establishing the Department of Energy, and airline deregulation. In sum, Carter has not necessarily proposed less innovative legislation than his recent Democratic predecessors.

Popularity

In one area President Carter did have an advantage over President Johnson: popularity. Carter's 1977 popularity averaged 64 percent, while Johnson's five-year average was 56 percent. However, Johnson's popularity in 1965 averaged 66 percent, which is very similar to Carter's 1977 figure, and they received almost exactly the same support from House Republicans and Southern Democrats and Senate Republicans and Northern Democrats (Carter did better among Senate Southern Democrats), despite Johnson's presumed greater legislative skills. Johnson also had the advantage, shown in Chapter 4, of winning election by one of the largest landslides in modern American history, while Carter won by a very slight margin.

Critical Votes

Perhaps the significance of Johnson's mastery of the legislative process as a source of influence is not reflected in aggregate Presidential Support Scores. This influence may have really mattered on the margins of coalition formation, that is, on gaining the last few votes needed to pass a program. After broader sources of influence, such as party affiliation and presidential popularity, had built up support, the more personal legislative skills of the president may have turned a sizable coalition into a victorious one by winning over the last critical few votes.

In a memo to President Johnson on gathering votes in the House in 1965, Lawrence O'Brien wrote, "Normally we enter into a tough count with a minimum of 175 votes, about which we need not worry, and we move from there with the active help of the leadership, the committee chairman, and the committee Democrats."[14] Consistent with our reasoning presented in Chapter 5, O'Brien's memo indicates that Johnson could depend in 175 votes out of the maximum of 218 necessary for a majority. If not everyone voted, which is usually the case, the number of votes needed to win was, of course, less than 218. So Johnson needed to add at most 43 votes to his dependable coalition— only about one-fifth of the total needed. We should also keep in mind that these figures are for "tough counts," not the typical vote. On less controversial measures he likely needed even fewer votes, if he needed any at all. In addition, Johnson had the help of the party and committee leaders and the committee Democrats, which was especially helpful since these people are important cue givers to other members of the House.[15]

If Johnson's legislative skills did gain him the few critical votes necessary to win, then he should have won at least a good number of votes by narrow margins. This would indicate the success of his efforts. Table 7.6 shows the victory margins of all the roll call votes on which the president took a stand in 1965, the year, observers generally agree, when Johnson was at the peak of his powers. As the figures indicate, Johnson did *not* win many votes by close margins, even when we use the generous definition of *marginal victory* employed here (a victory by twenty-five or less votes in the House and ten or less votes in the Senate). Moreover, the few marginal victories that did occur were not on major issues.

One might argue that 1965 is not a good year to choose for examining the success of Johnson's legislative skills, because in that year he was relatively popular with the electorate, averaging 66 percent approval for the year, and had an overwhelming majority of Democrats in Congress (295 in the House and 67 in the Senate, including 205 Northern Democrats in the House and 47 in the Senate). Thus, one could argue that Johnson's legislative skills were less necessary than when he was less popular and had a smaller Democratic majority in Congress.

This argument is contradicted by Johnson legislative aide Henry Hall Wilson, who said that when there was a "fat" Congress like that of 1965–1966, the White House increased its demands in order to exploit the favorable party balance. When the votes are not close, Wilson said, the White House is not doing its job. Johnson's approach, according to his aide, was to push each member of Congress to the limit in order to obtain the maximum output.[16]

If Wilson is correct, then 1965 should not have been an atypical year in regards to the margin of victory on presidential support votes. (We have seen above, however, that Wilson's description, which suggests numerous marginal victories, seems to be inaccurate.) Nevertheless, to cover all possibilities, we shall examine in Table 7.7 the margin of victories of presidential support votes in 1967, after

Table 7.6

Marginal Victories on Presidential Roll Call Votes: 1965

	NO. OF VOTES	NO. OF VICTORIES	NO. OF MARGINAL VICTORIES[a]	% MARGINAL VICTORIES
House	112	104	5	5
Senate	162	150	19	13

[a] Margin of victory no more than twenty-five votes in the House and no more than ten in the Senate.

Table 7.7

Marginal Victories on Presidential Roll Call Votes: 1967

	NO. OF VOTES	NO. OF VICTORIES	NO. OF MARGINAL VICTORIES[a]	% MARGINAL VICTORIES
House	127	96	11	11
Senate	167	136	23	17

[a] Margin of victory no more than twenty-five votes in the House and no more than ten in the Senate.

the Democrats had lost forty-seven seats in the House and three in the Senate in the 1966 election and when the president's average popularity dropped to 44 percent for the year. There are again few marginal victories (although there are more than in 1965), and those that did occur were generally not on crucial or controversial issues. Thus, Johnson's legislative skills are not proven to be very influential here.

Other Stages

Johnson's legislative skills might have been especially important in committees or in other stages of the legislative process preceding floor action. We probably shall never know for certain because we lack useful pertinent data. However, recent research finding that members of Congress vote on the floor consistently with their committee votes[17] casts some doubt on this argument. At any rate, roll call votes are important and worthy of study by themselves.

Proposals Altered

We also lack a measure of the extent to which a president's proposals are altered between introduction and passage. Even if we had such a measure, we would have to be very wary of interpreting it. Proposals by a president like Lyndon Johnson, who involves members of Congress in the drafting of legislation, may be changed less because congressional objections are considered *before* the proposals are introduced. Other presidents may meet objections after legislation is introduced. While the former approach may be more efficient and appear more impressive, the ultimate differences in policy may be purely cosmetic.

Johnson in Perspective

In sum, Johnson's mastery of the legislative process seems to have had considerably less significance than conventional wisdom indicates. Actually, many observers inside and outside the government agree that if Kennedy had lived, he would have gotten much the same out of Congress as Johnson did and at about the same time.[18] Senator Everett Dirksen, agreeing with then House Majority Leader Carl Albert, said, Kennedy's "program was on its way before November 22, 1963. Its time had come."[19] Legislative breakthroughs had taken place on several major bills before Kennedy's death, including those concerning Medicare and civil rights.[20]

Johnson, of course, was aware of the overwhelming importance of party affiliation in the passage of legislation. He called Lawrence O'Brien after the results of the Democratic landslide in 1964 were in and told him, "We can wrap up the New Frontier program now, Larry. . . . We can pass it now."[21] Johnson's chief domestic adviser, Joseph Califano, argues that the remarkable achievements of the Eighty-ninth Congress were due to the large Democratic majority and the fact that the House also had a *liberal* majority.[22] Other observers agree that the difference between Kennedy and Johnson in passing legislation was largely due to the smaller number of liberal Democrats in Congress under Kennedy.[23]

The reader must remember that the argument here is not that Johnson was unsuccessful in influencing members of Congress. Rather, it is that his legislative skills appear to have been less significant as a source of influence than the conventional wisdom suggests. The fact that he was more successful than President Carter in obtaining support from Northern Democrats in the House is of no small significance, however. Since there are (and were) so many Northern Democrats, the support of the typical Northern Democrat is of greater consequence for the passage of legislation than the support of the typical Republican or Southern Democrat.

Whether Johnson received more support than Carter from Northern Democrats because of his legislative skills is difficult to say. (Similarly, did Kennedy receive less support from Republicans than Johnson because he failed to seek it[24] or because Johnson's rapport with the opposition was greater?) On the whole, legislative skills don't seem to be the main factor. First, the less skilled Kennedy did better than Johnson among Northern Democrats. Second, House Northern Democrats have been the only group in either chamber whose support has steadily diminished for each succeeding Democratic president (see Tables 7.3 and 7.4). These representatives, being liberal, may have been the most affected by the war in Vietnam; being Democrats, were the most shocked by Watergate; and being in the majority (and thus with the most to lose from an oligarchic system), were most liberated by the reforms of the past decade. All of this would support the argument made earlier regarding the greater difficulty that Carter has in influencing Congress.

Republican Presidents

We might describe Gerald Ford's handicaps as being similar to Jimmy Carter's; also, he had the additional burdens of being the nation's first appointed president and having pardoned Richard Nixon (a very unpopular act). On the other hand, Ford had the most experience of the three modern Republican presidents in dealing with Congress and was probably the most legislatively skilled. In the discussion in Chapters 5 and 6 we found Nixon's efforts often to be negative and Eisenhower's often to be pleasant but bungling.

Tables 7.8 and 7.9 show the average presidential support figures of different groups in Congress for Republican presidents (1974 has been omitted because both Nixon and Ford served in that year).[25] Patterns relating to presidents' legislative skills are difficult to discern. Republican support in both houses is stable across all three presidents. Support by House Northern Democrats for Republican presidents steadily diminished, just as it did for Democratic presidents. In the Senate, Nixon and Ford did more poorly than Eisenhower among Northern Democrats and about the same as each other. In both houses, the more recent Republican presidents did better than Eisenhower among Southern Democrats, with Nixon strongest in the House and Ford strongest in the Senate.

The inexperienced, bungling, and apolitical Eisenhower (perhaps aided by his popularity) did better, albeit sometimes by only a small percentage, than the politically experienced Nixon and Ford among those at both ends of the ideological spectrum, Republicans and Northern Democrats, in both houses of Congress. Only among Southern Democrats did the later presidents have greater support. Nixon and Ford, despite their obvious differences in legislative styles, had similar records of support except for Nixon's greater support among House Northern Democrats. This support seems to have been due more to a change in the voting behavior of these representatives than to Nixon's legislative skills. Again we find

Table 7.8

House Members' Average Support for Republican Presidents (Percent)

	EISENHOWER (1953–1960)	NIXON (1969–1973)	FORD (1975–1976)
Democrats	49	46	35
Northern Democrats	53	44	31
Southern Democrats	42	50	46
Republicans	65	64	63

NOTE: Due to the change of administrations in 1974, the figures for that year are excluded.

Table 7.9
Senators' Average Support for Republican Presidents (Percent)

	EISENHOWER (1953–1960)	NIXON (1969–1973)	FORD (1975–1976)
Democrats	45	43	43
Northern Democrats	45	39	38
Southern Democrats	45	53	57
Republicans	69	64	66

NOTE: Due to the change of administrations in 1974, the figures for that year are excluded.

that the legislative skills of presidents do not seem to be related to the support that they receive in Congress.

Conclusion

Presidential legislative skills do not seem to affect support for presidential policies, despite what conventional wisdom leads us to expect. Sources of information about presidential-congressional relations, particularly the press, seem to have focused upon the more unique examples of these relations, implying that what they were presenting was typical. When we rigorously and systematically evaluate the evidence, however, we reach different conclusions.

While we have found that the support by Congress for presidents does not necessarily vary with the degree of presidential legislative skills, we are not suggesting that presidents should ignore these skills or that these skills never matter. Certainly presidents have successfully intervened with a phone call, bargain, threat, or amenity, occasionally winning a crucial vote because of such an effort. The important point is that these skills should be placed in their proper perspective. They do not appear to be a predominant factor in determining presidential support in Congress on most roll call votes and therefore, despite commonly held assumptions, they are not a prominent source of influence. Thus, what seems to be the most manipulatable source of presidential influence is probably the least effective.

Notes

1. "Text of Carter News Conference," *Congressional Quarterly Weekly Report,* April 22, 1978, p. 1007.

2. "Single-Issue Politics," *Newsweek,* November 16, 1978, p. 58.

3. For a discussion of the new importance of subcommittees, see Steven H. Haeberle, "The Institutionalization of the Subcommittee in the United States House of Representatives," *Journal of Politics* 40 (November 1978): 1054–1065.

4. For a good overview of recent changes in Congress, see Norman J. Ornstein, Robert L. Peabody, and David W. Rohde, "The Changing Senate: From the 1950s to the

1970s," and Lawrence C. Dodd and Bruce I. Oppenheimer, "The House in Transition," both in *Congress Reconsidered,* ed. Lawrence C. Dodd and Bruce I. Oppenheimer (New York: Praeger, 1977).

5. "Seniority in the 95th Congress," *Congressional Quarterly Weekly Report,* November 1, 1977, pp. 27–30. (A few of the new members had served previous terms in Congress.)

6. See, for example, Ornstein, Peabody, and Rohde, "The Changing Senate"; Dodd and Oppenheimer, "House in Transition."

7. Shirley Elder, "The Cabinet's Ambassadors to Capitol Hill," *National Journal,* July 29, 1978, p. 1196. See also William J. Lanouette, "Who's Setting Foreign Policy—Carter or Congress?" *National Journal,* July 15, 1978, p. 119; "Organized Labor Found 1978 a Frustrating Year, Had Few Victories in Congress," *Congressional Quarterly Weekly Report,* December 30, 1978, p. 3539.

8. "Shadowboxing," *Newsweek,* June 6, 1977, p. 18. See also William Colby, *Honorable Men: My Life in the CIA* (New York: Simon & Schuster, 1978); "Meanwhile, Back on the Hill," *Newsweek,* March 28, 1977, p. 16.

9. For an overview of this phenomena, see Arthur H. Miller, "Political Issues and Trust in Government: 1964–1970," *American Political Science Review* 68 (September 1974): 951–972.

10. Tom Wicker, *JFK and LBJ: The Influence of Personality upon Politics* (Baltimore: Penguin, 1969), p. 88. See also Harry McPherson, *A Political Education* (Boston: Little, Brown, 1972), p. 189; Francis M. Carney, "Kennedy and the Congress," in *Politics 1964,* ed. Francis M. Carney and H. Frank Way, Jr. (Belmont, Calif.: Wadsworth, 1964), p. 66; James L. Sundquist, *Politics and Policy: The Eisenhower, Kennedy and Johnson Years* (Washington, D.C.: Brookings Institution, 1968); Hubert H. Humphrey, *The Education of a Public Man: My Life and Politics* (Garden City, N.Y.: Doubleday, 1976), pp. 250–251, 253; George Christian, *The President Steps Down: A Personal Memoir of the Transfer of Power* (New York: Macmillan, 1970), p. 40.

11. Theodore S. Sorensen, *Kennedy* (New York: Bantam, 1966), p. 709.

12. Arthur M. Schlesinger, Jr., *A Thousand Days: John F. Kennedy in the White House* (Boston: Houghton Mifflin, 1965), pp. 709, 712. See also Sorensen, *Kennedy,* pp. 381–382.

13. Terrence Smith, "Carter's Courtship of Congress," *Houston Chronicle,* August 13, 1978, sec. 1, p. 12.

14. John F. Manley, "White House Lobbying and the Problem of Presidential Power," paper presented at the annual meeting of the American Political Science Association, Washington, D.C., September 1977, p. 27. For a similar argument regarding the Eighty-seventh Congress, see Neil MacNeil, *Forge of Democracy* (New York: McKay, 1963), pp. 258–259.

15. See John W. Kingdon, *Congressmen's Voting Decisions* (New York: Harper & Row, 1973), especially chap. 4; Donald R. Matthews and James A. Stimson, *Yeas and Nays: Normal Decision-Making in the U.S. House of Representatives* (New York: Wiley, 1975).

16. Doris Kearns, *Lyndon Johnson and the American Dream* (New York: Harper & Row, 1976), p. 235.

17. Joseph K. Unekis, "From Committee to the Floor: Consistency in Congressional Voting," *Journal of Politics* 40 (August 1978): 761–769.

18. See, for example, Sundquist, *Politics and Policy,* p. 482; Rowland Evans and

Robert Novak, *Lyndon B. Johnson: The Exercise of Power* (New York: New American Library, 1966), p. 364; Lawrence F. O'Brien, *No Final Victories: A Life in Politics from John F. Kennedy to Watergate* (New York: Ballantine, 1974), p. 106.

19. Eric F. Goldman, *The Tragedy of Lyndon Johnson* (New York: Dell, 1974), p. 68.

20. O'Brien, *No Final Victories,* p. 145. See also Sundquist, *Politics and Policy,* p. 481.

21. O'Brien, *No Final Victories,* p. 180.

22. Joseph A. Califano, Jr., *A Presidential Nation* (New York: Norton, 1975), p. 155.

23. Sundquist, *Politics and Policy,* pp. 476–480; Joseph Cooper and Gary Bombardier, "Presidential Leadership and Party Success," *Journal of Politics* 30 (November 1968): 1012–1027. Also see Goldman, *Tragedy of Lyndon Johnson,* p. 38; Aage Clausen, *How Congressmen Decide: A Policy Focus* (New York: St. Martin's, 1973), p. 146, for skeptical views of the importance of presidential legislative skills.

24. O'Brien, *No Final Victories,* p. 138; MacNeil, *Forge of Democracy,* p. 265; Stephen J. Wayne, *The Legislative Presidency* (New York: Harper & Row, 1978), p. 153.

25. It is best to omit the 1974 figures because those under each administration are not representative of the votes for the entire year.

Epilogue

We have traced the extent of presidential legislative success in Congress, finding that the president's policies often fail to be enacted into law. We have also shown that this conflict between the two branches is inherent in our system of government and, except in extraordinary circumstances, will remain a central feature of American politics. Finally, and most significantly, we have analyzed the impact of sources of presidential influence in Congress on the support by members of Congress for presidential policies.

The question now is What are the implications of this analysis for an understanding of American politics? The main implication is that the president is in a weak position with regards to Congress. His burdens are great and his assets are few. In Chapter 2 we discussed the many political factors that virtually guarantee that Congress will not readily acquiesce to the president's wishes. Every president must overcome these hurdles if he or she is to be successful in dealing with Congress. The rest of the book provides evidence that the president has relatively little influence to wield over Congress. Party affiliation is unreliable as a source of influence and applies only to members of the president's party (Chapter 3); presidential prestige, although it is a source of influence, serves more as a background factor than as an immediate cause of presidential support (Chapter 4), and legislative skills are of only marginal importance (Chapters 5, 6, and 7).

This conclusion may surprise readers who accept the notion of the "imperial presidency," which developed in the late 1960s and early 1970s during the Johnson and Nixon presidencies. Inappropriate analogies between the president's powers as commander in chief and his dealings with Congress undoubtedly confused the public about the extent of the president's influence in Congress. Another cause of confusion were analogies based on extraconstitutional exercises of power, especially by Richard Nixon (including impoundments, recess appointments, and the misuse of the pocket veto), which we discussed in Chapter 1.

Perhaps Nixon's disdain for Congress and his negative attitude toward much of the legislation that it passed further supported the view of the imperial presidency. Finally, Lyndon Johnson's extraordinary and well-publicized success in Congress naturally encouraged some people to assume that he had great influence. Congressional cries of being "walked over" by the White House further distorted the picture.

Of course, not all students of politics will find the conclusion of the weakness of the president with regards to Congress startling. Many close observers have consistently argued that the president does not enjoy great success in Congress. Data such as the Presidential Boxscores presented in Chapter 1 certainly support this view. It is important to note, however, that such conclusions are normally reached by examining the outcomes of presidential requests for support for policies. In other words, someone describes the president's success as being unimpressive. Thus, a second implication of our study is the utility of empirical methods and theory for studying the presidency.

This research offers several explanations of why the president has difficulties in gaining support from Congress. If we had relied upon traditional methods, we would not have been able to analyze the sources of presidential influence in Congress rigorously. While insight intuition, speculation, generalization from selected examples, and other means of inference found in traditional literature on the presidency certainly have a place in scholarship, they are not sufficient to provide us with analytical generalizations about presidential influence in Congress in which we can have confidence. Most of what we have learned about presidential influence in this book required the use of the theory and methods of behavioral political science. Indeed, many of our findings are counterintuitive. For example, our findings in Chapter 3 of the disappearance of presidential coattails in recent presidential elections, including 1964, would not have been expected even by many close observers of elections. Similarly, our findings of the relative lack of importance of presidential legislative skills in Chapters 5, 6, and 7 certainly run contrary to conventional wisdom.

Other findings here have not even been objects of speculation in the past. In Chapter 4, for example, we examined presidential prestige as a source of influence by disaggregating presidential popularity into partisan groupings in the public, disaggregating presidential support into partisan groupings in Congress, and further disaggregating presidential support by presidential administrations. The relationships we then tested have not even been suggested before. Traditional methods do not lend themselves to such careful conceptualization, measurement, and analysis.

Yet another implication of our study is that there is little the president can do about his degree of influence in Congress. He cannot affect the party affiliation of members of Congress to a large extent: Incumbents only rarely change their affiliations, presidential efforts at campaigning in midterm elections do not appear to have positive results, and the coattail effect in presidential elections has disappeared.

While we have found that presidential popularity is a source of influence in Congress, we must also note that presidents have generally not been popular in recent years. The only really popular presidents since World War II have been Eisenhower and Kennedy, and their presidencies ended a generation ago. Despite considerable efforts,* recent presidents have not been able to maintain high levels of popularity. Presidential electoral victories appear to be less a source of influence in Congress than the president's current popularity, especially for Republican presidents. More importantly, as the experience of Gerald Ford shows, presidents as candidates or as incumbents are hardly in control of voters' decisions.

Presidential legislative skills are inherently limited as sources of influence in Congress. In addition, as the case of Jimmy Carter shows, presidents do not necessarily learn from their predecessors. The office of the presidency seems to lack an institutional memory for congressional relations, and, as Santayana would have expected, presidents repeat the mistakes of the past.

---

*Discussion of some of these efforts can be found in George C. Edwards III and Ira Sharkansky, *The Policy Predicament* (San Francisco: W. H. Freeman and Company, 1978), chap. 3.

Index